LIQUIDA

1969-1970
A CHELSEA MEMOIR

MARK WORRALL

Liquidator
1969-1970 A Chelsea Memoir
Copyright Mark Worrall 2019
ISBN: 978-1694468581

enquiries@gate17.co.uk
Twitter: @gate17marco
cover design: GATE 17
www.gate17.co.uk

CONTENTS

A very special thank you to Kim Clark and Tim Rolls.
Honourable mentions: Keith Sanford, Rick Evans, George Skevington, Paul Hicks and Rod Miles.

Liquidator is dedicated to the amazing people you will read about in the pages that follow who are sadly no longer with us, and also to family members and friends that I hold dear who filled my mind with so many vivid memories as I was writing this book.

Life is short. Break the rules, forgive quickly, drink slowly, love truly, laugh uncontrollably, and never regret anything that made you smile.

IT'S THE HOPE THAT KILLS YOU
Monday 12 August 2019 11.45 a.m.

It's the hope that kills you. When it comes to football, I've experienced the meaning of this well-worn cliché a few times as I'm sure fans of the glorious game the world over have... some more than others. It's inescapable... long-in-the-tooth masochists would say it's addictive. Sugar-coated, pre-season optimism metamorphosing through stages of anticipation and expectation... hope building... reaching out... a glistening trophy in touching distance. Then it happens... a decisive goal is scored bringing with it one of two things... a rush as powerful as that experienced taking the best illegal party drugs... or a dagger to the heart.

It's the hope that kills you. Ah Chelsea... let me probe that wound. In my time of supporting the Club, Manchester United and Liverpool have been in a league of their own when it comes to cruel twists of fate that have shattered many blue-tinted dreams.

Yesterday at Old Trafford I'd witnessed the managerial reign of Blues legend Frank Lampard get off to a chastening start as Man U scored four without reply. Heading north, hopes had been high that Chelsea, riding on the crest of an optimistic wave generated by Lampard's appointment, might get something from the game... but the reality was harsh.

Despite being encumbered by a transfer ban, Super Frank's youthful team were the better side for much of the game and the outcome might have been different had the frame of the goal not thwarted Tammy Abraham and Emerson... if only eh! Instead, the heavens opened and the sky fell in. 4-0 is a horrible scoreline to lose by and walking out of the ground having to endure the *Chelsea rent boys* taunts of jubilant Mancs was as nauseating as it was familiar.

It's the hope that kills you. On the way home, I thought back to 1994... *We're the famous Chelsea FC and we're going to Wembley. Wembley, Wembley.*

At 36-years old, Glenn Hoddle was five years younger than Frank Lampard when he was appointed Chelsea player-manager in June 1993 when I'd sensed that the pendulum of fortune might swing the way of Stamford Bridge, and not before time. Former Blues owner Ken Bates had (and still has) his critics, but the hiring of Hoddle, a hate figure for Chelsea supporters during his time as a player with Tottenham Hotspur, proved inspirational... and the delicious irony has never been lost on me that a bona fide Spurs icon would prove to be the catalyst for a 10-year chain reaction that culminated in June 2003 with Bates selling-up to Russian billionaire Roman Abramovich and the unprecedented glories that followed.

Chelsea's Premier League form in Hoddle's first season was much more of a miss than a hit, although in true gloriously unpredictable fashion the Blues had beaten eventual champions Man U home and away by the same 1-0 scoreline with midfield maestro Gavin Peacock rippling the net in both matches. Victory at Old Trafford in March 1994 ended United's 34-match unbeaten streak that had commenced the very game after they'd lost to Chelsea at the Bridge the previous September. Symmetry comes in many guises and this was a simple yet beautiful example.

Chelsea's next game after winning at the so-called Theatre of Dreams was an FA Cup quarterfinal tie at home to Wolverhampton Wanderers who were plying their trade in today's equivalent of the Championship then known as the First Division. Hoddle ran the show on the pitch and had a pivotal role in the move that led to Peacock leathering the ball past Wolves goalie Mike Stowell which settled the match 1-0 in the Blues favour. A celebratory pitch invasion followed. Chelsea were in their first FA Cup semi-final since 1970 when they went on to win the trophy for what at this time was still the only occasion in their history... supporter anticipation was gathering momentum.

'It's our year. It's our year,' my friend Tommy Walker bellowed, his eyes sparkling with enthusiasm. He'd forgotten that at his age he was supposed to be blessed with greater decorum and joined me in excitedly bounding down the wide concrete steps of the old Shed terrace and vaulting the low wall onto the always-muddy perimeter track.

Skipping past the row of parked up ice-blue, fibreglass-shelled, AC Invacars, once given to disabled people for free by the British Ministry of Pensions, we were soon on the no-longer-that-hallowed Stamford Bridge turf. At this time, the ground was going through its phased 'Chelsea Village' redevelopment into an all-seated stadium.

Ordinarily, the attendance for the game might have been higher than 29,340... however the North Stand terrace had closed the year before and work would begin on demolishing The Shed after the last home game of the current season.

All of us on the pitch held arms aloft ten-to-two-style joining in with the rest of the crowd singing *When Wise goes up to lift the FA Cup we'll be there, we'll be there.* The Metropolitan Police and stewards weren't too concerned... this pitch invasion, unlike some in previous years, was good-natured. The whole match-going experience was evolving. Little did we know it though, as our exuberance calmed and the authorities funnelled us off the pitch into the East Stand, that very soon watching Chelsea at the Bridge would never be the same again.

At this time, Tommy was a veteran of the two FA Cup finals Chelsea had thus far contested at the home of English football. The emotionally-trying 2-1 (Bobby Tambling) defeat to Tottenham Hotspur in 1967 (20 May) and the tempestuous 1970 (11 April) final with Leeds United which ended in a 2-2 (Peter Houseman, Ian Hutchinson) draw after extra-time.

Tommy always said that if he'd known me back then, he'd have taken me to watch Chelsea though I doubt my mother and father would have allowed it. He would have been 18-years old at the time of the 1967 final, whereas I was just six... a primary school kid in short trousers just at an age when the Blues first snagged my interest.

The attraction for me wasn't hand-me-down as it had been for Tommy, nor was it a result of peer group pressure or geographical location. Collecting A&BC football cards held a shared responsibility with *Jimmy Hill's Football Weekly*... Peter Osgood on the cover of Issue 9 (22 December 1967) was the clincher. There was something indescribably alluring about the blue hue of the shirt Ossie was wearing and even though I was a small boy he didn't look that old. He wasn't of course, he was only 20. None of then manager Tommy Docherty's 'diamonds' seemed old to me. All of them just looked so smart. The blue and the blue of the shirts and shorts. That was it. Right there, the defining moment when I knew Chelsea were the team for me. I hoped one day I would get to see them play.

It's the hope that kills you. If only I had known Tommy way back when. I'd have idolised him more than I ended up doing anyway if he'd taken me to watch the mighty CFC when I was a nipper in the '60s. As it transpired, it took five years of pleading before my father took me to my first ever football game. 4 November 1972, Chelsea lost 3-1 to Liverpool at Anfield. Strange I know. An away game before a home game, but that was the order of things when it came to my baptism as a Blue.

First Division
Liverpool 3 Chelsea 1
Anfield
Attendance: 48,932
Referee: Ken Burns

Chelsea: Steve Sherwood, Gary Locke, Eddie McCreadie, John Hollins, David Webb, Ron Harris, Tommy Baldwin, Steve Kember, Bill Garner, Chris Garland, Peter Houseman.
Scorer: Baldwin 75.

Liverpool: Clemence, Lawler, Lindsay, Smith, Lloyd, Hughes, Keegan, Cormack, Heighway, Toshack, Callaghan.
Scorers: Toshack 34, 55, Keegan 50.

A lady I knew as Auntie Alice managed the long-gone Merchant Officers Hotel which was on Canning Street a couple of miles or more maybe from the Reds ground. We'd stayed there a few times when I was very young though oddly enough this was to be the last time. It puzzled me in later life why I'd never asked the reason for this and sadly it's a mystery that will forever remain unsolved as my father passed away when I was still young, well before I reached an age when you reflect back on your life and look for answers to such questions.

At the game, we stood on The Kop! Insane and funny thinking about it now. I remember I wore a green corduroy bomber jacket adorned with a tiny Chelsea lapel badge, the miniscule, smaller-than-5p-size ones that featured the lion rampant regardant which I'd read in *Shoot* magazine had been appropriated in 1953 from the coat of arms of then Club president Viscount Chelsea. The very same lion rampant regardant embroidered on the shirt Peter Osgood was wearing for that cover shot of *Jimmy Hill's Football Weekly*.

My father wasn't much of a football fan, in fact I think this might have been his first game as well which when I thought about the whole day years later explained why he clearly had no knowledge that away ends had been created with the safety in mind of those who might be betrayed by their accent and manners… or miniscule, smaller-than-5p-size Chelsea lapel badges!

Despite this, as we'd clicked through the turnstiles, I recall he'd been savvy enough to tell me to keep my mouth shut and not to cheer should Chelsea score which they did eventually, but not before John Toshack and Kevin Keegan, Liverpool's dynamic double-act of this era, had put the Reds into an unassailable 3-0 lead, Keegan's strike bisecting a Toshack brace.

It was still only the 55th minute when 'Tosh' headed a pinpoint Steve Heighway cross past 18-years old Steve Sherwood in the Chelsea goal. I wanted to cry.

Liverpool, Liverpool, Liverpool sang the Kopites swaying in that peculiar way you could only ever do on a vertiginous, proper old-school football terrace. Sherwood was only playing because legendary Blues custodian Peter 'The Cat' Bonetti was still in hospital having sustained a stomach injury in a midweek League Cup tie away at Bury.

Catty like Ossie was one of my heroes. I even had a pair of Peter Bonetti 'Starcraft' goalkeeping gloves that were yellow and green with the letter B detailed on them. Looking at them now, they actually resemble the type of gloves you might wear when gardening!

In that Bury game, Bonetti was stretchered off in the 53rd minute having taken an accidental boot to the stomach courtesy of Shakers outside-right John Connelly. David Webb went in goal leaving Chelsea down to ten men as Peter Osgood had been withdrawn as early as the 10th minute with a hamstring injury.

With only one substitute permissible at that time, and Marvin Hinton having replaced Ossie, it was Webb to whom manager Dave Sexton entrusted goalkeeping responsibilities. The centre-back was no stranger to the job having once kept goal and a clean sheet for Chelsea when playing the full 90 minutes of a First Division game against Ipswich Town that the Blues won 2-0 (27 December 1971, Steve Kember, Chris Garland).

Webb successfully auditioned for the role of stand-in goalie a week previously in an away match with Coventry City (17 December 1971) when Bonetti had been stretchered off with an injured ankle after 30 minutes. He acquitted himself well in the 1-1 (Peter Osgood) draw, but it was reserve keeper John Phillips who was called up to play in Chelsea's next game, the first leg of a League Cup semi-final tie with Tottenham Hotspur at the Bridge (22 December) which the Blues won 3-2 (Peter Osgood, Chris Garland, John Hollins).

Ahead of the Ipswich match, Philips joined Bonetti on the injured list and manager Dave Sexton had a telegram sent to rookie goalie Steve Sherwood who was enjoying the Christmas break with his family 185 miles away in Selby, Yorkshire. Sherwood left home at 11 a.m. and sped down the M1. A police escort detailed to expedite his progress through London somehow missed him meaning the last few miles of the journey to the Bridge were tortuous. Despite this, he still managed to arrive at the ground before kick-off. With just three minutes to go however, referee Anthony Oliver wagged his finger and said, 'sorry son, you're too late', and the rest as they say is history. Well it was for David Webb.

Sherwood would go on to make his debut in Chelsea's next game, a 1-0 defeat away at Derby County (1 January 1972). The young keeper played brilliantly and was denied a clean sheet by Webb of all people whose mistimed attempt at a headed clearance saw the ball fizz into Chelsea's net.

Back to that League Cup tie at Bury... and although Webb was holding the fort well, Bonetti, following 20 minutes treatment, was desperate to re-enter the fray. Remarkably, during his time off the pitch, Blues striker Chris Garland had smashed home what proved to be the only goal of the tie. "It was killing me to walk, let alone return to keep goal but I felt I just had to get back in the match," Bonetti said after the game. Maybe if he hadn't gone back on he wouldn't have aggravated the injury and been fit enough to face Liverpool. Instead he ended up hospitalised in Manchester Royal Infirmary having an operation to repair a grisly-sounding torn intestine that would side-line him for 12 games.

All of that said about missing Bonetti, at Anfield, I made Sherwood Chelsea's man-of-the-match... for trying if nothing else, and he did make three blinding saves from Heighway, Chris Lawler and Alec Lindsay which sportingly got him an ovation from the Kop at the final whistle which I joined in with.

But for Sherwood, Chelsea might have been on the receiving end of a serious thrashing. I wasn't too sure if my father was willing this to happen. I felt certain he made me stay to the very end as punishment for having traumatized him for so long to take me to a Blues game. I was glad he did though because in the 75th minute I saw my first ever Blues goal that I would have missed had we left when Liverpool went 3-0 up.

Bill Garner won the ball after Chris Garland had successfully challenged Reds keeper Ray Clemence strongly enough for it to break loose. Garner found Tommy Baldwin who lashed it back past Clemence into the net. My father looked down at me and winked. I looked down at my miniscule, smaller-than-5p lapel badge and smiled. I swear to this day that the lion rampant regardant was smiling back.

Reminiscing now, I marvel at the fact that as an impressionable young boy I could have had my head turned by Liverpool that day... but the thought never once entered my head. So that was my first Chelsea game... a resounding defeat, and given that like Bonetti, Osgood also missed out through an injury sustained against Bury I was deprived of seeing the player whose magnetic persona had originally drawn me to the Blues.

It's the hope that kills you. It would be almost two years before I got to see Chelsea play in person again... a game that saw me make my own personal debut at Stamford Bridge. 17 August 1974 The first match of what ultimately proved to be a disastrous season. The Blues hosted Carlisle United, and my father who lived and worked in Windsor where Peter Osgood hailed from had 'acquired' tickets for a pair of seats in the brand new East Stand which at an astronomical, constantly escalating, cost of £2 million was effectively bankrupting the Club.

Sadly, for all concerned... apart from the visitors from Cumbria, Chelsea failed to turn up and were soundly beaten 2-0. I felt crushed.

Worse was to follow. The Blues ended the campaign second bottom of the First Division, meaning they were relegated. The bottom club? Carlisle United. Victory over Carlisle in that opening game would have given Chelsea sufficient points to stay up and, even better, consigned Tottenham Hotspur to the drop... you couldn't make it up. What a nightmare. It was true... yes, definitely 100% true. After crushing your spirit first... it was the hope that killed you... but it didn't stop me hoping.

9 April 1994 Staging FA Cup semi-finals at Wembley wasn't yet the norm. In fact it was the preceding season that saw both semis played at the venue for the first time. Traditionalists punted the opinion that the stadium should be for major finals and England games only.

Geographically, Chelsea v Luton Town at Wembley sort of made sense. The next day however, Manchester United and Oldham Athletic supporters had to travel a couple of hundred miles to watch their teams face-off which was ridiculous and a sign of things to come.

Luton had Chelsea legend Kerry Dixon in their ranks. His name was chanted in unison by fans of both clubs... it was a nice touch. Once again Gavin Peacock proved his worth as a Blue scoring both goals in what was a routine win. Premier League brains undoing First Division brawn.

It's the hope that kills you. 14 May 1994 Ah the hope. I wasn't alone in feeling totally convinced this was going to be Chelsea's day. Singing *From Stamford Bridge to Wembley we'll keep the Blue Flag flying high* had taken on a new significance this season. It was a bit like the blind faith subsequently associated with belting out *Three Lions (football's coming home)* during the course of every major tournament England have contested since the track was spawned by the Lightning Seeds, David Baddiel and Frank Skinner ahead of the 1996 Euros.

Beneath leaden clouds bloated with rain, Chelsea took the game to Manchester United. 'If only Glenn Hoddle had picked himself to start,' Tommy often said when the final had cropped up in conversation in the years that followed.

There were lots of 'if onlys'. If only Gavin Peacock's half-volley had dipped a couple of inches lower instead striking the bar... the Blues might have had a vital first half lead.

Who's the wanker in the black? If only referee David Elleray hadn't been the subject of that chant things might have been different.

On the hour mark United scored the first of three goals inside ten minutes that broke Chelsea.

1) Eddie Newton upended Denis Irwin just inside the Blues 18-yard box... *Penalty!* Fair enough. Eric Cantona sent Dimitri Kharine the wrong way. Fair enough.

Chelsea, Chelsea, Chelsea, Chelsea (Amazing Grace version) Tommy led the chant. 'We can get back into this, I know we can,' he said optimistically. Of course I believed him.

2) Frank Sinclair made contact with Andrei Kanchelskis outside the box... the 'flying' Ukrainian, who had sprinted clear of everyone, most notably Elleray, tumbled to the ground. *Penalty!* Cantona scored again.

Elleray later admitted in his autobiography that he'd got it wrong but couldn't go back on his decision... really! It's the hope that kills you stone dead.

3) Boyhood Chelsea supporter Mark Hughes soon made it 3-0.
Yanited, Yanited, Yanited... chanted the Mancs.

It was only then that I became fully aware of the sheeting rain that would soak us to our leathery skins as we trudged disconsolately down Wembley Way shortly after Brian McClair had made it 4-0 to the Red Devils in the last minute.

Standing in the long queues to enter Wembley Park station, collective drowned rat misery overwhelmed half-hearted vocal attempts at raising morale.

Who the fuck are Man United? We'd just found out.

It's the hope that kills you. Fourteen years later, well it felt more like a lifetime... except when it all came on top it didn't, it felt like hours, minutes... seconds even, Manchester United got the better of Chelsea again. This time around the stakes were even higher, in fact they couldn't get any higher within the sphere of club football.

Fuck your history, we're going to Moscow had been the song of choice for Blues supporters gathered inside Stamford Bridge, 30 April 2008, when Liverpool were beaten 3-2 (Didier Drogba x2, Frank Lampard) in the second leg of a nerve-jangling Champions League semi-final. The first leg at Anfield, played 22 April, had ended in a 1-1 draw (John Arne Riise own-goal) meaning a 4-3 aggregate win for Chelsea and passage to the final. Man U, 1-0 aggregate victors over Barcelona in the other semi would be the opposition.

21 May 2008 On the flight out to Moscow, Tommy and I had discussed all our trophy-winning experiences supporting the Blues since that humbling by Man U at Wembley in 1994.

The FA Cup ghost that had haunted Chelsea since 1970 was finally laid to rest on 17 May 1997, a gloriously sunny day, when Middlesbrough were beaten 2-0 (Roberto Di Matteo, Eddie Newton).

The following season (29 March 1998), Chelsea won the League Cup beating Boro once again and by the same scoreline *2-0* (Roberto Di Matteo, Frank Sinclair)... *Two nil, we always win two nil...* became a popular chant sung when playing the Teessiders for many years thereafter.

At the end of the campaign, the European Cup Winners Cup was also won when Gianfranco Zola scored the only goal of the game as Chelsea beat Stuttgart 1-0 in Stockholm (13 May). What a fantastic trip that was... Euro aways were by now the ultimate football buzz, an expensive and addictive narcotic.

The FA Cup was won again in 2000 when a Roberto Di Matteo goal was enough to see off Aston Villa (20 May)... and then in June 2003 Roman Abramovich came along and bought Chelsea Football Club and turbo-charged the Blues into the silverware stratosphere.

Long-standing supporters pinched themselves regularly... was this really happening? Oh yes!

Back-to-back Premier League titles were won in 2005 and 2006. The League Cup in 2005 (27 February, Chelsea 3 Liverpool 2, Steven Gerrard own-goal, Didier Drogba, Mateja Kezman, and 2007 (25 February, Chelsea 2 Arsenal 1, Didier Drogba x2) the year when the FA Cup was also secured with a 1-0 win over Manchester United (19 May). Drogba scored the only goal of that game in extra-time. Did it feel like retribution for 1994? I wasn't sure to be honest... but it didn't half feel great singing *Who the fuck are Man United?* and watching John Terry lift the famous old trophy above his head.

By now it was the Champions League trophy that Mr Abramovich was coveting above all else, and we were right with him now. Oh the hope. It had killed us in 2005, a semi-final defeat to Liverpool when a solitary Reds goal at Anfield across the two legs (27 April, Chelsea 0 Liverpool 0. 3 May, Liverpool 1 Chelsea 0) ended Chelsea's challenge.

Worse still, in a pre-VAR-technology era, their was a huge question mark about whether or not Luis Garcia's goal-given shot actually crossed the line before it was hooked away by Blues defender William Gallas.

Infuriatingly, albeit more legitimately, the Scousers had repeated the feat at the same stage of the 2007 competition... this time via a brutal penalty shoot out.

Chelsea won the first leg at the Bridge 1-0 (25 April, Joe Cole) and

Liverpool the second leg at Anfield by the same score (1 May). After extra-time, the game went to penalties. Arjen Robben and Geremi failed from the spot and although Frank Lampard scored... Liverpool found the net each time and won the shoot-out 4-1.

Fuck off Chelsea FC, you ain't got no history was melded with nasally whining brays of *five times rent boys, five times.* No wonder then that a year later, *Fuck your history, we're going to Moscow* was sung so spitefully. Hope truly sprang eternal for all of us, our souls galvanized by the steely belief that now was our time.

'It's our year,' Tommy hollered. Instantly, I remembered I'd been on this journey before... that said, football has a unique way of distorting perception doesn't it!

It's the hope that kills you. Yanited fans still spitefully remind us every time Man U play Chelsea about John Terry's crucial miss in 'that' Moscow final penalty shoot-out.

Viva John Terry, he could have won the cup, but he fucked it up...

JT hadn't been in the first five to take a spot-kick should the game go to penalties, but Didier Drogba's earlier sending off for 'slapping' Nemanja Vidic meant a change to the game plan was required.

The match kicked off late on a Wednesday night, 22.45 p.m. local time, and 90 minutes plus extra-time later we were into the small hours of Thursday morning with the teams still locked at 1-1. I thought about it being the same shit, but a different day.

Cristiano Ronaldo headed Man U, much the better side early on, into the lead midway through the first-half, but Frank Lampard equalised just before the break slotting the ball past Edwin Van der Sar. Frank raised his hands to the heavens and looked up, a split-second dedication of the goal to his late mother Pat who had passed away the previous month. It was a beautiful and moving moment.

Super, Super Frank. Super, Super Frank. Super, Super Frank, Super Frankie Lampard.

Subsequently, Lampard and Drogba both hit the woodwork as Chelsea took the game by the scruff of the neck, but Man U were back in the ascendency as the game drifted into extra-time... a period which saw Terry miraculously head a goal-bound Ryan Giggs effort off the line and Drogba sent off. Bizarrely, the time was now 1:15 a.m. and the rain that had been falling incessantly for an hour or so had evolved into a deluge of biblical proportions... cascading from the black Moscow sky onto the Luzhniki Stadium's temporary natural grass pitch that had been laid for the final.

Rio Ferdinand won the toss for Man U and opted for his side to take the first kick. The shoot-out was at the opposite end of the stadium to where we were 'stood'… smack in front of United's travelling support.

Carlos Tevez stepped up and cooly beat Petr Cech. 1-0.

Michael Ballack drilled the ball hard into the roof of the net. 1-1.

Michael Carrick fired home confidently. 2-1.

Juliano Belletti, tidy. 2-2.

Cristiano Ronaldo… this was the one. In a bid to outwit Cech, before striking the ball, the Red Devils' talisman hesitated in his run-up. Cech dived to his right and saved magnificently. 2-2

Super Frank next. 'Nail this and we're going to win,' said Tommy. 'It's written in the stars.'

I bit my nails and said nothing. Lampard swept the ball into the net. 'Fucking get in there!' 2-3.

Owen Hargreaves. Okay, okay 3-3.

We could hear Ashley Cole being booed as he placed the ball…

'Come on Ash, do it…Yes!' 3-4.

Nani had to score for United to keep the Red Devils in the contest. 'Fuck it!' 4-4.

It's the hope that kills you. Chelsea's captain, leader, legend John Terry was going to win the Champions League for the Blues. Perfect!

Terry took a short run up to address the ball but he slipped and his standing leg buckled… his miss-hit still deceived Van der Sar sending the United goalie the wrong way, but the ball zipped off the right-hand post and went agonisingly wide. 4-4.

Anguished curses melded with distant cheers in a discordant cacophony. I knew right then we were done for. The die of misfortune had been cast.

It's often forgotten what happened next… that the shoot-out didn't end there… although I wished it had and the ground opened up and swallowed me whole.

Anderson scored for Man U. 5-4.

Salomon Kalou for Chelsea. 5-5.

Ryan Giggs for Man U. 6-5.

It was now Edwin Van der Sar versus Nicolas Anelka. I'd noticed that every Chelsea spot-kick had been to Van der Sar's left and wondered if Anelka was going to buck the trend.

Facing us, United's goalie pointed to his left post. Did psychology play a part… or did Anelka bottle it? Maybe it was a bit of both, that's what Tommy surmised later. Wherever the truth lay, it was a poor penalty. Instead of shooting to the keeper's left, Anelka aimed his kick to the right at a decent enough height for a diving Van der Sar to comfortably claw the ball away from the goal.

Game over… gutted! Dejected, we left the stadium. Still fell the rain, soaking every last stitch of clothing, permeating my skin, sapping my spirit. Tommy looked at me and I looked at him… I knew what he was going to say before he said it…

'It's the hope that kills you.'

THIS MORTAL COIL
Monday 12 August 2019 12.30 p.m.

'Okay Mark, you can go through now.'

Distracted from my drifting thoughts about Chelsea that I'd deliberately allowed to side-track me from the stark reality of where I was and why I was there, I looked over at Anna the receptionist who was herself another distraction.

What a beauty. Flawless porcelain skin, plump scarlet-lipsticked-lips, titian hair razor cut into a perfect bob just like Corinne Drewery the lead singer of Swing Out Sister. I wondered if Anna had any idea she resembled a 1980s pop star I'd had a massive crush on in my younger years? She was smiling at me just as she always did, her hazel eyes flickering as they met mine and momentarily held my gaze. There was an enigmatic yet compassionate quality to her expression that was Mona Lisa-esque, it gave her an air of feminine mystique that I found captivating which to be quite honest didn't sit right with me... not here, not now... not ever some might say. The thing is, I couldn't help myself and my mate Tommy who I had come to visit understood. He'd seen the funny side of it because if things were they other way around, he'd have been thinking exactly the same way. I didn't believe him, but that's what he told me.

I stood up and briefly contemplated wrestling with my conscience. I knew I had one. That was never going to work though... mainly because Tommy had laughed at my story and said not to worry.

I told him I'd mentally undressed Anna and had passionate sex with her within seconds of seeing her for the first time. That was a little over two weeks ago and the same had happened on each of the 12 occasions I'd seen her since then though the positions had changed to keep things interesting. Variety is the spice of love... especially imaginary love.

According to Tommy, my behaviour was nothing out of the ordinary. He said that conventional wisdom held that the male of the species thinks about sex every seven seconds and that basically I was as conventionally wise as they come.

'Are you okay Mark?' There was genuine concern in Anna's voice.

'I'm absolutely fine,' I replied hesitantly, wondering where our brief conversation might lead before shaking my head as I realised she was just doing her job.

'I know it's a difficult time. I'm here if you want to talk to someone,' she added, the sincerity in her voice making me suddenly feel deeply ashamed and disgusted with myself in spite of what Tommy had said to me.

'That's very kind of you. Thank you.' I waved at Anna as I spoke before I turned to walk down the long corridor leading to the double doors that opened out to the courtyard where the patient rooms were located.

The sound of my footsteps on the tiled floor echoed off the low ceiling providing a metronome beat which to my mind needed a tune to accompany it. The intro to *Sgt. Pepper's Lonely Hearts Club Band* by The Beatles filtered into my consciousness almost immediately, and I hummed it softly to myself breaking into the lyric at the appropriate moment.

*****

It's the hope that kills you. Well no, actually that's not true is it. The random absurdity of how I'd got to thinking about Chelsea while sitting in the reception area at the care home struck me again. Apprehensively, I took several deep breaths as I stared at the door in front of me. I didn't want to go in because each time I did I thought it was going to be the last time. I narrowed my watering eyes and focussed on the name neatly printed on the card snapped into the door sign holder.

Tommy Walker

A 30-year, three-pack-a-day Capstan Full Strength Navy Cut cigarette habit had gradually tarred Tommy's lungs and 15 years or so ago brought on emphysema and a steady deterioration of his general well-being. The diagnosis had stopped him smoking, but the damage was already done. Bouts of pneumonia became a regular occurrence in the winter months that followed and the strain of breathing brought on pulmonary problems. The "heart bloke", as Tommy called him, fitted a pacemaker that kept him ticking over and Warfarin thinned his blood so it kept circulating. The grim reaper could fuck right off. He wasn't taking our Tommy away just yet... life went on... but at an increasingly slower pace.

Last spring, a CT scan revealed Tommy had an abdominal aortic aneurysm... and subsequent scans that it was growing. Surgery was required, but because of his other problems the doctors were concerned his body might not be strong enough to withstand the rigours of an operation.

If this wasn't bad enough news, matters worsened when he found out he wasn't allowed to fly because the changes in cabin pressure might lead to the aneurysm rupturing which would cause severe internal bleeding with death the most probable outcome.

All Tommy had wanted to do was go on holiday to Pizzo Calabro, a seaport and commune in Calabria, southern Italy. Away from England, Pizzo was his favourite place in the world. He'd been going there for months at a time for many years, staying at the same place on each occasion, Villino Lo Zaffiro, a secluded beachfront bed and breakfast a couple of miles drive along the coast road out of town.

'Meraviglifuckingoso,' he'd always say when he returned from a sojourn there and I'd asked him if he'd had a good time. Tommy's bastardisation of the Italian word meraviglioso which means wonderful was... well it was meraviglifuckingoso!

My mother Giovanna hails from a village in northern Italy called Massa Finalese some 30 miles distant from Maranello home to the legendary Ferrari supercar dynasty and so Tommy's tales of his trips to Pizzo were well received by me as was his creation of a new word to add to my Italian vocabulary.

'They make the best Eggs Purgatorio in the world at Lo Zaffiro,' he'd always say, licking his cracked lips and smiling at the memory.

'Meraviglifuckingoso... ha ha.'

I'd argued with him many times that my Nonna Dirce made the best Eggs Purgatorio in the world. Dirce was my maternal grandmother, an extraordinary woman blessed with sublime culinary skills.

Now I know it's true that there are millions of Italians out there who will argue till the cows come home that their Nonna was, or even better... is, the best cook in the world... but I'm telling you now, my Nonna Dirce actually was the best cook in the world.

If I needed a spot of morning-after succour following a heavy night on the Peroni Gran Riserva and Limoncello, Eggs Purgatorio always did the job. The name of the dish made me wince a bit these days because it had become apt and not in the sense of sorting you right out if you had the mother and father of all hangovers. Roman Catholics believe that Purgatorio (purgatory) is the place where the spirits of the dead are punished for their mortal sins and purified before entering heaven.

Tommy Walker

I wiped the tears from my eyes and Tommy's name became less blurred. I still couldn't bring myself to open the door and so I continued to stand there facing it while thinking about Eggs Purgatorio. A psychiatrist would definitely have an opinion or two to share with me about why that was, I'm guessing I was just looking for anything to help me swerve reality.

I pictured myself sitting in Nonna Dirce's kitchen watching her at work. There was nothing complicated about preparing and cooking the dish. Cracked eggs cooked in a spicy tomato and Nduja sauce with Parmesan cheese grated on top served in a blisteringly hot skillet with a bread crostino.

As with all Italian home cooking, the secret to success lies in the sauce. Nduja is a fiery spreadable salami consisting of offcuts of pork, herbs and spices which include chilli peppers... my Nonna actually made her own, she'd form it into a football-sized globe and wrap it with fine gauze-type netting. I could see it now perched invitingly on the wooden worktop at the side of the ceramic butler sink.

Comforting distractions from the harsh realities of life are fleeting. That was my dear friend's name on the door in front of me. 'It's the hope that kills you,' I muttered to myself as I rocked back and forth on my heels.

If the inoperable abdominal aortic aneurysm hadn't been enough to contend with, Tommy's next diagnosis that followed more scans and tests in the summer swept away the last vestiges of faith he had in the principles of fair play. Lung cancer.

Tommy was given between nine months and a year to live. His underlying health problems meant surgery and radiotherapy weren't a realistic option. The doctors told him chemotherapy might help control the cancer and extend his life slightly, but the side effects would be unpleasant. Tommy opted for palliative care. He explained to me that he needed to be lucid for as long as possible because he had one last thing he wanted to do before he died... and then he told me that I was the only person he knew who could assist him and he'd explain everything in more detail the next time he saw me.

When he'd told me this we were both crying. Him because it was breaking him in pieces every time he had to tell a friend he cared for that he was dying... and me because he'd just explained the finality of his situation.

Given Tommy's quality of life had been steadily deteriorating for a longish period of time by now, I'd come to terms with the fact that one day he'd be gone... but it didn't make the sadness I felt any easier to bear. He'd faced every new diagnosis stoically... but now the brave face was gone.

Right from the very first minute I met him, Tommy was the hardest bloke I knew both mentally and physically... something that never changed. In his prime, nothing fazed him... but those days seemed distant now. The cancer, like untreated rust eating away at the chrome on a classic car, was corroding not only his body but his spirit as well.

*****

The night Tommy had told me about his terminal diagnosis, I'd laid in bed wondering what is was he wanted my specific help with. Some kind of bucket list maybe?

As sleep enveloped me, I was envisioning he had some grand plan that involved getting him to Pizzo Calabro one last time. A filmic final sojourn at Villino Lo Zaffiro where he could sit out on the sun-drenched olive-grove-bordered terrace every morning and breakfast on Eggs Purgatorio before taking a barefoot walk across the pearlescent white sand beach to the water's edge there to gaze out across the azure expanse of the Tyrrhenian Sea that mirrored the cloudless blue sky above it.

Heavenly and serene... I got that completely. I wanted to see it for myself, to understand better what it was about the place that my friend loved so much.

I've been to Italy so many times in my life I've almost lost track. Big city trips have had a Chelsea-in-the-Champions-League flavour to them. Cultural attractions ticked off, Milan, Rome, Turin and Naples evoke plenty of special memories like Dennis Wise scoring that song-inspiring late equaliser in the famous 1-1 San Siro draw against AC Milan (26 October 1999). The Blues rampaging 4-0 win over Lazio (4 November 2003, *Hello Hello Hernan Crespo*, Eidur Gudjohnsen, Damien Duff, Frank Lampard) in Rome's Stadio Olimpico was an unexpected blast.

A trip to Turin to see Chelsea play Juventus (10 March 2009, 2-2, Michael Essien, Didier Drogba) was made more memorable because we stayed in the Hotel Lingotto, a part of an old FIAT car factory that still had access to the rooftop race track which featured in the classic film *The Italian Job.* We were given a tour by a friendly waiter and spent the rest of the trip singing *this is the self preservation society.*

Chelsea losing 3-1 to Napoli in the cavernous and crumbling Stadio San Paolo (21 February 2012, Juan Mata) was a disaster from a football perspective, though the adverse result did contribute massively to the sacking of then manager Andre Villas-Boas... and we all know what happened next.

Naples was the furthest south I'd ever ventured in Italy, seaside holidays to the country had always been further north and been largely dictated location-wise by where 'la famiglia' were staying. Senigallia and San Benedetto del Tronto on the western Adriatic coast had been popular during my younger years, and when I was older my Aunt, Zia Luisa, acquired a flat in San Remo in the north-west Liguria region which was extremely easy to reach thanks to the availability of cheap and frequent two-hour flights to Nice in southern France and a meraviglifuckingoso 40-mile train journey along the coast skirting Monaco and crossing the France / Italy border which was roughly half way.

All three seaside towns had a 'dolce vita', sweet life, aspect to them that conjured up immediately those sun, sea and sand images I'd pictured for Tommy's Calabrian haven at Villino Lo Zaffiro.

The big question that suddenly started troubling me was how could we get there? It was too risky to fly, and going by boat was impractical, that left driving or getting a train or a combination of both. I quite liked the idea of a Trans-Europe Express-style rattler journey, but the more I thought about it the less practical it became. Tommy's emphysema had already made his breathing progressively difficult and restricted his ability to walk more than a few feet without having to sit down and he was steadfastly refusing to use a wheelchair meaning negotiating railway stations would be an ordeal. Then there was all his medication to carry, that would need a suitcase on its own. If we were going to go to southern Italy it would have to be by road.

It was 1500 miles door-to-door from our manor Cheam, on the

Surrey fringe of South London, to Pizzo. I knew that because Tommy had told me often enough about how quick he could get there. What a shame we couldn't take the three-hour flight from Gatwick, which was 30 minutes away, to Lamezia Terme which was only 20 miles or so from Pizzo. That said, with the right preparation and vehicle, the long drive could be a pleasant, sightseeing adventure. I'd speak to Square Tony about renting a motorhome. Tony was the local fixer when it came to cars. One less thing to worry about... however, the thought suddenly occurred to me about some kind of medical emergency occurring en-route. Anything could happen, and obviously there was no way Tommy was insurable.

I sensed for the first time that silver screen fantasy was creeping into my plan. Tommy could be that cinematic hero. One last hurrah, but this wasn't a time for heroes... common sense was needed. I'd call a medical employment agency about hiring a nurse to travel with us... that was a sensible idea. Why not?

As I drifted off to sleep, I considered writing everything down before my memory lapsed... I didn't, partly because I thought it might end up reading like the synopsis of a film script, but in the main because it suddenly dawned on me that I was making a big assumption that getting to Pizzo was what Tommy wanted my assistance with.

*****

'I've always fancied writing a memoir...' Tommy said, pausing for effect to gauge my reaction and grinning as I raised my eyebrows in surprise and clasped my hands behind my head.

'What did you think I wanted your help with?' he continued. 'Driving me to Pizzo for one last hurrah?'

I laughed out loud at this point and told Tommy that for the past couple of days since I'd last seen him I'd been thinking about what it was he wanted me to help him with and that's exactly what I'd presumed.'

Tommy laughed too, which was just as well. 'I did think about it, but not for long,' he said eventually, cracking the knuckles of each of the fingers of his left hand slowly and deliberately. 'It's a nice idea but not practical... the journey would be too stressful... and... well you know the rest.'

My brow furrowed as I nodded and then looked down at the floor to avoid eye contact. 'I'm really sorry mate,' was all I could think of to say.

'Don't be,' replied Tommy in an upbeat manner that surprised me. 'Now listen. I've wanted to ask you for a while if you'd be interested in writing up an absorbing tale I've got to tell. It's set around the time Chelsea first won the FA Cup. Maybe you could include it in a future book you write?'

Tommy's voice lost its croakiness as he spoke. He appeared instantly bolstered by the prospect of having something to focus on that was important to him. I didn't think twice about it. This project might provide him with a positive diversion off the negative psychological road he was travelling along which had to be a good thing.

Like all football supporters, young and old, Tommy had never been short of a story to tell about games, places and faces and everything in between... all of them normally embraced his other love, music. But these were snippets generally related to whatever was happening at a present moment in time.

The 1969/70 season he was referring to would be fascinating, well it would be to me at least, because obviously it was the period when I'd taken to the Blues and football in general though had yet to go to a game.

The 1970 FA Cup Final at Wembley between Chelsea and Leeds United was the first match I recall watching in its entirety 'live' on television and on a colour set as well. The father of a friend at school owned a chemist's shop and he invited a few of us round to his house for the whole day.

The coverage was brilliant. *Cup Final Grandstand* on the BBC started at 11.45 a.m. and was introduced by David Coleman. Frank Bough and Barry Davies did outside broadcasts at the team hotels with features on all the star players. Joe Mercer, Manchester City manager at that time, and Brian Clough who was the Derby County gaffer, provided expert analysis while Kenneth 'they think it's all over' Wolstenholme was the match commentator. I'm certain I never averted my eyes from the screen for six hours. The match and everything that went with it was totally enthralling.

I've often thought back to that day whenever the game crops up in a discussion and I'd heard Tommy talk about it... but not in the kind of granular detail that maybe he was going to treat me to as he told his story.

As a kid you're often curious about what it's like to be an adult and as an adult you're often curious about what it would have been like to be an adult in a different time and place. Now, half a century later, I was going to have my curiosity appeased and, far more importantly, help Tommy on his journey.

FRIENDS FOR LIFE
Friday 3 December 1976

It might seem an exaggeration, but I've always felt I owed my life to Tommy Walker. A chance first meeting that turned out to be very lucky for me as it happened.

3 December 1976 My mother and father were living apart and I was staying at mother's house near Manchester. As the journey wasn't too far, I decided to go and watch Chelsea playing away at Sheffield United. This was prime *Eddie McCreadie's Blue and White Army* time.

A youthful side, fashioned by legendary tough-tackling former Blues full-back turned manager Eddie Mac and followed around the country by a legion of feral kids just like me. Eddie's team were top of Division Two. They call it 'The Championship' now which makes it sound elitist. I think those who've experienced supporting Chelsea outside the top-flight refer to 'The Championship' as 'the old Second Division' or words to that effect. It avoids doubt. Division Two = not good enough to play at the top level though this didn't seem to matter back then to be honest.

Every other weekend presented a chance for new adventures and there were plenty had. With my father living 'down south' and my mother 'up north' (where I spent most of my time at this period of my life) there were lots of opportunities to 'travel'. From my mother's house it was easy to get to Division Two strongholds like Oldham, Burnley, Bolton, Blackburn and Blackpool. The latter, a couple of months previously, being the place where I'd lost my virginity! Not inside Bloomfield Road I hasten to add, but the Friday night before the Blues 1-0 victory over the Seasiders (25 September, Steve Finnieston).

Getting lucky in Blackpool whetted my appetite for the possibilities that Sheffield might offer because the Blues game against the Blades was scheduled for a Friday night. It was much less of a ball-ache getting from Lancashire to Yorkshire than it was from the Capital to the Steel City which is where the majority of travelling Chelsea supporters would be heading to Bramall Lane from.

At that time, Friday night football was a novelty… however looking back now it was an early taste of the awkwardness that has become an unwanted part of watching football in the 21st-century when selfish television company schedules regularly take zero account of the hardship match-going supporters endure following their team many miles away from home. Absenteeism from school or work comes at a price… as does the increased cost of weekday public transport.

I hadn't attended Chelsea's last away game at Nottingham Forest (20 November), but I'd read about what happened in and around the City Ground. The match, a 1-1 draw (Ian Britton), was made a sideshow by fierce fighting on the terraces between rival fans before and shortly after kick-off which spilled onto the pitch and forced referee Denis Turner to take the players off for a few minutes while order was restored. 26 arrests made on the day presented a familiar statistic to underline the lawlessness associated with football in the 1970s and with Chelsea's 'enthusiastic' away following growing week-by-week, seeking safety in numbers was a good code to follow for youngsters 'flying solo' like me.

Trouble was lurking on every street corner of every town. Smaller gangs, knowing they stood no chance in a skirmish with a large group of Chelsea supporters, looked out for stragglers and without provocation you could find yourself on the floor getting a boot wrapped around your head.

A popular Shed anthem of the day relayed a story about *the dark back streets of Liverpool, where the Mile End's never been...* there should have been one about the dark back streets of Sheffield, like the one I mistakenly found myself on an hour or so before the 7.30 p.m. kick-off.

If it hadn't been so perishingly cold, I might have waited at Sheffield railway station for the football special to arrive from London... that was my normal modus operandi, but having got an early rattler and arrived at 5 p.m. distinctly under-dressed for the Baltic conditions, I decided to walk to the ground which was less than a mile away and call into the first half-decent-looking café I passed on the way. A few minutes later, I'd found myself a tidy seat in an authentic greasy spoon next door to a post office on Shoreham Street.

Perfect! I wasn't going to get lost or risk my allegiance getting found out if I had to ask for directions to the ground as I could see the floodlight pylons that towered over Bramall Lane clearly out of the café window. Feeling relaxed, I got stuck into a piping-hot plate of double sausage, egg, chips and beans lashed with a massive dollop of HP Sauce... pausing occasionally to cool my mouth with a sip from a can of Tizer 'the appetizer'.

*****

Writing this now makes me think of a nostalgic conversation I had with Tommy last year about the mesmerising yet stark beauty of floodlight pylons and how disappointing their steady loss from the football landscape was as stadia were redeveloped into template-designed bowls with lighting built into the stand roofs.

In the days before you had *Google Maps* on your mobile phone to guide you to a chosen destination, floodlights were the shining beacons that led away fans to unfamiliar grounds on many a dark night like the one I experienced in Sheffield.

Coincidentally, in 1878, Bramall Lane had been the first ground to experiment with artificial lighting when it staged an exhibition match between two teams composed of leading players of the Sheffield Football Association.

A curious crowd of 12,000 turned up, and the following day *The Times* reported that the 'brilliancy of the light dazzled the players and sometimes caused strange blunders.' Now there's an excuse that current Liverpool manager Jurgen Klopp, who has variously blamed the wind, snow, a dry pitch and TV broadcasters for the Reds occasional high-profile blips under his stewardship, could add to his evolving repertoire.

'Salah was blinded by the light!'

*****

This was my first time at Bramall Lane and what I wasn't aware of was the fact that the big stand I could see out of the café window was The Kop end which housed Sheffield United supporters... away fans were penned at the opposite end of the ground meaning I'd made a fundamental error which only became apparent when I finished my scoff and decided to make a move.

I crossed the road and saw a huge painted sign which read:

HOME SUPPORTERS ONLY

Fair enough. Keep your head down, don't speak to anyone and walk round the ground. Easier said than done as I was about to find out.

'Nah then. Where art gooin lad?' asked the brick-wall-chested, claw-hammer-faced police constable stood in front of me in an accent so abrasive it could have mined a seam of Yorkshire coal all on its own.

'The visitors section,' I replied nervously.

'Visitor eh lad... Chelsea bastard ere fort agro art thee?'

I shook my head sheepishly. The policeman drew his truncheon and pointed at the far end of the road. 'Go darn theer,' he said to me, smirking as he spoke.

I should've known better. I walked up to the roundabout at the end of Shoreham Street and turned into John Street which skirted the north side of the ground and that's when it happened. I fell for the oldest trick in the football hooligan book.

'Ay-up cock. D'y know what time it is?' Suddenly blocking my way were five lads, probably around 18 or 19-years old. They were all wearing donkey jackets and had red, white and black bar scarves knotted around their necks.

'About half six,' I replied, realising two things immediately. Firstly, my accent was a giveaway to not being a local, and secondly, and of far greater concern, I was probably fucked!

'Blade or Blue?' As he growled his question at me, the gang's cadaverous-looking ringleader closed in on me.

'B-B-Blade,' I replied, stammering nervously and stepping back while wondering what was going to happen next. The low gate of the house we were in front of prevented any further retreat.

'Oose our goalie then?' asked one of the other lads, slowly and deliberately in a sneering tone of voice.

If only I'd bought a match programme before going in the café instead of at the turnstiles, I would have studiously read it cover-to-cover as I tended to do at that age. Of course I would have seen the Sheffield United team listed for the game and subconsciously noted their goalie was called Jim Brown. It might have bought me a little more time. Precious time to figure a way out of my situation, or some kind of divine intervention to take place, which would save me from getting a good hiding.

'Right you lot, on your way or I'll nick you.'

I couldn't believe my luck, or so I thought. In the sodium glow of a nearby street lamp, I caught sight of the burly policeman I'd encountered minutes earlier. As the Sheffield gang made off hastily, I felt relief wash over me... it was short-lived.

A truncheon-whack to the side of my head knocked me to the icy paving stones and then a highly-polished pair of black Dr. Martens boots came flying in. I curled up in a ball, instinctively protecting the precious collection of soft dangly objects between my legs that I'd recently found a new use for. Time stood still. It felt like I was taking a beating for hours, but it was a matter of seconds. My life swam around me and as the white lights of unconsciousness were sparkling brighter... suddenly it stopped.

'Leave the kid alone you nonce.'

I looked up from the floor and saw a man in his late twenties dragging the policeman off me. There was a flurry of punches and the flesh, bone and gristle-scrunching sound of a forehead meeting the bridge of a nose.

I rolled myself clear and noticed blood seeping down my left arm. While going to ground, I'd crashed through a couple of panes of glass that were propped up against the low gate I'd bounced off. As I tried to process what had just happened and how much worse my situation might have got, I was pulled to my feet by a tall, sharp-dressed, blonde-haired man with piercing blue eyes.

'You Chelsea then?' he asked, beckoning two other men who were stood nearby to come over.

He spoke with a London accent so I felt safe to say 'yes'. I patted myself down checking for any other blood injuries and winced as finally I touched the side of my head and the bruise that was forming where I'd been truncheoned.

'The filth are horrible up here son, you should be more careful.'

I nodded and looked at the policeman lying prone on the floor where I had just been.

'What's your name son?'

'Mark.'

'I'm Tommy and this is Rick... and this is Keith.'

Only now did I realise that my saviour wasn't alone. I looked at each of one them in turn. From top-to-toe they oozed Capital style. A Friday night in Sheffield watching Chelsea though... why the smart attire?

Tommy was wearing a black, three-quarter-length leather trench coat. Rick, whose brown hair was styled with a centre-parting like Steve Marriot sported in his Mod heyday fronting iconic 1960s rock group the Small Faces, wore a sheepskin jacket over a blue roll-neck jumper and Keith, whose skinhead-cropped sandy hair gave him a harder look, was wearing a dark blue gabardine-style mac over what looked like a suit complete with shirt and tie. All three had identical oxblood leather brogues on their feet. There was no point using flowery language to describe their collective appearance... they looked the absolute dogs bollocks. Fucking Chelsea! Yes!

'We'd better get going. He'll be properly conscious again soon and calling for reinforcements,' said Tommy, pointing at the policeman before rubbing his hands together and blowing on them. 'No doubt tell his mates he took on this lot,' he continued, pointing at a group of at least twenty men who were marching past us, four-abreast, military-style.

'The North Stand mob,' said Rick, raising hand to his head and saluting them.

'The fucking terrace SAS,' added Keith, laughing as the men continued on their way in silence. 'Let's fall in behind 'em. Come on, hup-two-three-four.'

The three men laughed, but I didn't understand the humour in what Keith was saying... and then suddenly I started shivering uncontrollably as the adrenalin that had been coursing through my system ebbed.

'I've been cut,' I mumbled, taking my coat off as we followed the North Stand mob down the street.

Tommy quickly examined my injury... decided I'd live, and advised the wound would need stitching... but not today unless I wanted to miss the game and worse still end up being stranded in a hospital waiting room for hours on end.

Fortunately, there was a St. John's Ambulance parked near to the entrance turnstiles. Rather than attract unwanted attention, Keith went and got some bandages and plasters and once we were in the ground Rick swiftly patched me up. The temperature had dropped again, now it wasn't just cold, it was bastard cold. I think it acted like an anaesthetic.

We stood right at the back of the terrace. Tommy had already suggested I stick with them in case the police came looking for further trouble. I felt a little nauseous and I knew my whole body was going to hurt in the morning but fuck it... as the players ran out onto the pitch and a huge cheer went up, there was only one thing on my mind right now.

Come on Chelsea! Come on Chelsea!

It may have been a Friday night... but that hadn't deterred Chelsea supporters from travelling in numbers and making themselves heard. Every Blues player had his name chanted. With the exception of veteran goalkeeper Peter Bonetti, now 36-years old, and 28-year old midfielder David Hay, Eddie McCreadie's team were a young bunch in their early 20s, the majority of whom had come through the youth ranks at Stamford Bridge. This was something the fans greatly appreciated even though it was largely due to the austere circumstances the club found itself in at that time.

The match itself was a shabby affair with conditions not at all suited to Chelsea's swift passing game. The icy pitch was both challenging and treacherous and Sheffield United as a team were mixing it in the tackle and being largely allowed to get away with murder by referee Brian Martin who was already having his parentage questioned in song by Blues fans long before the 65th minute when he disallowed an Ian Britton goal. It seemed harsh. Ray Wilkins, who'd provided the cross for Britton, was penalised for allegedly fouling Blades goalie Jim Brown... Jim Brown... Jim bloody Brown. If only I'd known his name earlier.

I told Tommy, Keith and Rick about my encounter with the Sheffield mob who'd tested my knowledge of the team I'd tried to pretend I supported and winced as their laughter made me laugh and my ribs that had taken a kicking began to ache... and then ache some more.

To make matters worse, a few minutes later, the home side went in front. Ray's slightly older brother Graham lost control of the ball trying to make a clearance under pressure in Chelsea's 18-yard box and United skipper Alan Woodward went to ground as he slipped past him. *Penalty!*

Referee Martin had no hesitation in pointing to the spot and by way of a cruel irony, up stepped a former Blues player in the shape of Ian 'Chico' Hamilton to make it 1-0.

Second Division
Sheffield United 1 Chelsea 0
Bramall Lane
Attendance: 23,393
Referee: Brian Martin

Chelsea: Peter Bonetti, Gary Locke, Graham Wilkins, Gary Stanley, Steve Wicks, David Hay, Ian Britton, Ray Wilkins, Steve Finnieston, Ray Lewington, Ken Swain.

Sheffield United: Brown, Franks, Garner, Longhorn, Colquhoun, Kenworthy, Woodward, Edwards, Guthrie, Hamson, Hamilton.
Scorer: Hamilton 68 (pen).

Tommy told me that Chico was the youngest player ever to feature for the Blues. 'He wasn't much older than you are now son. 16 years and 138 days old. Scored on his debut against Tottenham in a 1-1 draw at

White Hart Lane (18 March 1967). He'd come through the youth ranks and I swear I thought we'd found another Jimmy Greaves... and guess who put Spurs ahead in that game... yeah, Jimmy Greaves. We should never have sold Greavsie and maybe Chico too... he wanted that goal just now didn't he.'

I was impressed by Tommy's knowledge of Chelsea. He went on to tell me that Chico didn't live up to his early promise and was soon sold to Southend United before going onto play for Aston Villa for a few years and then signing for Sheffield United. Tommy also told me that the Chico nickname came about because he shared his surname with a famous jazz drummer called Chico Hamilton!

Chelsea laboured as the game went on and in the end could have no real complaints about the 1-0 defeat, although Blues fans saw it differently and continued to berate the ref with a chant that suggested he pleasured himself frequently.

That whole *the referee's a wanker* thing really made me laugh. I mean, shouting at people and calling them a wanker in a derogatory way. The inference being that if you were a wanker you were... well a wanker. Now I'm not about to go into details about my wanking habits, but I was a teenager. What a cheap hobby wanking was back then. Such pleasure to be had from self-gratification... and yet we all pretended we didn't do it... for fear of being called a wanker. Priceless!

In the closing minutes of the game, both sets of supporters traded *you're going to get your fucking heads kicked in* chants with the Sheffield fans at the opposite side of the ground also singing *it's a long way to the station* and *we'll see you all outside*.

Concern shrouded me as I contemplated what might be in store next. Maybe I was feeling that little bit edgier after my pre-match ordeal than I would have done normally as songs threatening violence were par for the course at this time... every club had fans who sang them, even Fulham! Alongside this, thoughts of getting lucky like I had in Blackpool had been kicked out of me. Now I was hurting, and I just wanted to get to my mother's house, get my head down and go to sleep... and, having mentioned it previously, wanking certainly wasn't an option that entered my head.

There was no urgency on the part of Tommy and his friends to leave the ground. Eventually, we sauntered out and they explained they had driven to Sheffield as they were en-route to Leeds where they were going to stay for the weekend as some friends of theirs were playing a gig at the Polytechnic on Monday.

I didn't have the presence of mind to ask who? I would have done so if I was thinking straight and, oh my God, looking back now, I would have walked to bloody Yorkshire barefoot over hot coals to join them if I'd known... but I didn't find out until the next time I ran into Tommy.

Right then, I just wanted to get home. It had been my luck that they had parked up in Charlotte Road not far from where I'd got into trouble and my good fortune continued because they offered to give me a lift to the railway station which I gratefully accepted.

Tommy had written down his telephone number on the back of my programme and told me to ring him over Christmas as I was hoping to get to the Chelsea / Fulham game at Stamford Bridge on 27 December (2-0, Micky Droy, Ken Swain). Unfortunately, I mislaid the bloody thing... for almost 40 years! I found it when sifting though a pile of old copies of long-defunct music paper *Sounds* when I was doing some general research for the *Eddie Mac Eddie Mac* book I co-wrote with David Johnstone, Kelvin Barker, Mark Meehan and Neil Smith.

Finding the programme all those years later immediately made me think of that night in Sheffield and what might have happened to me if Tommy, Keith and Rick hadn't been on hand to rescue me from a beating worse than the one I received. Then there's the scar on my left arm that has stayed with me, never fading... like an indelible tattoo. I used it like a badge of honour, rolling up my left sleeve was my party piece during the time when football discussions were as much about hooliganism and police brutality as they were about the game.

Things are a lot different now. On social media, today's Chelsea youngsters jokily and sometimes spitefully refer to older Blues fans as 'yer das'... walking, talking anachronisms who drink too much and live in the past. Is that so bad?

The *PlayStation* generation seem to have an unhealthy, almost perverted, obsession with statistics. Debating pre-assists, assists, completed passes, heat-maps, expected goals, sequences and possession percentages seems to be their thing. Some of those stats are interesting, but when I see tables drawn up saying Liverpool would have won the 2019 Premier League title ahead of Manchester City if it had been determined by their xG (expected goals projection) it makes me laugh out loud.

Each to their own though, what I will say is that one day, the current youthful crop will be 'yer das' themselves... what then? Time catches up with everyone.

*****

The next occasion I encountered Tommy wasn't at Chelsea, it was purely by chance almost nine years later at a gig. Football and music, music and football. Working class popular culture intertwined a lot more in the '60s, '70s, '80s and '90s than it seems to have done since the turn of the century... but maybe that's just an age thing on my part?

A newish group, The Godfathers, the reincarnation of a band called The Sid Presley Experience who I used to enjoy watching live, were playing at legendary music venue the Marquee Club (90 Wardour Street: sited at this location from 1964 to 1988 – currently residential use) in the heart of London's Soho.

It was a Tuesday night (9 September 1986), and the venue wasn't that busy. I walked up to the bar, and stood there having a drink and a smoke was Tommy Walker. I recognised him straight away. Tall, lean, dressed in black, and with a retro bowl haircut that oozed the type of Mod cool that I aspired to but couldn't match. He looked me up and down as I called out his name.

'I thought you were going to ring me,' he said, shaking my hand and laughing as I told him I'd lost the Sheffield United programme that he'd written his telephone number on. For several seasons after, I'd looked out for him at every Chelsea game I'd been to since that Friday night match.

Tommy said he'd had a break from going to football as he'd had a family issue to deal with for several years and also Keith and Rick had settled down into the wife and kids family routine and had less appetite for it.

We agreed the beauty about Stamford Bridge was that it was always there... and, when circumstances allowed, you could go and watch the Blues whenever you wanted.

By now, I was living and working in London and following Chelsea was a massive part of my routine. The Club had won promotion at the end of that season when I'd first met Tommy, but sadly manager Eddie McCreadie left his position and success was short-lived with relegation back to the second tier coming in 1979.

Come along, come along, come along and sing this song... we're the boys in Blue, Division Two and we won't be here for long was sung enthusiastically for five long seasons and the song might have had to be rewritten slightly had it not been for Clive Walker scoring the only goal of the game for Chelsea away at Bolton Wanderers (7 May 1983), a victory which proved pivotal in preventing relegation to the Third Division for the first time in the Club's history. *Boys in Blue, Division Three* didn't rhyme anyway, so Walker's goal brought an added bonus.

A month prior to this (2 April), Ken Bates bought debt-ridden Chelsea for £1 thereby ending a 77-year connection with the Mears' family who had founded the Club. Bates traded well in the transfer market and gave then manager John Neal the backing he needed to succeed and the following season an upswing in form and fortune saw the Blues win promotion as Division Two champions.

Despite Chelsea being back in the top-flight, Stamford Bridge was a football ground in disrepair and The Shed terrace a disintegrating, weed-encroached ruin whose roof had more holes in it than a cheese grater. It didn't bother me personally, because apart from that one time I'd sat with my father in the East Stand posh seats and several thrill-seeking 'transfers' to the concrete benches in the West Stand, I stood on The Shed and I bloody loved everything about it.

I recall coming up with the title for Tim Rolls' book *Stamford Bridge Is Falling Down* which tells the story behind the swift decline in Chelsea's fortunes in the early 1970s. From a stadium perspective, it was equally apt for the 1980s and into 1990s when Ken Bates' Chelsea Village development got underway... and even then it didn't stop visiting West Ham fans singing *Stamford Bridge is falling down, falling down, falling down. Stamford Bridge is falling down... poor old Chelsea.* That always made me laugh because the Hammers precious Boleyn Ground was hardly Buckingham Palace now was it. Oddly enough, since their move to the London Stadium, West Ham fans have resurrected the song... Chelsea's witty riposte to this being *You're not West Ham anymore.*

'What are you doing here then?' Tommy asked me, motioning the barman to set up a couple of Jack Daniel's shots as he spoke.

I told him about my interest in the Godfathers and music in general. 'How about you?' I asked, before downing the JD and grimacing as the fiery liquid coursed down my throat.

Tommy smiled as he listened to me witter on a bit about glam rock and punk rock and then without saying anything he necked his JD back and instructed the barman to pour two more shots. He then asked me if I remembered why he and his friends were going up to Leeds after the Sheffield game all those years ago. '

'You were going to a gig, but I can't remember who you said was playing,' I said, after quickly racking my brains without success.

'You never asked,' replied Tommy, sliding another JD across the bar to me. 'I thought you weren't interested.'

I shrugged my shoulders and felt a bit embarrassed. 'I would have been, but it had come on top for me a bit that night.'

Tommy laughed. 'Don't worry son, I never gave it a second thought.'

'Who was it then?'

'Well if you're clued up on punk... do you remember what happened on 1 December 1976?'

'Yeah. That was when the Sex Pistols guested live on ITV's *Today* programme and Bill challenged Steve Jones to say something outrageous and Steve said "what a fucking rotter" which upset quite a few people but catapulted punk into the mainstream overnight.'

Tommy nodded. 'Yeah, exactly that, and a couple of days later the Pistols were due to start a UK tour...'

I couldn't stop myself interrupting. 'The Friday Chelsea played away at Sheffield United!'

Tommy nodded again.

I continued. 'Promoters shat themselves and loads of the gigs were cancelled.'

Again Tommy nodded. 'Spot on. The first show they ended up doing was at Leeds Poly which was on the Monday. That was the gig we were going to. The Sex Pistols supported by The Clash, The Damned and Johnny Thunders and The Heartbreakers.'

I looked at Tommy and then at the JD on the bar... I picked up the glass and downed the shot in one go and asked the barman for two more. Purely by coincidence the Marquee disc jockey played the Pistols track *Did You No Wrong* which was the flip side of the band's 'controversial' hit *God Save The Queen.* I told Tommy I thought *Did You No Wrong* was the better song of the two and he agreed, going further by saying he thought it was their best effort of what ended up being a very short back catalogue.

Our conversation flowed... and so did the Jack Daniels. Tommy told me about that Leeds gig and how he'd got to know Sex Pistols manager Malcolm McClaren several years before he became seriously involved in the music business.

Back in mid-1971, McClaren was selling vintage rock and roll records at a boutique called Paradise Garage located at 430 King's Road, Chelsea, close to where Tommy said he worked at that time. The pair had been on nodding terms for a while before striking up a friendship in a nearby café called the Regent where Malcolm had spotted Tommy reading the sleeve notes on the back cover of the eruptive, self-titled debut album by the New York Dolls which he'd just purchased an import copy of from the Berwick Street Market branch of Harlequin Records. (Harlequin disappeared as a high street brand in the 1980s when the chain was acquired by the also long-defunct Our Price record shop empire.)

Malcolm asked Tommy what he liked about the band and he'd told him it was a combination of their trashy look and attitude. They were like an X-rated, transvestite version of the Rolling Stones and he'd been hooked by their performance on the legendary BBC TV music show the *Old Grey Whistle Test* (27 November 1973) when the Dolls performed *Looking for A Kiss* and *Jet Boy.*

Tommy was both surprised and impressed to learn that McClaren and his partner at that time, fashion designer Vivienne Westwood, had kitted out the band with some clobber from their *Let It Rock* clothing line that shared its name with the shop at 430 King's Road which they had swiftly taken over the lease and rebranded.

In 1972, Let It Rock metamorphosed into Too Fast To Live Too Young To Die then, in 1974, SEX, before a major revamp in December 1976 brought with it a change in moniker to Seditionaries. *Clothes For Heroes* was the marketing strap-line, but the punk look wasn't Tommy's style at all and he said Malcolm respected him for that.

'You have to be true to what you believe in Tommy.' Ha ha! That was funny, given the constant changes at 430. Maybe Malcolm was trying to find something to believe in and the New York Dolls gave him an appetite for what was possible when he sojourned in the United States and managed them briefly early on in 1975.

The next time Tommy saw Malcolm down the King's Road was later that year and this is when he learned about his next big project, the Sex Pistols. The band already featured one of his shop assistants at SEX, bassist Glen Matlock, and a couple of young vagabonds who were punters, guitarist Steve Jones and drummer Paul Cook, who also happened to be Chelsea supporters. The line-up that initially shocked the nation was completed when another SEX customer, John Lydon aka Johnny Rotten, a scrawny urchin with bad teeth and dyed orange hair grabbed Malcolm's attention. It mattered little that Lydon sounded like a cat being strangled during his audition which comprised 'singing' *I'm Eighteen* by Alice Cooper... he looked the part, the rest would follow and it did.

Tommy was invited along to one of the band's early gigs dragging Keith and Rick along for good measure. They appreciated the raw energy of the lads who reminded them of their favourite band The Who in their formative years. The Pistols couldn't match The Who for musicianship, but it was clear they had something about them, clearer still to Tommy when they'd created a real buzz right here at the Marquee when supporting Eddie & The Hot Rods at that gig (12 February 1976).

In the midst of Tommy concluding his story about the Pistols, The Godfathers atmospheric intro music, the theme from cult '60s TV show *The Persuaders*, began piping out of the Marquee's PA system.

What great timing and what a great story. I chinked glasses with him and then he asked me if I was going to Spurs on Saturday?

'Yes,' I replied. 'Are you?'

Tommy nodded, and as vocalist Peter Coyne led the gangster-chic-attired band out onto the stage we agreed to meet for a drink in Victoria near the station first and then get the tube up to Seven Sisters.

'If we get split up, make sure you know who the Spurs goalie is beforehand son... just in case,' joked Tommy. We both had a good laugh at that, at which point The Godfathers launched into their set with the still-visceral, twin-guitar-power-chord-crunching track *I Want Everything*.

Coyne's stripped-back, snarling singing style suggested his vocal cords might not endure and yet well over thirty years later he's still treading the boards and malevolently advising the audience in front of him that he wants it all. The band have been through a number of incarnations, but they still know how to rock and over time I got to know Mr Coyne who kindly allowed me to reproduce the lyrics to The Godfathers classic *This Damn Nation* in my novel *This Damnation* in which the group also feature.

Chelsea beat Tottenham 3-1 (13 September 1986) with former Spurs hero Micky Hazard netting twice for the Blues and Kerry Dixon also getting on the score sheet. Quirkily, the result would have upset Peter Coyne as he later disclosed to me he was a fan of the Lilywhites... but we've never let football rivalry get in the way of our friendship.

Victory at White Hart Lane eased the pressure on then manager John Hollins, a very popular former Chelsea player who had succeeded John Neal the previous summer and had a decent first season as Blues boss but was finding his second campaign in charge a chore.

The previous weekend (6 September), the Stamford Bridge faithful had been treated to a 3-1 home defeat at the hands of 'mighty' Luton Town. The low attendance, 13,040, reflected the general mood of dissatisfaction among fans who were left even more disgruntled when Chelsea fell apart after Kerry Dixon had opened the scoring in the 30th minute.

The Hatters defeat sent the Blues spiralling to 19th position in the First Division table and was the start of a maddening sequence of games that underlined the glorious unpredictability associated with Chelsea Football Club. Having bounced back against Spurs, the following weekend (20 September) at the Bridge, Hollins' side were battered 6-2 by Nottingham Forest. Ridiculously, Chelsea had been 2-1 up after 10 minutes thanks to goals from Pat Nevin and Johnny Bumstead.

It got worse. Three days later came an embarrassing 1-0 defeat in the First Leg of a Second Round League Cup tie with Third Division side York City at Bootham Crescent.

As a consequence, nobody gave Chelsea a hope in hell in their next game away to Manchester United (28 September), but King Kerry scored in the second minute and, thanks to goalkeeper Tony Godden miraculously saving two penalties, the Blues held out for a much-needed victory.

Surely this was the turning point? No, of course it wasn't. 4 October and back at the Bridge, Chelsea lost 1-0 to Charlton Athletic. I could go on, but I think you get the picture. I didn't go to the York game, but went to Old Trafford with Tommy and for a good few years after this we went to many games together.

The Finborough Arms on Finborough Road, a short stroll from Earls Court underground station and Stamford Bridge, was our drinker of choice for home games back then. The Finborough was, and still is, a decent watering hole that surprisingly has survived the long, grinding downturn in the pub trade which has seen so many matchday boozers vanish off the map.

It was here I'd convene with a group of lads, among them Ugly John, Chicken Plucker, Young Dave, Video Vic, Alright Pav, Big Chris, Roger Socks, Baby Gap Brian and Sir Larry who would eventually join me in getting season tickets in Gate 17, the infill section that bridges the Upper Matthew Harding Stand and the East Stand. Today, myself, Dave, Pav, Chris and Rog still sit in the same seats we have done for almost 20 years, and since 2013, when he tragically passed away, we've also kept Sir Larry's season ticket on in his name as a tribute to him.

If anyone ever asks me what it is about football that keeps me going to games I would probably give them a verbal snapshot of this chapter and throw in the line that cocky young Mod, Jimmy Cooper (Chelsea supporter Phil Daniels' character) in the brilliant film *Quadrophenia* blurts out when he's mocked about his unreliable scooter by Rocker, Kevin Herriot, (West Ham fan Ray Winstone). *I mean, it isn't the bikes, is it? It's the people.*

Chelsea Football Club has been the bedrock of numerous lifelong friendships, but the fact the Blues are now a hugely successful world-renown team has little to do with it. As Tommy Walker often said to me, Chelsea is the glue that binds mates together... for richer or poorer, in sickness and in health and every other wedding vow you care to mention... the big difference is... there's never a messy divorce or a secret affair to contend with. We are who we support... 'till death us do part. It amazed me that Tommy would joke about that now... 'what more proof do you need', he said to me. I had no words.

WORLD'S END
Saturday 23 April 1955

Sgt. Pepper's Lonely Hearts Club Band... John, Paul, George and Ringo at their finest, rinsed from the speakers as skewers of sizzling, seasoned swordfish duelled for the affection of my palate with sausages and steak fresh from the counter at Pinegar's butchers in Cheam Village.

70 degrees of balmy September sunshine and the ice-cold Peroni's were slipping down a treat. I shared Tommy's passion for music and I loved the fact he wanted to compile a playlist to accompany the story he was going to tell. It was like a soundtrack to his life... such a sweet idea. I imagined doing the same thing at some point, though I didn't want to contemplate the circumstances. Maybe I'd just do it anyway to relive the memories they evoked.

Editor's note: *Tommy's playlist can be found on page 208*

It was Tommy's idea to have a barbecue at his house to kick-off our writing project. Sat in the garden shaded by an umbrella, his mood, his appetite... and thirst were extraordinary all things considered. It was if the prospect of talking about the past had reversed his body clock... taking the 'miles' off, and the damage.

'The first time I heard *Sgt. Pepper's* was 4 June 1967. The original Summer of Love... I was a few weeks off my 18th birthday,' said Tommy, pausing to gaze wistfully up at the cloudless sky.

I poured my Peroni into a Peroni glass which made Peroni taste even better and sat down. I knew this was going to be good and waited expectantly for Tommy to continue which he did without being prompted.

'I spent a couple of months working 'on the dust' for Westminster Council. It was filthy work emptying bins but there were plenty of perks if you knew where to look and as I was bang into music I always had my minces peeled for bill posters, tickets and promo material discarded by West End pubs, clubs and theatres that put bands on.

The Saville Theatre at 135 Shaftesbury Avenue, it's an Odeon cinema now, always merited extra attention as it had been leased by Beatles manager Brian Epstein and was used as a venue for both plays and rock concerts.

Pink Floyd, The Rolling Stones, The Who, Cream... I saw them all there, blagging in for free thanks largely to what I'd found sorting out rubbish left out for collection.

4 June was a Sunday and I was down at the front of the stalls at the Saville to see Jimi Hendrix playing with the Experience. They always had a few groups on the bill. That night it was Denny Laine's Electric String Band, The Chiffons and Procol Harum, but it was Hendrix that everyone wanted to see.

Now as it happened, The Beatles had released their eighth studio album *Sgt. Pepper's Lonely Hearts Club Band* on the Thursday and I'd yet to hear the title track… not that I was expecting to that night. Back then, you obviously never heard anything that hadn't yet been recorded on the wireless. This was a few months before Radio 1 started broadcasting, so we just had the pirate stations like Caroline and London to listen to… but to be honest I never really had much time for that once I got to 16-years old. I was either out grafting, at the football… or at a gig.

Anyway, at this Hendrix show, Jimi only opened his set with *Sgt. Pepper's*. In a couple of days, he'd learned the track… and now here he was putting his own unique spin on it which blew everyone's minds… including Beatles Paul McCartney and George Harrison who were there along with Eric Clapton and Lulu, who I want to point out right now was a proper darling.'

It made sense that *Purple Haze* by Hendrix was on Tommy's playlist. Find it, play it… listen. We both strummed air guitars, expertly picking out the notes on our imaginary fretboards as the track kicked in.

'Jimi played a white Fender Stratocaster that night and of course he played it with his teeth before smashing it up,' advised Tommy, stopping short of mimicking the guitar legend's more extreme on-stage antics.

'Imagine if Hendrix had been a Chelsea supporter,' I said, more out of wishful thinking than wanting to steer the conversation in the direction of football and the story Tommy had said he wanted to share that was set around the time the Blues first won the FA Cup.

He laughed and nodded. 'Yeah, that would have been cool. Who knows, maybe if he hadn't died young, he'd have got into the game and maybe followed Chelsea as he did used to get down the King's Road.

I used to buy some of my threads from Dandie Fashions at number 161, I never saw Jimi in there but Judy my on-off girlfriend back then worked behind the counter at weekends and saw him a few times. He'd turn up to the after-club parties they held there. It was a pretty wild gaff and he got busted for drugs. Oddly enough, The Beatles bought it the following year and renamed it *Apple Tailoring* though that didn't last long. I think it's an art gallery now.'

Tommy went onto wax lyrical about the clothes of the day and how his personal style evolved. 'The suits were flamboyant and floral prints were everywhere particularly on silk shirts. This was the psychedelic period, the time when the '60s were really swinging. In my early teens when I first became aware of fashion I'd always liked the Mod look especially the suits.

For my 18th birthday I treated myself to a blue pinstriped, double-breasted number with two pockets on the right and four pairs of buttons down the front. If you wanted to get yourself noticed, you had to look sharp. I didn't want to be working on the dust for the rest of my life.'

I asked Tommy about his early years. He was an only child, born to Helen and George Walker on 29 Jun 1949. The family home back then was in Slaidburn Street, Chelsea. Adjacent to the King's Road in an area known locally as the World's End.

Living on Slaidburn (pronounced Slayburn) sounds very grand in the context of today's perception of the London property market, however this now fashionable cul-de-sac where gentrification has pushed house prices above the £2 million mark wasn't always a desirable place to reside.

'It's "one of the worst streets in London" Victorian-era social reformer Charles Booth once proclaimed,' Tommy said, laughing as he told me about his childhood. 'Booth hadn't finished cracking on either. "Drunken, rowdy people who were a constant trouble to the police. Broken patched-up windows, open doors, drink-sodden women," he'd advised. I don't remember it being that rough as a kid or what you might call a slum, but then I didn't know any different... and besides I was very happy.

We had a living room, two bedrooms and a tiny kitchen on the ground floor of the end terrace that housed four families across three storeys. There were communal bathrooms on the first and third floors, and a shared double toilet stall outside. The brick wall that blocked off the end of the street had a football goal painted on it and I'd be out there with the other lads playing at all hours. Games seemed to go on for days. I just joined in when I wanted to. I knew from an early age I wasn't much good though.'

World's End originates from what is now known as The World's End Distillery public house at 459 King's Road. There had been a 'tavern' in the locale since the 17th-century when King Charles II first sought out entertainment there. The evocative name is explained by the fact that during this period, the journey from central London to the 'house of fun' was arduous, the roads and pathways increasingly dangerous to traverse, and the surrounding properties infested with rats and inhabited by the type of people polite society was absolutely terrified of. "This is the world's end," King Charles is said to have snobbishly remarked as he gazed out on the poverty of the surrounds... and the name stayed with the place.

Equally hard to imagine now, but right through Tommy's childhood, World's End was an enclave noted for factories and industry that made use of its southern border frontage with the River Thames. He told me his mother worked at a bottling plant owned by the Watney's brewery which used to be located between Fernshaw Road and Gunter Grove, a couple of streets away from their house. Tommy recalled she used to wear wooden clogs as opposed to shoes as the floor of the plant was always swilling with water. When he played football in the street after school, he'd always hear her before he saw her as she clumped along the pavement.

'Mother always seemed to have her hair in rollers, and my father's face was mostly grimy. He worked at the power station at the river end of nearby Lots Road. We called it the Chelsea Monster. Its chimneys dominated the skyline and belched out smoke morning, noon and night as it generated the electricity required to power London's underground network.'

The Watney's brewery building is now known as Kingsgate House, a residential development where a one-bedroom flat will set you back £1 million. Lots Road Power Station was decommissioned in 2002 and the eight-acre site, renamed Chelsea Waterfront, plays host to landscaped gardens, glass towers, shops, restaurants... and exclusive apartments costing millions of pounds.

Tommy told me he went to Ashburnham School which at that time was located opposite the power station on Upcerne Road at the junction with Lots Road.

'I behaved myself at school,' he said, with a look on his face that expected me to express surprise. 'My father said it was important to show respect to my teachers, especially Miss Nobbs the headmistress... so out of respect to him that's exactly what I did... even though I thought they were all a pretty mean bunch. Cane first and ask questions later. It was standard back then.'

Tommy then explained how Chelsea Football Club first came into his life in his early days at Ashburnham.

'I was five-years old. Ted Drake, the manager at that time, visited the school with goalkeeper Bill Robertson. They said a few words after assembly. I can't remember what exactly, but I do recall telling my father about them that night and him saying that Robertson had been really busy at the weekend picking the ball out of the net five times. He also said lots of people joked about Chelsea being rubbish saying we would never win anything and that the "Ducklings" as Drake's team had been nicknamed by the press waddled and quacked a lot but couldn't play football.

Memories tend to blur a bit at that age, but when I was a little older I figured out by a process of elimination that the game my father was referring to was a 5-6 home defeat to Manchester United (16 October 1954, Seamus O'Connell x3, Jim Lewis, Ken Armstrong). That must have been some game to watch, and the result probably underlined why Drake's team weren't rated. It was a scoreline not too dissimilar to our matches out on Slaidburn Street! That defeat left Chelsea marooned in mid-table in the old First Division and looking a fair bet to maintain their unwanted record of never having won a major trophy since the club was founded in 1905!

Oddly enough, around this time I was told I was old enough to know why I'd been christened Tommy and the fact it was Tommy as opposed to Thomas and that being changed to Tommy as a nickname as it often is. Of course, being only five, I'd never asked and probably never would have to be honest. What's in a name anyway eh... it's just a name... something to get called by.

I was just a kid, but I felt quite pleased when I found out that Tommy was a nod to Tommy Walker, a Scottish international inside-forward who made 105 appearances for Chelsea between September 1946 and December 1948 scoring 24 goals.

My father later said that him and mother had started thinking of boys and girls names as soon as she found out she was pregnant. That was early on in October 1948 and the last Chelsea game my father had been to was against Burnley. A 1-0 win (25 September) in which Tommy Walker had scored the only goal from the penalty spot. Since the family surname was Walker it made good sense... and mother didn't disapprove. The funny thing was, many years on I found out that Tommy Walker had actually been christened Thomas and I pulled my father's leg about that. He replied, saying the other name he'd come up with was Johnnie as in Johnnie Walker the Scotch whisky brand which was his favourite tipple. If I'd been born a girl I would have been named Helen, just like my mother, her mother and her mother before her. Some tradition that... and thankfully it ended there because my mother was an only child just like me.

I know you often hear it said that people who lived in this part of London would religiously go and watch Chelsea one week and Fulham the next, but I wasn't really aware of that when I was a kid. Chelsea were in the First Division and Fulham the Second. My father was a regular at Stamford Bridge... but not so much for the football, he was a betting man and he would go along to the greyhound racing meetings that had been held at the stadium since 1933. I got to know when he'd won a few quid because it would be the only time I'd hear him and my mother rowing. There was a pub at the end of Slaidburn Street called the Wetherby Arms, sadly and un-coincidentally it's a branch of the bookmaker Paddy Power now. When he had money in his pocket, my father found it impossible to walk past the place without going in and emerging three sheets to the wind several hours later. He was a happy drunk though and never raised his fists to my mother when she scolded him.

My interest in music came from my father who was into jazz and blues. Incredibly, the first time I ever saw a band playing live was in the back room of the Wetherby. I would have been around 12-years old then. A group called the Blues Boys, good name eh, some of whom lived in a flat in nearby Edith Grove used to rehearse at the pub. They used to play cover versions. The one that sticks in my mind is *Come On* by Chuck Berry. In 1962 they changed their name to the Rollin' Stones which soon after became The Rolling Stones.

I remember my father used to tell a story that he was drinking in the pub around December 1962 when Bill Wyman came in carrying an expensive-looking amplifier. He wasn't in the group yet, he'd come down to meet Mick Jagger, Keith Richards and Brian Jones and have a jam with them. My father reckoned Wyman could play a bit even then, but the reason he got to join the Stones was because he had a flash amp. In June the following year, The Rolling Stones released their first single... a cover of *Come On*.'

The track of course made Tommy's playlist. I wasn't familiar with it at all, though that's because, similarly to The Beatles, The Rolling Stones early stuff never really chimed with me. Unlike The Beatles who stopped playing live not that long after they started, the Stones are still gigging today though *Come On* hasn't featured in their sets since 1965. It's worth sparing the one minute and 53 seconds it lasts to have a listen mainly because Jagger's fake cockney drawl is all over it... the backbeat though is unrecognisable as the band had yet to hone its unique sound

I asked Tommy about his first experience of watching Chelsea. He told me that by the mid-1950s, the century-old Factory Act of 1850 had long since changed the life of the grafting classes in the World's End. The working week legally ended early on Saturday afternoons and the culture of heading straight to Stamford Bridge to watch football had been ingrained in generations of the same families from 1905 when the Club had been founded and played its first games in the old Second Division.

'My father was taken to his first game at the Bridge as a six-year old in 1926 by my grandfather, Big Paul. Chelsea played South Shields and drew 0-0 (27 February). Sadly, I never met Big Paul. He lost his life fighting for King and Country in Burma in 1943.'

Tommy got up and beckoned me to follow him into the living room of his house where he pointed at three framed black and white photographs hanging on the wall above the fireplace.

'That's Big Paul in the middle wearing his Army uniform,' said Tommy, sighing as he spoke.

I wanted to ask him more about his grandfather, but it didn't feel right especially as he'd never mentioned him before. Instead, I looked at the photos either side of Big Paul's.

'On the left, that's my father George when he was a kid and Big Paul,' continued Tommy, clocking my interest and sighing as he pointed at the photo on the right. 'That's me and my wife Sophia on our wedding day wth my parents and her parents. All of them long gone... waiting for me.'

I studied each face intently and said nothing. It was a peaceful and respectful moment and I wasn't going to break it. I wondered if Tommy was going to talk further about his family. His parents had passed away within a couple of months of each other in 2009 and his wife Sophia succumbed to ovarian cancer aged just 42 a year before I'd become reacquainted with him in 1986. That's why he stopped going to watch Chelsea for a few years. They never had children and he never remarried. I remember years ago him saying she was that she was incomparable... the love of his life, but since that time he'd always closed up and changed the subject if her named cropped up in any conversation he was engaged in.

I think maybe that's why friends, Chelsea and music were so important to Tommy... they were a distraction from the immense sadness of losing Sophia that haunted him. I waited, not saying anything and after a minute or so he shrugged his shoulders, clicked his fingers and walked back out into the garden. I followed him and we sat down again, him back under the umbrella and me in the sunshine... and he settled into telling a fantastic story about the first time he'd seen Chelsea play.

'My father never walked briskly, and so neither did I. It was less than a mile to Stamford Bridge from our house... a 15-minute stroll for my eager almost six-years-old legs... but we took a lot longer to get there... and looking back now I can understand why I hadn't been taken to a game when I was younger, not that I'd been clamouring to go.

Saturday 23rd April 1955... St. George's Day. We left the house at midday, 30 minutes or so after my father had woken up. He'd finished a week of late shifts the night before and had slept in after more than likely having had a few after-hours whiskies at the Wetherby on his way home.

The route? Well we took a right turn at the end of Slaidburn Street onto the King's Road and when we got to Stanley Bridge, my father made me wait outside the antique shop on corner of Wandon Road while he crossed over to the Nell Gwynne public house (currently known as The Jam Tree) which took its name from King Charles II mistress, the lady who it's said encouraged him to have the King's Road built.

This, as I would come to learn was a regular routine. My father wasn't having a quick pint or gold watch (Scotch whisky), he was placing bets with an illegal bookmaker called Nick Hill... a villainous character who led the Latchmere Lot, a gang hailing from the south side of Battersea Bridge.

Eventually my father emerged smiling from the Nell and we made our way along Wandon Road to the Fulham Road and there it was... Stamford Bridge. I'd never seen so many people.

'Happy St. George's Day! Three cheers for the Blues.'

My father was shaking hands left, right and centre. I thought for one minute he must be famous and then I could see everyone was doing the same thing. There was a buzz in the air that made me tingle and I found it hard to contain my excitement. It was the last home game of the season and if Chelsea won it they might become champions of England for the first time in their history. There'd been talk of nothing else at school. All my classmates had said they were going, well the boys anyway... but on the day I never saw any of them.

I glanced round and there was the Rising Sun public house (currently The Butcher's Hook). I remember Ted Drake telling us when he'd come to the school that this is where Chelsea had been founded. 10 March 1905... so back then the Club was just over 50-years old and in its Jubilee Year. Being a kid, trust me, fifty years seemed like an eternity. Imagine not winning anything for that long. Even though I was a small boy, I understood the significance of what might happen... and then I became distracted by the huge sign fastened to raised pillars high above the gates to the stadium that read...

STAMFORD BRIDGE GROUNDS
CHELSEA FOOTBALL & ATHLETIC CO. LTD.
GREYHOUND RACING

I was craning my neck to take everything in. Beyond the crowds adjacent to the railway line I could see the original East Stand with **CHELSEA FOOTBALL CLUB** painted on the side in massive letters. My father distracted me thrusting a programme for the game at me.

'Something to read while we wait for the match to start,' he said, after we'd queued for what felt like an hour to click through the turnstiles... except I didn't click through, well not properly. 'Right son, under you go.'

Instinctively, I crouched down at my father's instruction. He paid at the turnstile and as he clicked through I scrabbled in on my hands and knees... nobody said a word. The official attendance for Chelsea's home game that day with Sheffield Wednesday was given as 51,421. As years went by and I found myself a part of visibly similar-sized crowds that were obviously more genuine in regard to the quoted attendance, it became clear that there were plenty more than 51,421 packed into the Bridge on my first visit.

My father had been at Chelsea's previous home game, an Easter Saturday match with Wolverhampton Wanderers and the official attendance that day was 75,043 (1-0 Peter Sillett) and he later said he was sure the crowd wasn't far off being a similar size for the Sheffield Wednesday game.

Clambering up the concrete steps at the back of what then known as the Fulham Road End anticipation was building. I felt giddy with excitement.'

Tommy pinched the end of his nose momentarily before continuing. 'That horseshit and hamburger smell many people talk about when they go on about their first experiences of watching football, well it was different then. When you breathed in, the aroma was more stale sweat, cigarettes, beefy Bovril and steak and kidney pies... definitely no horse shit and the hotdog and hamburger stalls on the Fulham Road were a few years away yet.

What happened next stayed with me forever... I reached the top of the steps... and suddenly, there it was in all its sprawling magnificence. If I'd been old enough to swear, I would have done. Briefly, my father lifted me up so I could get a full panoramic view of the huge cavernous bowl that was Stamford Bridge. Apart from the East Stand, the rest of the structures made no immediate sense. In the north east corner, protruding up from the adjacent East stand was another all-seated stand that looked like it was on the verge of collapse. Stretching round from there was an expanse of people stood on sloping open terracing.

My father pointed at the wooden tower at the back of the north terrace which was a jumble of letters and numbers and explained that was the TOTE board used during the greyhound meetings to display the odds and payoffs for the dogs in each races. The TOTE board worked via a manual alphanumeric system in similar fashion to the horizontal board just along from it which he said was used to display scores from other football matches. The letters corresponded to the fixtures detailed on the back page of the programme I'd been given. Father said the letters that were important today were, C, F and J.

The large advertising hoardings caught my eye as well. BOVRIL, OXO, WATNEY'S, NEWS OF THE WORLD. Even at that young age I understood their value. You couldn't miss them. The rest of the ground was open to the elements... apart from the quirky roof that covered a smallish part of the steep terrace that dropped down to the pitch just in front of us.'

C   Cardiff v Portsmouth
F   Manchester City v Blackpool
J   Sheffield United v Wolves

'Although in fourth place and six points off the lead, Portsmouth had two games in hand over Manchester City, Wolverhampton Wanderers and Chelsea above them who each had each had two games left. With the Blues holding a four point advantage over Man City and defending champions Wolves, in this era of two points for a win, a victory over Wednesday would eliminate them from the race and effectively end Pompey's challenge also... although if the south coast outfit won they could in theory keep the challenge open although they had a vastly inferior goal average.

My father marched me down the terrace to the front of the low white wall that skirted the pitch which now weirdly seemed distant because of the greyhound track. Significantly as it turned out, this was the first time I met Keith and Rick as I found myself pressed up next to them on the terrace. I recognised Keith as he was in the year above me at Ashburnham. Rick I would learn later was Keith's cousin. Both of them had football rattles. I was jealous. They were with Rick's father, Fred, who was holding a large placard that had picture of a Chelsea pensioner complete with an RH (Royal Hospital) cap. At the top of the placard it read **Up The Pensioners** and at the foot it said **Good Old Chelsea** and **Chelsea Supporters Club**.

I remember Ted Drake saying that he'd got rid of the old Chelsea Pensioners crest and replaced it with a lion and that Chelsea were now to be known as the Blues and so the Pensioners placard puzzled me, but I was only five-years old so I didn't really think about it and besides the players were soon on the pitch. They looked smart in royal blue shirts, white knickers (as they were called then) and black, blue and white hooped socks. I didn't recognise any of them... but then why would I?

I asked my father why Chelsea's goalkeeper wasn't Bill Robertson who'd come to the school with Ted Drake. He said that Chic Thompson was now in goal. I told my father that Drake had said that Robertson was the best goalkeeper in the country. I remember my father laughing and saying well he wouldn't have said he was the worst now would he.

I protested for a better explanation but he was more interested in sharing a joke, a smoke and a twist or two of snuff with Fred. This was the beginning of an enduring friendship which saw them go to many Chelsea matches together in the years that followed and of course I was allowed to tag along and that's how I got tight with Keith and Rick.

Wednesday were bottom of the table and already relegated. My father had said Chelsea would win easily, but that wasn't the case. That's Eric Parsons, he said pointing at Chelsea's number 7. He's our most skilful player and he fought for King and Country during the war. A footballer and a soldier! Immediately, Parsons was my hero and I wanted him to score. It took a while but lo and behold it was indeed Parsons who put the Blues in front, acrobatically heading home a Frank Blunstone cross. I knew it was Blunstone because he was our number 11 and I'd cross-checked the details in the programme. I liked the names of the positions though I had no idea what they meant. Parsons – Outside-right, Blunstone – Outside-left.

The pace of the game and my line of sight made it difficult to understand if Chelsea were playing well. The fact mine and Rick's fathers and lots of other grown ups around us were swearing a lot suggested to me it wasn't as easy for the Blues as it was meant to be.

At half-time, everyone was looking at the A,B,C board waiting for the scores from the key games affecting Chelsea to be posted up. I did wonder how they came by this information and a couple of years later I found out that on 40 minutes the man in charge of operating the A.B,C board ran to the Club office which was out by the East Stand car park and telephoned the Littlewoods Football Pools office in Liverpool. He then had to run all the way back to the north terrace and operate the board... which eventually displayed the important scores.'

C   0-1
F   1-1
J   1-1

'There were some curses but not many amid cries of "Pompey are winning at Cardiff." It wasn't ideal and my father pointed out that Chelsea needed to score another goal to consolidate their lead and kill off Wednesday's chances of equalising.

'"It's the hope that kills you... remember that," said my father as he lifted me up so I could stand on the white wall and have a better view as the players came out for the second half. Next to me, Keith and Rick twirled their rattles and everyone else around us clapped and cheered.'

Chelsea! Chelsea! Chelsea!

Tommy's fervour for his story was infectious. I found myself joining in with his *Chelsea! Chelsea! Chelsea!* cheer which made me smile when I played back the recording I was making using my mobile phone to help with the writing process. He really got into full flow and his memory was brilliant considering he was just a kid at the time. He told me that he'd spoken about the day many times since then with his father, Fred, Keith and Rick which emboldened the finer details in his mind that he might not have remembered otherwise.

'Not long after the match restarted Blues number 9 Roy Bentley and Wednesday goalkeeper Dave McIntosh collided and McIntosh was carried off on a stretcher. There were no substitutes then and so Wednesday left-back, number 3, Norman Curtis, went in goal and the visitors were down to ten men. After 25 minutes of what I sensed was growing impatience, Chelsea were awarded a penalty. We were almost level with the penalty area and I saw clearly that when the Blues number 6, Derek Saunders, had a shot on goal which was deflected by Wednesday number 10, Jackie Sewell.

People around me shouted *hand ball!* but it didn't look that way to me and I told my father. He told me to shut up because the referee William Ling had refereed the World Cup Final between Hungary and Germany the previous year and obviously knew what he was doing.

Rick's father laughed and said Ling was bent because he'd disallowed what would have been an equaliser for Hungary when Ferenc Puskas put the ball in the back of Germany's net with a few minutes left and the score 3-2. Germany won the World Cup. My father said he didn't care because he'd had a bet on Germany and he'd had a bet on Peter Sillett scoring for Chelsea today... and who was taking the penalty Ling had just awarded? Chelsea number 2, Peter Sillett.

I held my breath as Sillett placed the ball on the spot and coolly slotted it low to the right of Curtis and into the Wednesday net. *YES!* My father understandably was happier than anyone else, screaming and shouting with joy and then turning to pick me up and hug me which I don't remember him ever doing before though I'm sure he must have done when I was a tiny baby.

Rick tried to clamber over the wall but was pulled back by his father. The applause was deafening and so was the chanting.

Come On Chelsea! Come On Chelsea!

For the first time it sounded like every single Blues supporter in the ground was shouting their encouragement to the players.

A cauldron simmering with excitement boiled over five minutes later when Parsons, whom my father kept calling Rabbit, scored his second of the game. Blunstone again was the provider, but Parsons' shot was a tame effort which Curtis fumbled and allowed to bobble over the line. I asked my father why he called Parsons 'rabbit' and he said it was his nickname given him because he was so fast. I said there were faster animals than rabbits, like the greyhounds that he liked to bet on that ran around the track that circled the pitch and he clipped me round the ear. I still think it was a fair point.

Sillett scoring the penalty had been a cue for the first proper chant from the home crowd of the afternoon and Parsons goal was the catalyst for their first song. I'd heard a few people singing throughout the game, but it was just a few people here and there and I was too wrapped up in what was happening on the pitch to pay attention. Now though, it seemed as if everybody in the ground was singing.

Shoot high, shoot low, away then we will go.
We'll go away with the Chelsea away. Away we'll go.

The words were easy to remember, it was like a nursery rhyme. I sang it the next day when my mother was giving me my weekly hot bath and she told me the song was actually called *Blow High, Blow Low* and it came from a musical called *Carousel* written by Richard Rodgers and Oscar Hammerstein II that she and my father had been to see at the Theatre Royal in Drury Lane. She promised to take me to see it when I was a little older. This didn't happen, though she took me a couple of years later to see the film version starring Gordon MacRae and Shirley Jones.

It was the first time I ever went to the cinema. We went to the Gaumont Palace Theatre at 206 King's Road. Back then this was a huge building with 2000 seats. This was scaled down over time though it remained a cinema. It was an Odeon from the early 1960s to the early 1980s. Then I remember it as the Chelsea Cinema before it became the Curzon Chelsea. Last time I went past there it was being redeveloped.

When referee Ling blew the final whistle, there was a massive cheer and lots of people invaded the pitch among them Keith and Rick who tried to take me with them, but my father pulled me back. I asked him why he wasn't as cock-a-hoop as everyone else, he said that until we knew the Portsmouth score the championship wasn't confirmed. The stadium Tannoy then crackled into life saying as much and asking people to get off the pitch. Pitch invasions and Chelsea eh. Who knew?

We waited… and waited… it must have been a good 15 minutes. I spent the time studying the programme my father had bought me which cost sixpence in old money (£0.025) and had an aerial image of Stamford Bridge on the cover. I tried to memorise the Chelsea team. I couldn't manage it then, but funnily enough I can remember it now... Chic Thomson, Peter Sillett, Stan Willemse, Ken Armstrong, Stan Wicks, Derek Saunders, Eric, the greyhound ha ha, Parsons, Johnny McNichol, Roy Bentley, Les Stubbs and Frank Blunstone... there you go and with sequential shirt numbers 1 to 11 to match, none of these fancy squad numbers that run into high double figures.

First Division
Chelsea 3 Sheffield Wednesday 0
Stamford Bridge
Attendance: 51,421
Referee: William Ling

Chelsea: Chic Thomson, Peter Sillett, Stan Willemse, Ken Armstrong, Stan Wicks, Derek Saunders, Eric Parsons, Johnny McNichol, Roy Bentley, Seamus O'Connell, Frank Blunstone.
Scorers: Parsons 23, 75, Sillett 70 (pen).

Sheffield Wednesday: McIntosh, Martin, Curtis, McAnearney, McEvoy, Kay, Finney, Quixall, Froggatt, Sewell, Marriott.

"Here is the result from Ninian Park." Finally, the stadium Tannoy fizzed and popped as the announcer spoke. "Cardiff City 1 Portsmouth 1... Chelsea are the Football League Division One champions."

Memories of the sound of the crowd cheering that news still makes the hairs on the back of my neck stand on end. We stayed in the ground for at least another hour and looked on as Ted Drake accompanied by Chelsea's players made their way into the front row of the directors' box in the East Stand. They had a microphone rigged up to the Tannoy system. It was the first time I'd ever seen anyone address a large crowd in this way. Drake spoke as did Chelsea captain Roy Bentley and Chairman Joe Mears, respectively the son and nephew of the Club's founders, brothers Joseph and Gus Mears.

When we eventually left the ground, we walked back the way we came. My father disappeared into the Nell Gwynne to collect his winnings from the bets he'd placed with Nick Hill. He showed me the cash and said there was more there than the £20 Chelsea's players got paid each week for their services. I would have said I was impressed, but a few years later my mother told me he lost it all later that night playing cards in the Wetherby!

So there you have it. That's how I became a Chelsea supporter... at the top. I was the original Johnny Come Lately glory hunter ha ha ha.'

Tommy smiled at me before getting up to walk into the house. He returned with a yellowed copy of *Sunday Mirror* forerunner the *Sunday Pictorial* dated the day after the Blues title triumph.

After 50 inglorious years as football's laughing boys, Chelsea are League champions was a memorable line Tommy pointed out to me.

Football's laughing boys... We read that out together and then remarked on the fact it would be another fifty years before the title was won again and in the intervening years there were times when Chelsea were football's laughing boys once again.

*****

The next day, when the haze of drunkenness had finally cleared from my afternoon in the garden with Tommy, I started the writing process and then I'd meet up with him regularly so he could share more information and I could also read each new chapter back to him. Inevitably, he'd remember something else, a game, a gig, an incident and I'd edit the content as we went along before moving on.

Sadly though, I knew that at some point in the not too distant future the time would come when Tommy's illness would make matters increasingly difficult... and this is the stage on the journey we had now reached. As you can see, I was struggling to come to terms with it. He'd finished telling me his story that tied in with Chelsea's 1970 FA Cup-winning season and I'd typed it up... now it was time to read it back in full to him... which is where this book started with me at the care home and later finding myself staring at his name on the door...

Tommy Walker

I bit my bottom lip and swallowed hard, struggling to clear the lump in my throat as I wiped the tears welling up in my eyes with the sleeve of my jacket and opened the door.

Tommy was weak now, the cancer had ravaged his body. Sometimes communication was difficult however his hearing wasn't impaired. When his pain medication was balanced enough for him to stay awake, Anna the care home receptionist would call me to let me know and soon I'd be at his bedside to read back what I'd written.

In truth, Tommy had dealt with the enormity of his situation far better than I had. It was soul-destroying to see a close friend, renown to me for his sheer physicality and presence, fading away from this life in such a cruel way. I walked across the room, meeting midway my shadow created by a freestanding lamp next to the chair by his bedside. With the curtains closed, the subdued lighting always felt eerie... it had a supernatural quality that was unnerving.

Tommy was lying on top of the bed with his eyes partially open. His once powerful and tanned frame, propped up on a cushion at a 30-degree angle, had withered through lack of exercise as the illness took hold and his skin was sallow with a parchment-like fragility to it.

'Hello mate,' I said, sitting down slowly and reaching out my left hand to place it on his right arm that was folded across his chest that was rising and falling rhythmically as he breathed. I studied Tommy's face that was partially obscured by a nasal cannula delivering oxygen to his failing lungs. A faint knowing smile flickered there, briefly colouring his ghostly pallor.

'I'm here to read for you again,' I continued, reaching into my jacket pocket for the iPad Mini on which the manuscript for this book was stored.

Tommy widened his eyes and blinked a couple if times before closing them. I switched the iPad on, cleared my throat and pushed the spectacles I was wearing onto the bridge of my nose so the words on the screen came sharply into focus.

'Once upon a time,' I said… Tommy laughed… that was good… and then I got started.

TOMMY CAN YOU HEAR ME?
Saturday 30 August 1969

Worming their way into the heart of the crowd, any crowd, came easy to Tommy, Keith and Rick. Jostling skills subconsciously honed since childhood on packed football terraces were put to good use as the trio pushed, shoved, elbowed and shouldered themselves to a spot 15 feet or so from the front of the stage where they believed the optimum position to watch and listen to their favourite band performing was located.

'This'll do,' said Tommy, staring down the protesting looks he and his two friends were getting from a group of hippies they'd barged out of the way who were now stood behind them.

'It's the perfect spot,' replied Rick, reaching out his arms to embrace Tommy and Keith.

2nd Isle of Wight Festival of Music 1969 proclaimed the banner above the empty stage they were now staring expectantly at.

'Yeah, spot on,' confirmed Tommy, unshackling himself from Rick and arching his back which was still aching from the crouched driving position he'd had to adopt behind the wheel of the Hillman Imp that Keith had borrowed from his girlfriend Sheila to drive them down from London to Portsmouth.

As the name suggested, the Imp wasn't a large car, and at six feet, three inches tall Tommy's posture had been a cramped one for the entire three hours it had taken to drive the 80 miles that separated the Capital from the coast... or more specifically the car park at the Southsea terminal where they'd got the Isle of Wight ferry across the Solent to Ryde. Return tickets cost 12 shillings and sixpence (£0.63). From there it had been a tortuous, stop-start, four-mile bus ride to the sprawling 100-acre festival site that overlooked Woodside Bay.

Originally, they'd planned to get the train. Tommy didn't own a car yet. Since acquiring a colour photograph of Jimmy Greaves, his boyhood Chelsea idol, posing with the Jaguar 240 he owned outside Stamford Bridge, he'd had designs on what was popularly known as a Mark 2 Jag.

Funnily enough, the photo had been taken in 1965 when Greavesy was already playing for Tottenham Hotspur, but that hadn't mattered... well not much anyway. The sight of him lining up for Spurs against the Blues a couple of years later in the 1967 FA Cup final at Wembley well now that was different... it hurt, as did the result... massively.

The car though, well that was a beauty and maybe the photograph should have been retaken, this time with one of Chelsea's current stars like Peter Osgood standing beside it.

Rick was doing the Knowledge. Now that would have been handy if he'd already got through it and had a trusty black taxi to drive them around in when he wasn't working.

Keith wasn't interested in cars or driving them. He hadn't bothered taking his driving test yet, though he'd recently admitted he should do for practical reasons and also he reckoned that hanging onto Sheila who was starting to pick up an increasing amount of modelling work might depend on it. Sheila often spoke about having a manager and Keith was worried that if he didn't take the job on himself whoever did would soon be trying it on with her.

She was a dolly bird alright. A real looker. Legs all the way up to her armpits. Alan Holston one of the owners of Dandie Fashions on the King's Road had been the first to suggest she should be a clothes horse when they'd all been invited to a party at the shop after a raucous evening at the three-storey Cromwellian 'cocktail bar and discotheque' opposite the Natural History Museum in nearby South Kensington (3 Cromwell Road, London SW7, now residential apartments on two floors with the ground floor vacant).

Sheila started modelling clothes for magazine features on the shop and it went from there. Her latest shoot had been with Terrence Donovan, who along with David Bailey and Brian Duffy were to fashion photography what Peter Osgood and Charlie Cooke were to Chelsea Football Club... supreme talents with a maverick streak who knew how to enjoy themselves. Twiggy, Jean Shrimpton and Penelope Tree, the top models of the day, had better watch out, there was a new girl on the block with that all-important slim silhouette and a spikey girl-about-London attitude to match.

As he surveyed the scene, Tommy randomly thought he might be in love with Sheila, but she was Keith's girl and so that was the end of it and besides he had other plans which didn't involve having someone needy wrapped around him.

There were people everywhere. The size of the crowd had to be on a par with the 100,000 he'd been one of at Wembley for that Chelsea / Spurs Cup Final choker. This was far more easy-going though. There was a sense of freedom and community that seemed to have evaporated at football matches which were far more edgy now than they had been when he was a boy. Here, young people were into getting stoned and making love as opposed to throwing stones and sticking the boot in. The vibe was clannish peace rather than tribal aggression. It was youthful rebellion with a different dynamic.

Serious money was being made as well. Keith said the organisers of the festival, three local lads who were brothers, Ray, Ron and Bill Foulk, and a rock promoter called Rikki Farr were all in their early twenties, so not much older than them. It was 25 shillings (£1.25) for a ticket to the

Saturday concert and £2 for Sunday when Bob Dylan was headlining. An extra 10 shillings (£0.50) would cover the whole weekend, but that was never going to appeal to three townies like Tommy, Keith and Rick.

Campsites were for refugees and Boy Scouts and besides they were only here to see one act, a band that were now so big they'd been flown to the site by helicopter. The pilot must have been as stoned as the majority of the festival goers given the alarming way he'd just landed the chopper.

'Here we go lads!' exclaimed Tommy, clenching his fists and punching the air in an identical manner to when he celebrated a Chelsea goal.

"Please welcome on stage, the greatest rock band in the world... The Who!" The MC appeared startled by the volume of his voice booming through the huge PA system as vocalist Roger Daltrey, guitarist Pete Townshend, bassist John Entwistle and drummer Keith Moon scrambled onto the stage. The cheering from the crowd was raucous... there was definitely a parallel with being at a football match in this respect.

Daltrey had taken to wearing a fringed jacket that seemed inspired by the clobber worn by cowboys in the Wild West. His hair had grown into a big frizzy mop. He didn't look like the ace face Mod that had been an inspiration to kids like Tommy, Keith and Rick who lived and breathed the lyrics to what was still the band's signature track, *My Generation.*

Tommy wasn't that bothered though to be perfectly honest. He hadn't over-thought Daltrey's appearance because he still packed the couldn't-give-a-fuck-attitude that really mattered. Immediately, he owned the stage. His searing vocals demanded attention and admiration. Keith always said, "You never realised how good a singer Roger was until you tried to mimic him." That was so fucking true.

Pete Townshend garbed in a white boilersuit was a textbook foil for Daltrey. His guitar was like a machine gun, spraying out power chords instead of bullets, arm whirling windmill fashion as he cranked out thunderous riffs.

Keith Moon matched Daltrey and Townshend's energy and stagecraft from behind his kit. The power, invention and brilliance of Moon's drumming was extraordinary... even more so given it was common knowledge that these days he played every gig wasted on booze and pills.

The murderous tempo mustered by Townshend and Moon was welded together by John Entwistle's frenetic virtuoso bass playing. Entwistle didn't move about like the other three... but he didn't need to... the notes he wrenched out of his bass did it for him.

As a quartet they were consummate. Hendrix came close, but he was effectively a solo performer and his aggressive stage act that included trashing his guitar wasn't original... Townshend had done it first.

The band opened with high-octane renditions of *Heaven and Hell* and *I Can't Explain* before doing a couple of cover versions, *Fortune Teller* and *Young Man Blues* that Tommy wasn't that fussed about. *Young Man Blues...* he'd laughed at the connotations of the song title and then the story behind his own name.

Tommy being named Tommy after Tommy Walker who'd once played for Chelsea wasn't too fanciful. Unless you were a Blues supporter who'd followed the club in the 1940s, you'd never make the connection.

"Did your parents call you Tommy after Tommy Walker the Chelsea player?" was a question that nobody had ever posed him nor would they ever do so in the future. Tommy had however worked out a fantastic chat-up line related to his name that wasn't just whimsical, it was bordering on the outlandish... and it was true.

The main part of the set The Who were about to launch into, was taken from their new album *Tommy* which had been released in May. It was billed as a 'rock opera' conceived by Pete Townshend. *Tommy*, the fictitious deaf dumb and blind kid brainwashed by his mother, tormented by his cousin, sexually interfered with by his uncle and packed off on a mind-bending LSD trip by a gypsy before becoming a pinball wizard and messiah was actually the son of a soldier... Captain Walker... which made his full name Tommy Walker!

What a coincidence... except that Tommy Walker named after Tommy Walker the former Chelsea footballer had a theory that Pete Townshend had come up with the surname for his *Tommy* character after a couple of gigs The Who had played on the same day at his favourite old haunt the Saville Theatre.

The band had trod the boards at the venue on 22 October 1967 and Tommy had been to both gigs... on his own as it was a Sunday. Before the matinee gig, he'd got talking to Pete outside. Being four years his junior, it meant that Tommy had been an awestruck 15-year-old when he'd first seen The Who play live at the Goldhawk Club in Shepherds Bush in 1964 and he'd admitted this to Pete and asked if he went home after the first show and got his LPs *My Generation* and *A Quick One,* would he and the rest of the band sign them? Of course he would and not only that, he'd said, "I'll get you on the guest list now so you don't have to blag your way in later."

'Great!'

Pete had a notebook in his pocket. 'What's your name then?'

'Tommy.'

'Tommy what?'

'Tommy Walker.'

'How are you spelling your surname?'

'W A L K E R.'

'Nice to meet you Tommy Walker, see you later.'

That was cool. Tommy saw the gigs for free without having to try and bunk in and he got his LPs signed. Ordinarily, that would have been the end of it in Tommy's mind however in January 1968, The Who recorded a track called *Glow Girl* which yielded the line *it's a girl Mrs Walker* which Townshend had used again in the track *It's A Boy* that follows the melodic *Overture* intro at the beginning of the *Tommy* album!

Tommy had his signed LPs, what more proof did he need? Who's to say it wasn't true that the surname Walker and Christian name Tommy hadn't seeped into Townshend's subconscious following that brief meeting outside the Saville Theatre. It was a conversation that Tommy had already decided he never wanted to have with the guitarist... just in case it wasn't true. He was simply living the dream it could be true and that's all that mattered to him, the real walking, talking Tommy Walker... and that's exactly what he was thinking when he laid eyes for the first time on Sophia Fossati.

The Who were midway through an exhilarating version of *Pinball Wizard* when Tommy felt a tug on his arm.

'Mind if I stand in front of you, I can't see,' shouted the girl pulling at him. Her hair, a natural black colour, was backcombed in such a way it gave her an aura. Her face was naturally tanned and she was wearing huge wrap-around sunglasses like the ones modelled by Marianne Faithful in the film *Girl On A Motorcycle* which was still fresh in his mind as he'd only seen it a couple of weeks previously. This was a new experience at a Who gig... being sidetracked... by a girl... an impossibly cool girl.

'Yeah – sure, er what's your name?'

'Sophia... and before you say anything else don't call me Soph.'

Sophia raised her arms as she gyrated to the music and turned to face the stage. Tommy immediately wanted to put his arms around her waist. He looked at Rick and Keith who were totally immersed in the gig and hadn't noticed his new friend. She was wearing a purple dress with paisley detail stitched into it. It could have come from Dandie, his girlfriend Judy could have sold it to her. She should have been here but preferred to stay in London, they weren't that close anyway.

Tommy admired Sophia's contours and couldn't help imagining her naked. He did this countless times with pretty much every attractive girl he saw... it was normal... well Keith and Rick had always said it was when they were a lot younger. The thing is, he couldn't remember his eyes lingering that long and wondered if she was high as a kite like all the other hippie chicks at the festival seemed to be.

The '60s psychopharmacological revolution had expanded and blown the minds of plenty of people he knew, especially some of the lurkers and the shirkers that frequented the King's Road. A rite of passage or a recipe for addiction? Prescription medicines for insomnia, anxiety and depression were being nicked, sold-on and necked in vast quantities. Try this, try that. Tommy, Keith and Rick had given just about everything a go bar skin-popping.

Amphetamine uppers, barbituate downers. Tommy's father had told him he'd heard that Winston Churchill, who'd died four years ago aged 90, had banged down Drinamyl which was a mix of both for years. In the early '60s, the little bluish-coloured triangular tablets were prescribed as a "pick me up" to tired housewives and along the way were christened "purple hearts" and found their way into the burgeoning nightclub scene where they became a part of the new Mod culture that The Who had once been at the epicenter of. *I hope I die before I get old...* no thank you.

The Rolling Stones rhythmic paean to the calming drug Valium, *Mother's Little Helper,* released as a single in the USA in 1966, went to No.8 in the Billboard Hot 100 probably on back of sales to the mothers who sought a little tranquilizing help from Doctor Feelgood.

It was easy to tell what type of drugs people were taking... easier still if they were smoking marijuana like the hippies behind them. Love and peace man. In the middle of Roger Daltrey singing *I Can't Explain* which was the first single the group had released as The Who he'd scared the shit out of them, turning around staring at each one in turn. Widening his eyes and pretending he was pilled up.

On the ferry across the Solent, a couple of leather-clad Hells Angels had been selling blotting paper LSD trips. If there was a danger to taking drugs aside from the fact you could overdose and die, it was the deep psychological trauma you could put yourself through by overdoing Acid. A couple of tokes on a joint, half a pill... you could ease yourself in... discover your tolerance level. LSD was an all or nothing thing. You either took a trip or you didn't.

A couple of years ago, Tommy had taken a trip with Judy at one of the Dandie after-parties and had a psychedelic experience that had swiftly veered from cheery and colourful to terrifying. Hallucinating about being chased down the King's Road by the Devil sat behind the wheel of the multicoloured 1956 Bentley that was usually parked outside the shop had brought on anxiety and panic that had taken days to recover from.

There was another boutique called Granny Takes A Trip which was located across the road from the World's End pub. Every time he passed the shop front, which at that time featured a huge mural of a yellow-haired girl with long eyelashes and red lipstick who looked uncannily like Judy, especially when he'd had a drink, Tommy had a flashback... now just the name was enough to bring him out in a cold sweat.

People taking acid carried on dancing when the music stopped which was a bit of a giveaway. Pill heads made chewing motions with their mouths.

For those who could afford it, there was cocaine. Cocaine was a drinkers' drug. The first line made you feel confident and charismatic for an hour or so and then you just kept chasing that high within shorter time frames and all the while you drank like a fish, didn't feel drunk... but talked an increasing amount of shit as if you were pissed. An expensive combination that. Fine if you were running your lifestyle tab with Daddy's money, tricky otherwise.

Then there was Heroin… a part of the new "bohemian subculture"… that's how it was glamourised. All that "trendy junkie" expectation led to addiction though… and sometimes death. Needles? Sleeping? Dying? Fuck that!

Tommy looked at the sea of people around him pumped up with artificial energy and then beyond them out to the bay and the expanse of blue water… how many would end up skinny-dipping later? Deep water and drugs were a dangerous combination.

While people were chasing illegal highs around him, Tommy was about to experience euphoria of a different kind for the one and only occasion in his life. As Pete Townshend crunched the final power chord to *Pinball Wizard*, Sophia span round and took her sunglasses off allowing Tommy's eyes to lock onto hers. His brain went into overdrive, its core elements synchronising like never before as they released a heady chemical cocktail of dopamine, adrenalin, oxytocin and vasopressin. Whoosh! Love at first sight!

Tommy pulled Sophia towards him and then slipped his arms behind her back lifting her off the ground as he embraced her. It wasn't premeditated; he hadn't given it a second thought. He wasn't a player; he was too young. 20-years-old… just another chancer trying his luck with a pretty woman? No, it wasn't that. It was impulsive, hormonal... human nature at its most basic. He wasn't aware of Keith and Rick catching sight of him and Sophia in a passionate clinch that as the minutes flew past was verging on becoming pornographic. If The Who had been ripping through the type of hard-edged set they had grown up with they might not have noticed, but the sonic chicanery of *Do You Think It's Alright, Fiddle About, There's A Doctor, Go To The Mirror* and *Smash The Mirror* wasn't doing it for them at all. Keith and Rick were distracted… Daltrey, Townshend, Entwistle and Moon were being upstaged!

Tommy and Sophia were French kissing with such ardent urgency they were both already subconsciously sensing they were going to go all the way... but not here, not with an audience. Salivating, snaking tongues separated, they opened their eyes as they untwined arms from bodies and her bare feet found the floor.

'Who's your new friend?' asked Keith, patting Tommy on the back as Rick pointed down at the two of them with his hands held high and smiled.

Before Tommy had a chance to reply, Sophia had grabbed his hand and was leading him away from his friends through the crowds to the treeline at the edge of the field where the longer coarse grass struggled to root itself and felt springy underfoot.

'Here will do,' said Sophia, face flush with anticipation as she paused to catch her breath. 'Lie down.'

Tommy's mind was whirring as he got down on his knees. It felt like they'd been walking for ages. He could hear the muffled sound of The Who tearing though *My Generation*... he thought about dying before he got old. Fuck that!

'On your back boy.'

Briefly, Tommy felt nervous, but he complied and was soon fumbling with the fly buttons of his jeans in a bid to undo them. Success! The sandy soil was gritty and felt cold and damp against his buttocks as he pulled his jeans down but the discomfort he experienced was immediately overridden by the sexual urge overwhelming him. Drugs? Who needed drugs? Momentarily he closed his eyes. What a buzz!

Sophia moved quickly, pushing herself up on her haunches and squatting over Tommy. He bent his neck forward and opened his eyes. Her hair was loose now, strands hanging over her face. Pointed tongue licking lasciviously across plump pouting lips; eyes, heavy with mascara, wide open and staring at him. She laughed as he winced when she roughly grasped at his straining cock and guided it inside her. They both groaned as she ground herself down hard taking every inch he had to offer.

Tommy had never experienced an erection feeling larger or harder than now. He'd never fucked in this position before. He thought men fucked women not the other way round. Sophia was in complete control, gripping his wrists, digging her nails in. Tommy bit his lip... they were only seconds into it and he felt his stomach tensing, he didn't want to come yet but this was sex beyond his wildest fantasies.

Judy was hot, but she was a bit of a princess between the sheets and wanted all the attention lavished on her. By comparison, Sophia was a wild-hearted woman who selfishly wanted to get herself off as quickly as possible. He admired the contours of her sylphlike body, he wanted to suckle on the oversize nut-brown nipples on her soft, smooth pert breasts, to nip at the downy hair on her flat stomach and stroke her shaved pubic area... but there was no time.

Sophia started to buck and moan gutturally, her eyelids fluttering as the orgasm building up inside her burst forth. Tommy screwed his eyes shut; he could take no more. Instinctively, he raised his knees up and squeezed his thighs together growling her name, *S O P H I A,* as he ejaculated. Skin glistening with sweat, Sophia allowed herself to fall forward onto Tommy's prone body. As she did this, his softening cock flipped out of her and he felt their combined secretions flood out onto his stomach.

Nuzzling in the afterglow, Tommy wanted to ask Sophia if she always fucked men so soon after meeting them for the first time?... But instead he started chatting shit about The Who probably because as he'd reached the point of no return they were closing their set with a very early version of *Naked Eye* which lyrically, by strange coincidence, would eventually reference finding a woman and laying down on the ground.

Orgasmic synchronisation didn't get much better than coming in time with Keith Moon crucifying his drum kit and Pete Townshend trashing his guitar... feedback from the PA system that screamed for attention faded quickly leaving just the sound of the crowd and Sophia's slowing heartbeat to compete for his hearing and then that receded also and it was just him and Sophia... and she asked him what he was thinking... and the first thing he thought of to say was, '*Pinball Wizard* the machine and the boy. If you've played pinball Sophia, you'll know what I mean. The kid is deaf dumb and blind so he becomes part of the machine. It's like life isn't it. It's about action, scores and results.'

As Tommy randomly blurted out his take on The Who track, Sophia started laughing.

'Do you think sex is overrated then?' she asked, sitting up and widening her eyes as she looked at him.

Puzzled, Tommy hoisted his jeans back up his legs and reached into the pockets for his cigarettes and matches. 'What err... what do you mean?' he enquired, nervously feeling himself blush like a foolish schoolboy with a crush.

'I've just fucked you senseless... I suppose... that must be it.' Sophia nodded at Tommy. 'That's it isn't it. I mean what else could explain it?'

Tommy tapped out a couple of cigarettes from the slightly flattened packet and handed one to Sophia. He was lost for words. He wondered briefly about making some other kind of small talk.

Last month (3 July), Rolling Stones founder Brian Jones had been found dead in the swimming pool of his home at Cotchford Farm, East Sussex and then of course the other big news was Neil "That's one small step for man, one giant leap for mankind" Armstrong, the Apollo 11 astronaut. Imagine being the first man to walk on the moon (20 July). What a chat up line!

'Don't worry my senseless lover boy, I'm just teasing you,' said Sophia, smoke billowing from her nostrils and mouth as she spoke.

Tommy looked at her and smiled as relief washed over him. 'Thank fuck for that. So what team do you support then?'

Sophia shook her head and laughed. That was a good sign. Women liked men with a sense of humour. Fleetingly, Tommy contemplated football. Chelsea had played Crystal Palace at home today. He wondered how they'd got on (1-1, Peter Osgood). He went to their games week-in-week-out with Keith and Rick... loyal supporters.

It hadn't been a brilliant start to the season. The Blues had been hammered 4-1 by Liverpool at Anfield on the opening day of the campaign (9 August, Ian Hutchinson) and had only won once (16 August, Chelsea 1 Ipswich Town 0, Ian Hutchinson) in the five games that followed up until today.

Ordinarily, they would have been at Stamford Bridge for the visit of Palace, but The Who headlining at the Isle of White festival, well that was a landmark event... a bit like Neil Armstrong walking on the moon...

it was something that wasn't going to happen every week.

'I like Peter Osgood. He's really good looking isn't he.'

Sophia's declaration was a bolt from the blue... literally. Tommy gave his head a shake and asked for clarification.

'Do you mean Peter Osgood who plays for Chelsea?' Then he laughed out loud because he knew there wasn't another player called Peter Osgood.

'Yeah. That's him. What's so funny?'

'Nothing. Er nothing at all. I support Chelsea. I live down that way. Ossie's one of my favourite players.'

'You gonna take me to a game so I can watch him play then?'

Sophia's request felt like a marriage proposal. Any trace of post-coital awkwardness Tommy felt was lingering after their impromptu coupling disappeared in an instant.

'Fucking yes!' he replied, his face beaming with a child-like smile.

'Just a yes, would have done nicely lover boy.'

Inside the next hour, he learned from Sophia that she lived in Clerkenwell near the Sadler's Wells Theatre right in the heart of London and that her father was Italian. He'd come to England to find employment after the war and settled at a job on Smithfield Market where he'd met her mother, Frances.

Sophia was a PE teacher at the City of London School on the nearby Barbican Estate. Just as well it was girls only thought Tommy, she'd have teenage boys in a right lather. It was the middle of the school holidays and she'd come down to the Isle of Wight for a week with some old college friends. They were staying in a bed and breakfast... which might come in handy if he couldn't find Keith and Rick later.

Tommy told her about his childhood and growing in the World's End and how every weekday morning at 6.30 a.m. he walked up the King's Road to Nel's greengrocers where he always bought an apple and an orange and then caught the number 22 bus and rode top deck into the West End alighting at Berkeley Square. He didn't get the opportunity to tell Sophia anything about his job as their privacy was invaded by a group of hippies who had decided that a small clearing nearby would be a good place to pitch several small tents. Bob Dylan was headlining the festival the following day and people were still arriving on the site and looking for opportunistic places to camp relatively close to the stage.

Tommy stood up and lit the cigarette that had been stuck at the corner of his mouth for too long and took a couple of drags before passing it to Sophia. He only had a couple left on him and cursed at the thought of having to go without if he couldn't buy a packet from somewhere.

"You'll smoke yourself to death one day," his father always told him... but you don't think about things like that when you're carefree and young do you?

'Come on lover boy.'

Sophia grabbing at Tommy's hand startled him. He wasn't used to being in the company of such an assertive woman. Yeah, that's what she was… a woman. She may only have been four or five years older than him at a guess, but the difference between what he was used to… and what he was experiencing now reminded him of the film he'd been to see a couple of years previously with Judy. *The Graduate,* that was it. Dustin Hoffman playing the part of a young kid out of college getting seduced by an older woman, Mrs Robinson. That Anne Bancroft who portrayed Mrs R… well she was proper crumpet. The older type. Sophia wasn't as old, but there was something similar about her… well basically, she was a woman younger men would lust after because she had smouldering sex appeal and looked like she knew what they wanted and how to give it to them.

As he followed Sophia's lead back through the long grass and trees the Simon and Garfunkel track *Mrs Robinson* wormed its way into his ears.

'Fuck off! Get away from me.'

Sophia stopped in her tracks.

'No not you! Simon and Garfunkel.'

'Have you taken something?'

'Ha ha no.' Tommy looked in Sophia's eyes. They were welcoming. They gave him confidence. Go on my son… ask her then. 'Can I stay with you tonight?'

LIQUIDATOR
Saturday 18 October 1969

Tommy had taken a fair bit of stick from Keith and Rick following his disappearing act on the Isle of Wight. They'd waited by the stage for an hour or so after The Who had finished their set before leaving.

In the modern world of mobile phones, email and social media, communication is taken for granted. Today, Tommy, Keith and Rick would have their own *WhatsApp* group... 'Lads. I've got lucky. I'm staying with this bird Sophia'... add a couple of Emojis, press send... and there, in an instant, everyone knows what everyone else is doing.

In 1969, even though technology had advanced enough to propel three men to the surface of the moon, when it came to human interaction if it wasn't face-to-face, you had the choice of the good old-fashioned Bakelite telephone, writing a letter or sending a telegram... none of which were practical in a field with a 100,000 plus revellers many of whom were tripping their tits off.

The next time the trio met up after the festival was in the Wetherby a couple of weeks later. Chelsea were playing Wolverhampton Wanderers at the Bridge (13 September, 2-2, John Dempsey, Peter Osgood) and Tommy told them about his adventure with Sophia and explained he'd been keeping a low profile on the manor because Judy his regular squeeze had been on his case since he'd finished with her on his return to London. Keith and Rick had laughed at him and said he should have played them both... but he couldn't do that because he was smitten with Sophia. He didn't tell then that because the ribbing he'd have got would have been worse than it was already.

'Sophia this, Sophia that, Sophia the other... you'll be introducing her to George and Helen soon.' Keith was in his element.

'Wanker!' Wankers the pair of them because Rick was just as bad.

'You'll be bringing her to Chelsea next. That'll be it then.'

Tommy couldn't bring himself to admit he'd already planned to take Sophia to a game, mainly because he was going to swerve his two mates beforehand and do something that he'd never done before... enter Stamford Bridge early... like an hour before kick-off... and he'd already purchased tickets in the West Stand for the game he had in mind, Chelsea v West Bromwich Albion (18 October).

It was okay, sitting in the stands was going to be a one off because Sophia had made it clear that she wasn't too keen on being around "football ruffians" who she'd read in the newspapers were always fighting each other on the terraces.

The difference in price was quite a lot really, 17 shillings and sixpence (£0.88) for a West Stand seat compared with five shillings (£0.25) to stand on The Shed, but Tommy could afford it and besides Sophia had a point. It was unlikely there would be any disorder against West Brom, but then you never really knew what might happen.

Three days before the Baggies game, Tommy, Keith and Rick had trekked over 300 miles north to watch Chelsea play Second Division side Carlisle United in a Fourth Round League Cup tie (15 October). The Cumbrians pulled off a shock beating a strong Blues side 1-0 in a game that was marred by serious disorder!

Tommy and his friends had been on the fringes of a skirmish which took place just before kick-off and traded a few punches with a Carlisle mob intent on chasing a handful of Chelsea out of the Warwick Road End at Brunton Park... which was fair enough as it was the home terrace. Paying 11 shillings (£0.55) for an advance ticket to sit in the stand allocated to away fans had little appeal to this small band of travelling Blues supporters who regularly stood on The Shed. A couple of coach-loads of fans had opted for seating though and, to be fair to them, they'd got behind the team... repeatedly chanting *Chelsea! Chelsea!* Common sense prevailed as far as Tommy, Keith and Rick were concerned and they melted into the crowd and kept a low profile.

In the 25th minute of the game, Peter Bonetti was felled by a piece of slate thrown by an idiotic Carlisle fan, an incident which led to the game being held up for almost five minutes and irate referee Kevin Howley making a loudspeaker announcement to the crowd. "I'm not going to abandon the match no matter what the score is, but I'll tell you what I will do, I'll empty the ground if there is any more trouble and then finish the game." Howley also advised that Bonetti had sustained a cut head.

Keith and Rick argued that this might have affected The Cat's judgement for the rest of the match and maybe they were right. With a little over 10 minutes remaining, Carlisle right-back Derek Hempstead fired a daisy-cutter from fully 30-yards out which zipped through a crowded Chelsea penalty area, through Bonetti's legs, and into the net. Game over! Just the League and FA Cup to contest now!

On the arduous train journey back to London, Tommy decided it was for the best if he told his friends about taking Sophia to the West Brom game. He was surprised at their reaction which was low key, though that might have been down to the fact it was midnight and Chelsea's defeat had subdued all their moods.

Tommy couldn't sleep, so he used the idle time to plan the day. Meet Sophia at Sloane Square station at 10.30 a.m. Stroll down the King's Road to the Markham Arms for a quick drink before having an early lunch next door at Alexander's. Sadly, now a branch of the

Santander bank chain, the Markham was an interesting place to be on a Saturday as it was frequented by the gay community so he'd get more attention than her, that would be funny. It was also a pub used by Chelsea players during weekday afternoons after they'd finished training. He'd seen Peter Osgood, Charlie Cooke, young Alan Hudson and Tommy Baldwin having a decent drink in there on a few occasions, and a couple of weeks previously he'd asked the landlord Davey Casey who knew his father to introduce him to Osgood when the striker had been in there on his own.

They'd had a decent chat and Ossie had laughed when he'd mentioned Sophia and that she fancied him and would he be up for pretending he was a really good mate at some point in the future if he was out with her and their paths crossed. Of course that would be no problem at all. Nothing was ever a problem when you were in search of the craic like Ossie was... like he was. Young men enjoying everything swinging London had to offer.

Before going into Alexander's which was in the basement, Tommy expected Sophia would want to have a look round *Bazaar*, fashion designer Mary Quant's boutique. Keith's girlfriend Sheila had done some modelling for Quant when she'd come up with her early 'hot pants' designs. While Sophia looked at clothes, he'd probably get distracted by strikingly attractive, mini-skirted shop assistants and customers. No wonder Chelsea's footballers drank in the Markham. He'd never thought about that before.

If the Markham was a bit camp on Saturdays, Alexander's took it to another level... but it would be enjoyable fun and the food was good. Pepe and Manuel the waiters were stark raving bonkers, but they would make a massive fuss of Sophia and that's exactly what Tommy wanted. He wanted her to feel special, because she was special and besides, what was going to follow at Stamford Bridge might not be to her liking. He thought about introducing her to his parents, maybe he could do that after the match... play things by ear though eh Tommy. One step at a time.

*****

'What do you think then?' Tommy held out his arms and looked around Stamford Bridge. He was surprised how many supporters were already in the ground considering it was well over an hour before the scheduled 3 p.m. kick-off time. He'd never been in that early, not even when he was younger.

'Could do with a lick of paint,' Sophia replied wrinkling her nose and smiling before pointing at a group of players going through their warm-up routines on the pitch over to the left in front of the North Stand. 'Is Peter Osgood down there?'

'No, that's the West Brom team, He's over there.' Tommy nodded in the direction of The Shed.

'Oh right. The music's good.'

'Yeah, it is.' Tommy lit a cigarette and handed it to Sophia before lighting one up for himself. Pete Owen and Dave Scott the disc jockeys behind what was known as *Pre-match Spin* played some decent tunes and also read out requests. He'd written in to them on the off chance he might get a dedication to Sophia read out.

Space Oddity by David Bowie was currently burbling from the Tannoy, the sound was actually okay. Pete Owen had dedicated it to Chelsea supporter Neil Armstrong. Was that a joke or a coincidence? Someone whose name was the same as the first astronaut who'd just walked on the moon requesting *Space Oddity*? Ha ha.

Bowie was an interesting character, a Mod who looked like he could start a trend of his own. He was on Tommy's radar to take Sophia along to one of his gigs.

Next up came *Bad Moon Rising,* a No.1 chart hit last month for Creedence Clearwater Revival. There seemed to be a moon theme developing here. Tommy had been chatting with Sophia when the dedication for that track had been made and he couldn't help cutting his banter short and singing along with The Shed who'd reworked part of the lyrics slightly to, *don't go out tonight, there's sure to be a fight, Chelsea boys are back in town.*

This was a penny-drop-moment. The early birds in the ground were listening to the hits being played and thinking up ways to Chelseafy them. The successful ones like this had been reprised during matches and caught on. Manfred Mann's *Mighty Quinn* from last year was another great example. *You go in on your feet, you come out on your head. You ain't seen nothing like the mighty Shed.* There was another version which appealed as well. *Come on and see, come on and look. You ain't seen no-one like Charlie Cooke.*

Tommy could see that Sophia was enjoying the atmosphere in the ground building as more supporters filtered through the turnstiles, onto the terraces and into the stands. She was also enjoying watching Ossie and his teammates going through their warm-up.

Oh Well by Fleetwood Mac had her up on her feet dancing which was funny. The view from the West Stand was decent… so it should be given the price of the tickets, but it wasn't The Shed… and basically once you'd sat down, you weren't meant to stand up, let alone dance.

'Excuse me young lady, do you mind sitting down, one can't see.'

The cut-glass accent and received pronunciation from the stuffed shirt moaning behind them reminded him of being at work in Berkeley Square. Tommy didn't respond, instead he stood up and started dancing with Sophia. They stayed on their feet as the track faded and Pete Owen started speaking.

'That was Peter Green leading Fleetwood Mac through *Oh Well* and now another track that's getting a lot of requests on *Pre-match Spin, The Liquidator* by Harry J. All Stars. This is for Tommy Walker who's brought his girlfriend Sophia to her first Chelsea game today. Tommy says he loves you Sophia.'

Sophia, who was never short of a word or three, was stunned. Tommy smiled.

'I shall summon the stewards to have you two ejected if you don't sit down immediately.'

Tommy ignored the 'threat'. Right now he was only interested in *The Liquidator*. What a great track! A reggae instrumental that demanded immediate, on-your-feet-and-groove attention. Jamaican record producer Harry Zephaniah Johnson's session band had conjured up a magical mix of rocksteady beats and an eddying Hammond organ melody... no vocals were required to complement Winston Wright's keyboard playing, the man was out there on his own.

Tommy first heard a white label version of *The Liquidator* on the jukeboxes in the Rising Sun and the Wetherby over the summer. Pete Owen and Dave Scott played it for the first time at the Bridge before the Wolves game last month and every home match thereafter and he'd heard about the reaction it had been getting and now he was seeing and hearing it too... and joining in at the rippling point where Wright's organ subconsciously invited those standing on The Shed to clap their hands four times and shout *Chelsea!*

It was brilliant, and looking at the bemused West Brom fans absorbing the atmosphere being generated, as no-doubt the players, managers and officials of the visiting club were, Tommy sensed *The Liquidator* would soon be getting an airing at The Hawthorns and many other grounds as well.

First Division
Chelsea 2 West Bromwich Albion 0
Stamford Bridge
Attendance: 34,810
Referee: Tommy Dawes

Chelsea: Peter Bonetti, Ron Harris, Eddie McCreadie, John Hollins, David Webb, Marvin Hinton, Charlie Cooke, Alan Hudson, Peter Osgood, Alan Birchenall, Peter Houseman.
Scorers: Osgood 40, Cooke 45.

West Brom: Cumbes, Fraser, Williams, Cantello, Talbut, Kaye, Brown, Suggett, Astle, Hartford, Hope.

Rockin' Crickets by the Rockin' Rebels, another instrumental which this time featured a swirling saxophone churning out an engaging hook completed *Pre-match Spin* as the players ran out onto the pitch. Tommy thought they should run out to *The Liquidator* as it would be motivational for them to hear the *(clap, clap, clap) Chelsea!* refrain. It was a nice idea. But right now it was all about the game. He turned round to the stuffed shirt who'd protested at him standing up and surprised him by offering a handshake, an apology and a very loud *Come On Chelsea!*

The Blues went into the game sitting in 12th place in the table. Having finished fifth the previous season, the start to the current campaign had been viewed as disappointing and the League Cup exit hadn't brightened the mood at Stamford Bridge though Tommy wasn't too concerned.

Bonetti, having fully recovered from the head trauma suffered at Carlisle, was making his 362nd appearance for the Blues surpassing Ken Armstrong's club record. To mark the occasion, manager Dave Sexton made him captain for the day.

The Cat made an outstanding early save from Tony 'Bomber' Brown and from that point on it was all Chelsea as Peter Houseman, Charlie Cooke and Alan Hudson terrorised the West Brom defence.

The deadlock was broken in the 40th minute when Cooke flighted a ball into the Baggies box for Peter Osgood to head home superbly. Tommy leapt up and cheered and turned round to the stuffed shirt with his hands raised high before hugging Sophia who was also on her feet applauding the King of Stamford Bridge.

'I think I'm in love,' she said breathlessly.

'Me too,' replied Tommy, before looking wistfully over at The Shed which was a sea of bobbing heads and twirling blue and white scarves. His father would be in there with Rick's father and Keith and Rick. It felt strange not being with them... he felt detached somehow.

Chelsea doubled their advantage in first half injury time when Ossie nodded on a Houseman corner ball to Cooke who rifled it into the net off the underside of the bar.

The goal was a cue for The Shed to burst into song with a revamped version of The Scaffold hit *Lily The Pink* which had topped the charts the previous year.

> *We'll drink, a drink, a drink, to Charlie the King, the King, the King,*
> *The saviour of the Chelsea team.*
> *For he invented professional football and now we're gonna win the league.*
> *Peter Houseman, played terrible football, and The Shed all called him names.*
> *So they gave him a kick in the bollocks, and now he plays in every game.*

Tommy sang along and nodded when Sophia asked him if Chelsea supporters had a song for every player which wasn't strictly true in fact it wasn't true at all, but he couldn't be bothered explaining that at the very least, they each had their name chanted before kick-off.

During the halt-time break, Sophia went to the toilet and Tommy struck up a conversation with the stuffed shirt behind him. His name was

Edward Jones, but he said he preferred to be called Ted. Ted, who was probably in his mid-fifties, lived in nearby Eaton Square and owned a company that provided secure printing solutions, a line of business related to, though far more interesting than the West End magazine publisher that employed him as a typesetter.

It was a decent job, the pay was good and he could get time off during the week to go to football like he had just done because he had to work every other Sunday which was a chore sometimes especially if he'd had a late Saturday. Even so, Tommy had never contemplated moving on... especially now as he was enjoying his life. But when he'd told Ted he was a typesetter, out had come the business card with an instruction to call on Wednesday next week. He'd even shook hands on it. His father had told him when he was a child that if you shook hands on a 'deal' you had to honour it.

The second-half of the game was mundane. West Brom goalie Jim Cumbes, also an accomplished First-Class cricketer who'd represented Lancashire and Surrey as a fast-medium pace bowler, gave Peter Bonetti a run for his money in the cat-like agility stakes and kept the score to 2-0 with a string of decent saves.

At the final whistle, Tommy had planned to introduce Sophia to Ted, but when he turned round he'd already left. He scanned the steps either side of the block of seats they were in and caught sight of him just about to walk through the exit at the top that led to the back of the stand.

'Made a new friend?' asked Sophia looking a Tommy intently.

'Maybe. He works in the print. Wants me to call him next week.'

'You should.'

'I will.'

'Funny how things turn out. He was going to have us thrown out and I thought you were going to thump him... which would probably have got us thrown out too.'

'Yeah. Well we're both Chelsea aren't we.'

'Does that make a difference then?'

'Seems to doesn't it.'

'Maybe they should send a group of Chelsea supporters out to Northern Ireland to bring an end to The Troubles, or how about negotiating peace in Angola, or Vietnam?'

'Very funny.'

'What are we doing now?'

'I'm going to take you home to meet my mother.'

MANCHESTER UNITED AWAY
6 December 1969

Chelsea's victory over West Brom proved to be a turning point for the Club form-wise and Dave Sexton's side had kicked on winning four games and drawing two out of the six that followed, results that helped propel the Blues up to fifth in the table.

Momentum had been lost slightly when their next fixture, a home match against Stoke City (29 November) had been postponed because of heavy snow, but the lack of football had created an additional buzz for Tommy in the days leading up to what he always viewed as one of the biggest games of the season, Manchester United.

Even though legendary Red Devils manager Sir Matt Busby had retired at the end of the previous campaign, and their form under new boss Wilf McGuiness saw them languishing mid-table, Man U at Old Trafford would be a tough nut to crack. That said, Chelsea had thrashed them 4-0 up there the previous season (24 August 1968, Tommy Baldwin x2, Bobby Tambling, Alan Birchenall). United had won the European Cup just three months previously, so the victory was all the more impressive.

Tommy, Keith, Rick and Fred (George was working) were in a relaxed mood on the British Rail 'special excursion' train from London Euston to Manchester Piccadilly. The fare, 60 shillings (£3) return, was double the cost of going by coach, but the journey-time was much shorter... less than three hours, and you had freedom to move around... and you could have a decent drink and a game of cards with your mates without feeling cramped.

They'd started playing a few hands of three-card-brag when the train departed at 10.25 a.m. Fred seemed to win most of the hands, but he'd bought the cans of lager they were drinking so losing a few shillings to him didn't feel like theft. He worked in the licensed trade now and could get hold of Tennent's whose cans were adorned with photos of glamorous ladies. They'd started out featuring just one model, Ann Johansen, but earlier in the year a bevy of beauties, the 'lager lovelies' had been introduced. Sex appeal and beer, what a clever marketing idea that was!

An hour into the journey, bored with playing cards and the football chatter that had gone with it, Keith, Rick and Fred had their respective heads buried in the *Daily Mirror*, *Melody Maker* and *Racing Post*, Tommy hadn't brought anything with him to read intentionally as had plenty to think about. The West Brom matchday hadn't just been a watershed for Chelsea, but also for him for a couple of reasons.

Firstly, meeting Ted Jones had proved to be a fortuitous stroke of luck. He'd telephoned Ted as requested and been invited over to his work premises located in Dovehouse Street, Chelsea, at the King's Road end close to the fire station… a 15-minute walk from his home in Slaidburn Street. Ted's company, TJ Print, started life printing bespoke business forms, but following requests from of a number of high-profile clients he'd invested in the latest magnetic ink technology that enabled them to produce branded and secure banking stationery such as single cheques, cheque books, paying in and deposit slips.

Ted was looking for someone who understood the print game and would also be prepared to assist with deliveries… there were risks associated with manufacturing and transporting products that were a target for organised criminal gangs.

Tommy didn't need much convincing this was the job for him, the fact that Ted was willing to pay £45 a week plus overtime which was a rise of £8 per week on what he was earning was a bonus as was the news that the business was always closed at weekends. He'd handed his notice in at work the next day and started his new role the following Monday.

Secondly, his friendship with Sophia became a relationship. Their big day out together went swimmingly from start to finish. Tommy's meticulous planning paid dividends although it's fair to say he wasn't expecting any kind of return beyond some extra sexual gratification. Sophia enjoyed going to watch Chelsea and told him, maybe she'd go again… now and then, but Saturday daytimes were difficult because most of the mornings during term time she was supervising the sports teams her school fielded. Perfect!

After the match, he'd taken her to the Nell Gwynne. His father was out back with Fred, both of them had done well betting and were drinking their winnings. They were 'charmed' to meet her. Fred especially! Keith and Rick weren't there, they'd headed straight to the Lord Palmerston, on the corner of the King's Road and Brittania Road.

The Palmerston, last known as the Morrison (a bathroom showroom currently occupies the site), was a cavernous drinker and an established favourite with local faces largely thanks to the landlord for many years having been legendary boxing figure Dennie Mancini who considered running the pub his day job! It was also a select local watering hole favoured by Chelsea players post-match. Often they would stay way past last orders when the curtains would close to prevent prying eyes outside from looking in.

Tommy never really understood the point of licensing hours. Either the police turned a blind eye to them or they simply weren't bothered. Every pub on the manor had a lock-in on a Saturday night.

Tommy had taken Sophia home to meet his mother who'd been far more impressed with her than she had been with Judy. He'd left them together to chat over a cup of tea while he went and got changed out of the Levi's and pullover he'd been wearing, had a wash and a shave... and smartened up his appearance.

Out of his wardrobe came a button-down blue tartan Pendleton shirt and a navy Baracuta G9 (Harrington) jacket, both purchased from the Squire Shop on Brewer Street, Soho with his first week's wages from his new job. White flat-front pants from Lord John on nearby Carnaby Street and a mail-order pair of black G.H.Bass & Co. Weejuns loafers completed the look. Tommy didn't need to check himself out in the mirror, staying true to his Mod roots he knew he looked sharp.

The Baracuta had become a must-have item of clothing initially for Modernists following a surge in popularity when John Simons, responsible for the Squire Shop, had started stocking the jacket at his Ivy Shop in Richmond. Essentially a smart, practical, golfing jacket with an elasticated waste and cuffs and a Fraser tartan lining, Simons had noticed it was often worn by Rodney Harrington a character played by Ryan O'Neal in the television drama *Peyton Place*. When dressing the Ivy Shop window with a Baracuta he added a label which read *The Rodney Harrington Jacket...* word spread... and almost overnight the Baracuta became known as the Harrington.

Tommy loved the detail behind that story because he was addicted to minutiae... football... music... clothes. If he'd lived nearer to Clapham Junction he'd probably have taken up train spotting. The devil was definitely in the detail... but not in the precise way the age-old saying meant it.

Maybe he should try and be more like Sophia, she was always happy with what she was wearing and never questioned anything. She had a different mindset, that hippie thing he couldn't really get to grips with. It wasn't a bad thing though, being at peace with yourself and your environment. She was so trim and pretty she could carry any look off and she'd come to the West Brom game garbed in a black double-breasted military-tunic-style coat with big silver buttons that was long enough to almost meet the tops of her knee high boots. Underneath was a Biba miniskirt and ribbed roll-neck top. Sophia turned heads wherever she went and Tommy's head most of all which was how he liked it.

Musically, they weren't completely aligned... but that was okay. That night they hadn't gone far. The Pheasantry at 152-154 King's Road (now a Pizza Express restaurant) was an interesting place, a Georgian building steeped in history that had once been the home of an 18th-century butcher and game dealer called Samuel Baker who bred pheasants for the royal household. Guitarist Eric Clapton, currently playing with Blind Faith, had lived on the top floor when he'd been in his previous group Cream... the groundfloor and basement was a nightclub which must have been full of some very obvious attractions for him.

The previous month Sophia had been to see a new band known as

Group X because they didn't yet have a name who'd gatecrashed a talent night at All Saints Hall in Notting Hill. She'd gone with the hippie crowd she'd travelled to the Isle of Wight Festival with as one of them was friends with their guitarist Mick Slattery.

Group X played one song, a long noodle based around the Byrds track *Eight Miles High* and their sound she'd over-enthusiastically described as a "turbulently psychedelic fusion of folk-rock and electronica." Tommy wasn't keen, but she'd insisted he came to one of their gigs.

There was quite a buzz at the Pheasantry, BBC Radio 1 disc jockey John Peel had been at the All Saints Hall gig and told the organiser to sign the band as he thought they had great potential. Group X now had a name, Hawkwind Zoo (shortened later to Hawkwind). Their set was better than Tommy thought it was going to be, the tracks *Hurry On Sundown* and *Mirror Of Illusion* which had vocals were decent enough but the experimental instrumentals he struggled with even though the excellent light show came into its own during these tracks. If you were high on hallucinogens or smoking the reefer then this early stage Hawkwind gig would have been a blast!

Sophia threw plenty of shapes on the dancefloor while Tommy kept a safe distance at the bar and watched her. She was athletic enough to be a go-go dancer. It brought back memories for him of being 15-years old and blagging his way into Mod haunt the Scene Club in Soho and seeing Sandy Sargent who'd been a dancer on the music television show *Ready Steady Go!* seriously getting into the beat. It was a shame that both the Scene Club and *Ready Steady Go!* were no longer a part of popular culture. Fashions changed quickly and interest in the so-called *Beat Boom* had faded. As he'd noticed at the Isle of Wight Festival, the changing look of The Who provided clues to the shifting sands of what was in and what was out threads-wise... which was fine... but he'd long since made his mind up he was a Mod for life.

Taking Sophia back to Slaidburn Street after their night at The Pheasantry had run its course hadn't been an option Tommy had seriously considered. Even though it was nearby, it didn't feel right sleeping with her in his single bed with his parents a wafer-thin wall away. It made him smile that they'd had sex within an hour or so of first meeting and then a couple of times back at her bed and breakfast, but since then, back in London, opportunities had been few and far between.

A couple of furtive knee-tremblers on the fire escape at The Speakeasy, a late-night West End drinking club near Oxford Circus (48 Margaret Street, London W1. Now a members club called Beat), had been fun and there had been a sleep-over at Sophia's house one night when her parents had gone to visit relatives but that was the end of it.

Frustrated didn't even begin to describe the way he'd felt about not being able to spend more skin-on-skin time with her... and then he had a bright idea. His new place of work. He had keys to get in. The room behind Ted's upstairs office was very well appointed. Tommy hadn't figured out yet what his new boss used it for, but it looked great for entertaining. A brand new Chesterfield sofa, drinks cabinet, coffee table, chaise longue, radiogram and television all standing on a plush, deep-pile carpet. Perfect!

Fortunately, Sophia had thought so too. Their coupling had been frantic. Tommy hadn't meant to say the three magic words 'I love you', but he'd just blurted them out as she was straddling him and his eyes were glazing over.

'What did you say?'

'I love you.'

'I love you too.'

'Fuck!'

'Yeah... let's do it again.'

Sophia was insatiable. The hours flew by. On Sunday, after they'd tidied the place up, he put her in a taxi to Clerkenwell and as he walked home he thought about the ramifications of what he'd said. 'I love you.' She'd said it as well. He meant it though and he wondered if she did. He wasn't sure what was supposed to happen next. He wasn't going to ask her to marry him, not yet anyway, but maybe they could talk next time they met about getting a place together or at least making a plan for the future. All of it was a bit crazy to comprehend... true love, if that's what it was, had a lot to answer for.

First Division
Manchester United 0 Chelsea 2
Old Trafford
Attendance: 49,344
Referee: Bill Castle

Chelsea: Peter Bonetti, David Webb, Eddie McCreadie, John Hollins, John Dempsey, Ron Harris, Charlie Cooke, Alan Hudson, Peter Osgood, Ian Hutchinson, Peter Houseman.
Scorers: Hutchinson 12, 38.

Manchester United: Stepney, Edwards, Dunne, Burns, Ure, Sadler, Best, Kidd (Ryan 65), Charlton, Stiles, Aston.

"Stand your ground" and "keep it tight" were orders regularly barked out by the leader of The Shed, Danny 'Eccles' Harkins. A stylish, clip-guard cropped skinhead who stood out from the crowd in his trademark olive green Harrington jacket. Eccles wasn't a sawdust caeser like a lot of the gang spearheads at other football clubs, he was the real deal and the highly-polished toe caps of his black ten-eye Dr Marten's boots regularly connected with the bollocks of those who crossed him either at Stamford Bridge or on Chelsea's travels.

Blues supporters had travelled to Old Trafford in good numbers and had taken up what looked as far as Tommy could see as almost three quarters of the uncovered East Stand, colloquially known as the Scoreboard End. Shortly after Ian Hutchinson had given Chelsea an early lead in the 12th minute, a small pocket on the far side of the terrace had opened up where a small group of battle-ready United fans had made their presence known.

Fred said he thought he'd heard a few distinctive Manc accents as they'd clicked through the turnstiles, but that had soon been forgotten as Chelsea took the game by the scruff of the neck. John Hollins, playing on the right side of midfield, had already tested Man U keeper Alex Stepney with a thunderous 30-yard volley when he decided to drift over to the left flank and try his luck again. This time though, Hollins saw Hutchinson making a marauding run forward and picked him out with quality centre which the Blues forward, with his back to goal, headed past Stepney.

Chelsea supporters leapt in the air causing a surge forward down the terrace. When you watched games on television and saw this phenomenon, it looked like the end, typically behind a goal, was falling. With gravity seemingly defied, the only thing that eventually kept people on their feet as they appeared to dive headlong down the terrace was the sheer volume of people in front of them and the presence of intermittently-spaced iron crush barriers which were embedded into the concrete, stepped floor.

As a kid, Tommy had been terrified when he'd been on a section of terrace when it happened, but now he loved it. His father and Fred didn't though, they always made a point of taking up a position where they could either rest their backs against a crush barrier or be stood right at the back or side of a terrace.

'Keep it tight Chelsea! Keep it tight.'

Tommy, Keith and Rick applauded as the gap on the terrace closed up. Blues supporters obeying Eccles' military-like instruction went shoulder-to-shoulder like Roman Legionaires and forced the United mob intent on causing agro to retreat back through a single-file line of police officers and the yard-wide area of no man's land which was there to segregate home and away fans.

Those were the days my friend, we took the Stretford End…
We took The Kop, we took the fucking lot.
We'd fight and never lose, then we'd sing Up the Blues…
Those were the days, oh yes those were the days.

The song, which reworked the chorus of Mary Hopkins No.1 hit from a year ago *Those Were The Days*, was as boastful as it was entertaining and pretty much every Chelsea supporter, including Fred, who had also been known to sing along to a different version which went *We'll see you all outside, we'll see you all outside…* joined in.

On the pitch, United regrouped and Georgie Best began to do what Georgie did best... traumatise the opposition defence... in this case Chelsea's. Blues skipper Ron Harris appeared to be paying heed to Eccles on the terraces... having previously afforded Best too much space he started keeping tight to the Red Devils' dangerman. A chance fell to Bobby Charlton, but Peter Bonetti was equal to the United striker's rasping shot leathered from outside the penalty area.

Tommy smoked his way through a couple of Capstan and marvelled at the pace, skill and vision of midfielder Alan Hudson. He was two years older than Huddy which felt strange. When you're a kid going to football, everyone on the pitch seems so grown up. Now though, here was this young lad of 18 who lived in one of the prefabs on Upcerne Road, less than a five-minute walk away from his house in Slaidburn Street, actually playing for Chelsea... at Old Trafford. He'd had that dream as a child, to pull on the blue shirt and play for his local team, and Hudson, having come through the junior ranks at Stamford Bridge and signed a professional contract in July 1968, was actually living the dream for him.

There was one slight difference. When he was at school, young Alan had dreamed of playing for the team he supported... Fulham. He wanted to emulate his idols Johnny Haynes, George Cohen and Rodney Marsh but the Cottagers had knocked him back when his father had taken him down there for a trial... the Bridge was the next port of call.

'Go on son,' shouted Fred at Hudson as he went in for a 50/50 challenge for a loose ball with Man U left-back Franny Burns and came out on top. 'What a player!'

Hudson split the United defence wide open with an inch-perfect pass that Charlie Cooke, having read his young teammate's mind, had advanced far enough to latch onto. Cooke fired a low, blistering drive at the Red Devils' goal. Stepney got down to the ball, but there was too much pace on the shot for him to deal with and it skidded away. Racing in and evading the attention of United defender David Sadler was Ian Hutchinson to prod it over the line. *YESSSSS!*

Tommy, Keith and Rick surged down the terrace. Fred leant back on the crush barrier and punched the air with his fists.

That second goal, coming just before half-time, knocked the stuffing out of the home side and silenced their supporters.

Entertainingly, during the break, a couple of records were played. *Sugar, Sugar* by The Archies which was No.1 in singles charts and *The Liquidator* which had crept up to No.13... presumably on the back of being bought by tens of thousands of football supporters.

(clap, clap, clap, clap) Chelsea!

'I bet they don't play that again here,' said Keith, sticking two fingers up at the distant Stretford End.

After the re-start, United tried to make a game of it. Bobby Charlton twice forced decent saves out of Peter Bonetti and substitute Jimmy Ryan had a shot hooked off the line by John Hollins, but Chelsea were always hustling forward. Hutchinson might have had a hat-trick but for the bravery of Stepney and young Alan Hudson a goal but for the linesman's offside flag. Charlie Cooke hit the post with an absolute belter and Huddy had netted the rebound... Tommy had gone diving down the terrace thinking it was 3-0 to Chelsea, but it wasn't. It was a shame because Hudson's fine performance would have been rounded off nicely with a goal to remember it better by. Not only that it would have been his first for the senior side.

Even though the goal was ruled out, the sight of Huddy beating Stepney was enough for thousands of disillusioned Man U fans to give up on their team for the afternoon and head home early.

Easy, easy, easy was followed by a repetitive chant of *Chelsea!* that continued until referee Bill Castle blew his whistle to signal full-time.

The return journey to London proved uneventful. A taxi, hailed and paid for by Fred, meant that possible problems with any United fans intent on causing trouble en-route from Old Trafford to Manchester Piccadilly Station were avoided. There were no further problems after their initial Trojan horse 'attack' had been repelled. Running the risk of getting a kicking or worse still being nicked by Old Bill had no appeal whatsoever. Imagine spending a night in a piss-stinking, freezing cell and then being kicked out at 6 a.m. on a Sunday morning... no thank you.

Arriving back at Euston just before 10 p.m. they made for the Prince of Wales Feathers on Warren Street. A proper drinker with a real sense of history about it, the Feathers was a short walk from the station and one of Fred's favourite pubs in London. He hadn't said anything, but he must have won some money betting because he insisted buying three rounds before calling a halt to proceedings.

Tommy had thought about telephoning Sophia earlier in the day to make a plan to meet up with her when he got back to town, but he was glad now he hadn't. It had been a long enjoyable day, but he was tired. He laughed at the fact that his big head appeared to be ruling his little head. That was a first. Time to get off home now son, tomorrow's another day.

SOUTHAMPTON
26 December 1969

Tommy was awake early on Boxing Day morning. It was still dark outside, and as he lay in bed with the blankets pulled right up to his neck he contemplated the latest turn of events in his life. He was enjoying the festive period more this year than he could ever remember.

Christmas Eve had been spent, as it always was since he'd looked old enough to be allowed to join them, in the Wetherby with his parents. This was a tradition that he was glad to continue to honour even though he'd been tempted by an invitation that had come via Keith from Sheila to a private party at the Cromwellian. He'd already been invited to have dinner on Christmas Day over at Sophia's with her family. That was an early start, he'd been told to be there at midday so even in his happy-go-lucky 20-year old mind he'd figured out that staying out till dawn at the 'Crom' and having a shocking hangover to accompany him to Sophia's wouldn't be the smartest move he could make... especially given what he had planned when he got there.

Was it too soon? Tommy had thought about it a lot for a few days before making his decision. The idea had come to him on the rattler back from Manchester. He hadn't mentioned it to Keith, Rick or Fred... in fact he hadn't discussed it with anyone apart from the very helpful shop assistant he'd met in Ogden, an up-market jewellers located in Mayfair's Burlington Arcade where he'd inadvertently found himself sheltering from a heavy rain shower. He'd parked the TJ Print company van nearby in Burlington Gardens and was in the process of delivering a carton of branded security cheques and associated stationery to the department store Swan & Edgar on Piccadilly Circus (later, more famously perhaps to a slightly younger generation, Tower Records, and currently vacant) when the heavens had opened. Water and paper weren't a good combination at the best of times.

Have a cigarette Tommy, look in a few shop windows. Clothes, jewellery, perfume... nothing you can afford here. It's where the West End toffs do their shopping. A jewellers window display caught his eye. A tray with blue rings, seduced him... each beguiling gemstone catching the light exquisitely... and the colour of course... it had to be the blue... it was exactly the same shade as the blue of the shirts Chelsea wore. This was meant to happen.

Tommy stepped inside and soon learned from the shop assistant, a slender middle-aged lady with grey hair, a hawkish face and an upper-crust accent identical to his boss Ted's, that an engagement ring should cost around three months salary. He laughed at the prospect of being paid monthly and did the maths based on 12 weeks wages.

'That's over a monkey!'

'A monkey?'

'£500.'

'Consider it an investment in the future sir.'

'How much is that one?' Tommy pointed at the ring that had originally caught his eye. An oval sapphire set in a slim gold band.

'475 Guineas.'

'And how much is that?'

'Almost a monkey.'

Tommy laughed. The shop assistant had a decent sense of humour. He asked her to try the ring on so he could see what it looked like when worn. She wasn't wearing a wedding band. He didn't want to ask. Beneath that severe-looking exterior there was clearly a funny, warm human being. He thought about his boss Ted, a widower of ten years whose wife had been killed in a road accident. There was someone for everyone, that's what his mother always told him.

'It looks beautiful, but I can't afford it.'

'How much can you afford?'

It was a very good question and one that Tommy politely asked for more time to answer before thanking the assistant for her time and leaving.

The discussion he'd had with Ted had been entertaining, especially as it had taken place in the room behind his office at work. Sitting on the Chesterfield, sipping a Laphroaig single malt and talking about work... every time he blinked, for a fraction of a second he saw Sophia's svelte naked form. He'd taken her to the room on three occasions now and each time they'd had sex and Ted was none the wiser. Why would he be?

The job was going well, Ted was pleased. In the new year there would be deliveries to make further afield as the company had taken on some new clients. Tommy seized on the opportunity to be up front with his question. Ted shook his head and laughed.

'How old are you again?'

'20.'

'How old is Sophia?'

'25.'

'She's a grown woman, you're still a young pup. What makes you think she'll say, "yes"?'

'If she says "no" I'll get my money back... I mean, I'll get your money back.'

Tommy made a point of being generous with his description of the assistant in the jewellers, he could tell Ted was interested... well curious perhaps. Ted didn't know that he knew about his wife's death, the men on the shop floor had told him when he'd first started. They were a decent bunch. Five of them... all Fulham supporters!

In the past two seasons, The Cottagers had suffered back-to-back relegations and were now plying their trade in Third Division. Tommy had wound them up about how good Alan Hudson was up at Old Trafford.

If Fulham had taken Huddy on as a kid, how would his career have started out? He might have got more chances last season instead of just the one first team appearance for the Blues (1 February 1969, Southampton 5 Chelsea 0), but what then? Football was strange like that. Luck and ability were intertwined... you needed both... but sometimes fate could be cruel. Look at Peter Osgood. Aged 19, he'd broken his leg in a challenge with Liverpool's Emlyn Hughes who was playing for Blackpool at that time (5 October 1966, League Cup, Third Round, Blackpool 1 Chelsea 1, Peter Houseman). The injury sidelined Os for almost a year meaning he missed out on playing in the1967 FA Cup Final defeat to Spurs. Had Osgood played, Chelsea might have won... the margins were fine and the debates intense. Huddy by contrast seemed to be blessed with both luck and ability... he'd become a Blue and he was in the first team now. Poor old Fulham.

The week before Christmas, Ted had been invited to a party by the directors of Swan & Edgar and he'd asked Tommy to drive him into town and on the way told him he'd worked out a deal regarding the engagement ring. The shop assistant in the jewellers was surprised to see Tommy again. The ring was still for sale and Ted told him to wait outside while he concluded the transaction. He didn't disclose the price paid, all he told Tommy was that he wouldn't be paying him for the overtime he worked until he'd decided that he recouped his outlay... and if he left the business before that happened he'd have to repay the price he'd originally been quoted in full... at once!

Ted's handshake was firmer than usual when the deal was agreed and he'd stared deep into Tommy's eyes as he explained the terms to him. This was the first time he considered there might be more to Ted than first thought. Beneath the hoity-toity, stuffed shirt, "I shall summon the stewards," flimsiness there was a more steely personality. Perhaps it was because money was involved now.

Tommy respected Ted, he also felt sorry for him. A lonely man perhaps. Who went to watch football on their own at his age? There were a lot of questions he wanted to ask his boss, but they could wait or maybe he should just curb his curiosity full-stop and be thankful for his good fortune.

At 11 a.m. on Christmas morning, with the sapphire ring in his pocket, and a BOAC shoulder bag containing some gifts for Sophia's parents and a bottle of champagne to hopefully celebrate the acceptance of his proposal to their daughter, Tommy drove across town in the TJ Print company van that Ted had given him permission to use privately on the proviso he logged the mileage and journey details.

Sophia's father Enrico was a giant of a man with a formidable frame whose looks belied his age. He was almost 70-years old but still had a full head of tousled jet black hair that was as thick as it was lustrous. His olive-skinned face was strong with defined features that looked like they had been chiseled from Italian granite and his gnarled hands were as big as shovels. As a young man, he'd boxed at a high standard and been a sparring partner of future World Heavyweight Champion Primo Carnera before Carnera moved to the United States to further his career.

Even though Tommy had only met Enrico three times, on each occasion the old man's welcome at his front door had been hearty giving the impression he was genuinely pleased that his daughter had met someone she liked. Maybe it was the Italian way. They'd never had a proper conversation, but that would change over Christmas dinner and then later especially when Tommy asked him a question that he realised in hindsight you should never ask any Italian unless you have a few hours to spare. "Do you like football?"

Sophia's mother Frances was a small, slender, softly-spoken woman with a make-up-free pale complexion. Her lined face was edged by a lifeless mane of grey hair, combined they made her look older than Enrico though she was ten years younger than him.

She frowned when Tommy had asked her husband if he liked football. There's was perhaps a similar relationship to that which his parents enjoyed. Longevity borne out of tolerance for each others shortcomings and a dedication to unity that eventually ironed out creases of anger caused by perceived and actual wrong doings.

The highlight of the five-course lunch that Enrico had prepared was the main course which featured a capon stuffed with ground meat, Parmesan cheese, mortadella and egg served with a spicy candied fruit condiment called mostarda di Cremona. The taste was extraordinary, like something you would eat in a fine Italian restaurant only better.

Tommy could tell Sophia was delighted he was making conversation with her parents. Asking about their lives, talking about them rather than himself. A box of Charbonel et Walker luxury chocolates for her mother and a tin of Corvanna Regina cigars for her father were well received. Along with the champagne, they had come from the Swan & Edgar Christmas Hamper all the TJ Print employees had been given by Ted last week.

Frances didn't permit smoking in the house which was unusual and Sophia had warned Tommy previously that her mother didn't know she enjoyed the occasional cigarette and it would be for the best to keep it that way. Enrico had built a large shed in the far corner of the back yard of their property. It wasn't just used as a storage space, there was room enough for a table, four chairs... and an ashtray.

Illuminated by three large candles that wouldn't have looked out of place in a church and warmed by endless large glasses of fiery grappa, Enrico and Tommy smoked and Tommy tried his luck with his football question. Enrico laughed, got to his feet and raised out his hands before making a grand delaration... in Italian.

'Questa notte splendida darà i colori al nostro stemma: il nero e l'azzurro sullo sfondo d'oro delle stelle. Si chiamerà Internazionale, perchè noi siamo fratelli del mondo.'

'Inter Milan?' asked Tommy.

'Internationale... please... because we are brothers of the world.'

'What does the rest mean?'

'It's a speech that was made the night the club was founded. 8 March 1908. This splendid evening grants us the colours of our crest. Black and blue set against a background of gold stars.'

Enrico explained that although he hailed from Calabria in southern Italy he supported Internationale because his great-uncle, Virgilio Fossati, had been the player-manager of the team in the early years after its formation. Virgilio, who also represented the Italy national side, was called up by the Army to fight in World War I and was killed in action on 29 June 1916 during a battle between the Italian and Austrian armies at Monfalcone.

Since the first time he'd been to see Chelsea, Tommy had heard a lot of football-related stories... but Enrico's was right up there with the best. He asked him if he followed the fortunes of any English clubs and his question was met with laughter.

'I look for Chelsea. Not because Sophia tells me they are your team or because she likes Peter Osgood but because once they wore the strip of my Internationale.'

It was true. Before the 1966 FA Cup semi-final tie at Villa Park (23 April, Sheffield Wednesday 2 Chelsea 0) then Blues manager Tommy Docherty had asked the players what strip they wanted to wear and Terry Venables suggested Inter Milan because the kit which comprised blue and black striped shirts, black shorts and black socks with a blue turnover looked very smart. At that time, Internationale were an awe-inspiring side having won back-to-back European Cups in 1964 and 1965. Unfortunately for Chelsea and their supporters, looking like the champions of Europe and playing like the champions of Europe were two different things.

Tommy was pleased when Enrico applauded his knowledge of his club. He hoped this would be the first of many conversations about football he would have with the old man... maybe he'd invite him to Stamford Bridge. It was a sound platform to steer the conversation in a direction that might make it practical to ask him if for his only daughter's hand in marriage, but before he could they were disturbed by a knock, knock on the shed door. It was Sophia providing a glimpse of one aspect of what future married life might look like... a brusque summons to both of them to come back into the house.

'Tal madre, tal figlia.' Enrico stood up, laughed and finished his drink motioning Tommy to do the same. 'Like mother... like daughter. Come on. Let's go inside… we can talk more there.'

Tommy was surprised at Enrico's reaction. He'd lost count of the number of times he'd seen his mother try and fail to get his father to cooperate with her when he'd had a drink. Enrico paused at door and turned to face Tommy. 'Was there something you wanted to ask me?'

Tommy was surprised. Was it that obvious? Fortified by drink and with nothing to lose he made his play. 'Well er yeah. I wanted to ask if you'd be okay with me asking Sophia if she'd marry me?'

Enrico smiled. We hava another saying in Italy… 'Il colpo di fulmine è la cosa che fa guadagnare più tempo… It means love at first sight buys you more time. It was the same for me with Sophia's mother. I knew from the first time I saw Frances that she was the woman for me and we are still together. After Sophia was born, she couldn't have any more children so I never got to have the son I also wanted… but now my daughter has brought me a son.'

Enrico didn't ask Tommy about the minor details regarding his intentions towards his daughter which was just as well because he hadn't thought them through. When would they get married and, more importantly perhaps, where would they live? They weren't minor details at all. But why let them spoil the romance of the moment?

The wedding proposal when it came was funny. At first Sophia thought Tommy had gone down on one knee to tie his shoelace when he knelt down in front of her.

'I've asked your father and he says it's okay for me to ask you to marry me.' Tommy rooted in his pocket for the box with the engagement ring, pulled it out, opened it and handed it to Sophia. 'Will you marry me?'

The silence that followed could have been construed as awkward, but it was momentary and ended when Frances burst into tears! Sophia's reaction was a mixture of genuine surprise, shock even, and joy. She stared at the sapphire ring in the box then placed it on the table and flung her arms open wide. Leaning forward, she embraced Tommy who was still down on one knee in front of her.

Happiness comes in many forms and as far as joyful family occasions went, this was one of the best if not *the* best that Tommy had experienced… especially when Sophia finally said 'yes!'

They toasted the engagement with the champagne he brought with him and although he'd been asked if he wanted to stay over the night, Tommy explained that he wanted to get home and spend some time with his parents. There was an element of truth in this of course, but also he didn't want to run the risk of getting delayed the next morning. Chelsea were playing Southampton at home with an 11 a.m kick-off scheduled as it was a Bank Holiday. Sophia's family didn't need to know that, though he was sure Enrico would understand.

*****

Chelsea followed up their resounding victory over Manchester United at

Old Trafford with a disappointing 3-0 defeat away at Wolverhampton Wanderers (13 December). The Saturday before Christmas (20 December), good form returned at Stamford Bridge where the Blues ran out 3-1 winners (David Webb x2, Ian Hutchinson) over Manchester City. The result meant Dave Sexton's side replaced City in fourth place in the table and there was plenty of enthusiasm for Chelsea's prospects for the remainder of the season.

The Shed wasn't packed, but it felt busier than it had done during the Man City game. Ever since his first Chelsea game, Tommy hadn't paid too much attention to the quoted attendance figures. He went with a gut feel... and today he reckoned the crowd was around 40,000.

'Only 34,791 here for City,' said Fred coincidentally, peering up from the matchday programme he was reading. 'Biggest home crowd so far this season was Derby. 51,421 here for that (11 October, Chelsea 2 Derby County 2, Peter Houseman, John Hollins).

George laughed. 'Dunno why you bother analyzing them. I've never believed those attendance figures since that crazy three-all draw with Dymamo Moscow after the war ended (13 November 1945, Reg Williams, Len Goulden, Tommy Lawton). 74,496 they said. Ha ha... more like 124,496.'

It was great everyone had turned out for the game. His father George. Fred and Rick... Keith. They were all going to have a drink together in the Ifield Tavern (closed in 2009 and converted for residential use) after the match. A brisk 10-minute walk from Stamford Bridge, the pub, located on the corner of Ifield Road and Cathcart Road was another favoured haunt of Chelsea players who enjoyed a few sherbets after the rigours of football.

The Ifield was so close to the ground that occasionally the players would be in there before supporters arrived. It was great they mixed with the fans. Tommy always recalled Boxing Day a couple of years ago after a 2-1 win over Arsenal (26 December 1967, Alan Birchenall x2) seeing Chelsea striker Tommy Baldwin already standing at the bar when they arrived after the match.

Shortly after Baldwin had signed for the Blues from the Gunners the previous year (1 October) he'd been christened 'Sponge' by John Hollins. Hollins had played alongside Arsenal midfielder Jon Sammels for the England Under-23 side in an 8-0 rout of Wales (12 October) and after the game Baldwin's name had cropped up in conversation they'd had and Holly found out from Sammels that his new teammate's capacity for drink was so extraordinary he must have a sponge in his stomach to soak it all up.

Boozing didn't seem to affect Baldwin's performances. He was one of the hardest working players in the Chelsea team. Maybe grafting on the pitch made him thirsty. It was a shame he was out injured at the moment having fractured his left leg in a goalless draw away at Sunderland earlier in the season (4 October).

'I miss the Sponge,' declared Tommy as they applauded the players onto the pitch.

'Yeah but look how good young Hudson is,' replied George. 'Taken his chance well since coming in the side after Baldwin got injured.

Tommy nodded. His father was right about Hudson.

Come on you Blues! Come on you Blues!

First Division
Chelsea 3 Southampton 1
Stamford Bridge
Attendance: 41,489
Referee: Pat Partridge

Chelsea: Peter Bonetti, David Webb, Eddie McCreadie, John Hollins, John Dempsey, Ron Harris, Charlie Cooke, Alan Hudson, Peter Osgood, Ian Hutchinson, Peter Houseman.
Scorers: Hutchinson 31, 61, Hollins 68.

Southampton: Martin, Kirkup, Byrne, Fisher, Gabriel, Stokes, Paine, Channon, Davies (Kemp 46), Walker, Jenkins.
Scorer: Channon 86.

Early kick-off Boxing Day games always came with a bit of a hangover or a touch of indigestion or both for supporters and the early stages of the game suggested that Chelsea players too might have overindulged the previous day.

'Come on Blues liven up! I was happier about doing all the washing up from Christmas dinner this morning than you lot are about playing football against this lot.' With half-an-hour gone, Fred was getting impatient... but as was often the case, no sooner had he made a critical comment, Chelsea scored a goal and what a goal it was.

Peter Osgood stroked a lovely ball through to Ian Hutchinson who evaded a challenge from Southampton keeper Eric Martin and curled a sweet shot just inside the far post. From that point on it was a question of when Chelsea might score again not if.

Shortly after the hour mark, Charlie Cooke, who after the break had steadily increased the degree of torment he was meting out to the Saints backline, found Hutchinson with a smart 30-yard pass and the Chelsea striker doubled his tally with a decisive finish.

'Some player, young Hutch eh,' said Fred, who'd now changed his tone completely. '£5,000 to buy him from Cambridge United last year (23 July 1968). What a bargain!'

'You should get him round to do the washing up after the game Dad,' replied Rick, patting him on the back.

Fred was absolutely right about Hutchinson. The papers reckoned that Southampton's star striker Mick Channon was worth £100,000. If that proved to be true, how much was Hutch worth now then?

Man-of-the-match Hutchinson turned provider for Chelsea's third goal, skillfully working a return pass move with John Hollins who volleyed the ball past Martin. There was hope for more from the Blues, instead Channon popped up with a late consolation goal for the Saints but that didn't take the gloss off what was a fine victory.

*****

The Ifield was packed and, sure enough, Tommy Baldwin, who had by now recovered from his broken leg and was looking for a return to first team action, was already at the bar when Tommy, George, Fred, Rick and Keith arrived.

'Maybe Dave Sexton has set him this as a fitness test,' said Keith. 'Run to the pub, drink five of the best and then run back.'

'Not sure about drinking five of the best,' replied Rick. 'I doubt Sexton's that keen on them boozing, plus we've got Palace away tomorrow.'

The idea of playing games on consecutive days always seemed a bit mad, but it was a fairly regular occurrence around the Christmas and Easter holiday periods. It was okay when the games were at the Bridge or elsewhere in London but a challenge if they involved travel and travel on public transport in particular.

Tommy hadn't told his parents he'd asked Sophia to marry him. He thought it might be nice to do it when she was with him and once they'd made plans for the future. None of that had been discussed the previous evening. There was no big rush anyway. He certainly wasn't going to tell Keith and Rick yet. They still teased him about that West Brom game... not that he was too bothered. He didn't rise to the bait, and besides Sophia said she wasn't that fussed about going to another match so it wasn't going to happen again.

The afternoon was spent listening mainly to Fred and George trading stories about watching Chelsea at Christmas in years gone by. Fred had a good yarn about trying to go to see the Blues during the World War II years which he'd spent working for the London Fire Brigade.

Regular senior football competitions were abandoned shortly after the declaration of war on 3 September 1939. From 1942 until the end of the conflict in 1945, a Wartime League operated regionally across the north, south and west of the country with Chelsea fielding a team in League South.

On Christmas morning 1944, the Pensioners as they were still known then, were due to play West Ham United at Stamford Bridge and Fred was determined to go to the game. Arriving at the ground he was dismayed to find the fixture had been called off because of fog which didn't appear too bad.

The following day he decided to go to Upton Park for the return game, but this time it was seriously foggy, a real pea-souper. Despite this, a big crowd had congregated outside West Ham's 'famous' 'Chicken Run' enclosure which was without a roof having taken a direct hit from a German V-1 flying bomb. Again though, the match was called off. As it was Boxing Day, Fred went to the pub and got drunk instead.

The best story was told by George. Tommy especially enjoyed it because it concerned the first game he'd ever watched on Christmas Day at Stamford Bridge. In fact they'd all attended the match together. Chelsea beat Portsmouth by an extraordinary scoreline of 7-4 (25 December 1957, Jimmy Greaves x4, Ron Tindall, Cyril Rutter own-goal, Peter Sillett).

Greaves, just 17-years old, scored a first-half hat-trick. It was 5-1 at the break and he would end up with four goals. His prowess as a striker was no surprise, he'd found the net 114 times playing for the youth team the previous season. They all agreed it was a tragedy when Chelsea sold him to AC Milan (2 June 1961) and an even bigger tragedy when they failed to re-sign him six months later after he'd swiftly become disillusioned with life in Italy.

There were collective head shakes and curses about Greaves signing for Tottenham and for the first time in a while Tommy thought about the photo he had of the striker with the Mark 2 Jag outside the Bridge. The car was a distant dream now he was getting married.

George wrapped up his tale with a reality check. Having thrashed Pompey at home, the next day Chelsea played the reverse fixture with Portsmouth at Fratton Park... and lost 3-0. They hadn't gone to that game as the journey on Boxing Day would have been a nightmare but Crystal Palace away at Selhurst Park tomorrow presented no problem and hopefully the team would turn up as well.

BIRMINGHAM CITY
3 January 1970

In the days between Boxing Day and the New Year, Tommy had changed his mind about the timing of announcing his engagement to Sophia. The planning associated with a wedding could come in the months that followed, and besides Sophia had explained to him that she was considering a new teaching role at a girls school in Cheam. If she took a job there it would make sense for them to find a house to live in that area where it would certainly be cheaper. They could even consider buying a property instead of renting. That was enough common sense information for him to feel comfortable telling his parents and Sophia didn't need to be there.

'You haven't knocked her up?'

Tommy had thought his father might react in this way at the news. He might not have done if Sophia had been with him… but there was always that risk. His mother was far more relaxed about it all and she had good reason to be as it transpired.

'What if he has George? You have a short memory.'

You could have heard a pin drop in the Walker kitchen until Tommy started laughing. 'Well well. Shotgun wedding was it then?'

George rubbed his hands together and smiled. 'Not quite. Nobody could afford a shotgun. Sophia's a nice girl, son. Your mother and I are really pleased you've met someone decent… she isn't though is she?'

Tommy shook his head. "Love at first sight buys you more time," that's what Sophia's father said. He might have wondered if I'd got her pregnant when I spoke to him about it… but he never said anything.'

His father looked relieved… so did his mother. Both of them were impressed with his level-headed approach to the process and explanation about possible future plans.

When it came to his friends, that had been easier. Keith's girlfriend Sheila had been given tickets to a New Years Eve party at The Speakeasy Club in the West End where Tommy and Sophia had previously stolen a few moments of passion.

It was a great evening. In the run-up to midnight, Tommy held up Sophia's left hand and pointed at the sapphire ring on her third finger. The Beatles track Come Together, recently released as a double A-side single with Something, had been blaring out at peak volume making conversation difficult which was handy as it didn't give Keith and Rick an opportunity to make any kind of remark other than say 'congratulations'.

Sheila, all smiles, waved her left hand in front of Keith's face... she might have been joking, maybe she was being serious... Tommy didn't care, he got embraced by Sophia and they grooved to the sound of John, Paul, George and Ringo.

As 1969 became 1970, Rick, conscious perhaps of becoming a gooseberry now Tommy had joined Keith in having a serious girlfriend, found himself some female company he couldn't keep his hands off on the dancefloor... Margaret, a tall, slender, long-lashed, green-eyed beauty with a shock of red hair cropped into a bob. If Rick had said she was a model like Sheila, none of them would have been surprised... but he told Tommy and Rick when they went to the bar that she worked for the BBC as a radio broadcast assistant which didn't mean much and wouldn't have been that exciting apart from the fact that she'd also said that later on New Year's Day (Thursday) she was going to be involved in a recording session at the Paris Theatre which was going to be aired on John Peel's brand new Radio 1 *Sunday Show*... on Sunday.

Tommy had never been to the venue, but he'd heard plenty about it. A former West End cinema in the basement of Rex House at 12 Lower Regent Street, London SW1 (now a part of the PureGym chain of health and fitness clubs), the Paris Theatre had hosted the Beatles frequently in the early 1960s.

Come 2 a.m. Rick had an invite he was never going to turn down. Margaret lived on the Peabody Abbey Orchard Estate in Westminster. If they couldn't find a taxi, it was only a 20-minute walk. As they left, Margaret said that if collective hang-overs weren't too bad they should come along to the Paris as she could get them on the guestlist.

Family, a rock band that Tommy, Rick and Keith had seen a few times at the Marquee and weren't that fussed about to be honest, were scheduled to play, but according to Margaret, vocalist Roger Chapman was touch-and-go having gone down with stomach flu over Christmas and so Tyrannosaurus Rex, Marc Bolan's band, had been added to the bill

Tommy's interest perked up markedly. No disrespect to Family, but Bolan was far more attention-grabbing even with a hang-over. Like David Bowie, he'd started out on his musical-style journey as a Mod and like Bowie he seemed to be metamorphosing constantly in a bid maybe to find a unique look and sound that would see him recognised as a trendsetter rather than a dedicated follower of fashion.

*****

The Paris Theatre wasn't packed, it looked about ¾ full if that. Margaret said the capacity was 400, so 300 people wasn't a bad turnout considering the public transport difficulties associated with New Year's Day. Tommy nudged Rick and told him he should hang on to her as there could be some brilliant acts lined up for these John Peel show broadcasts.

With Chapman unable to sing, Family would only perform a couple of instrumental numbers *93's OK J* and *Here Comes The Grin* although interestingly enough when Tommy tuned into Peel's show on the Sunday, he padded out their set with several tracks from their *A Song For Me* LP.

Bolan on guitar, accompanied by percussionist Mickey Finn, was mesmerising. The stage, such as it was, was more of a platform raised a few inches off the floor. It felt like they were in someone's front room. Tyrannosaurus Rex played a 30-minute set opening with *Hot Rod Mama* and working their way through *Debora, Pavillions Of The Sun, Dove, By The Light Of The Magical Moon, Elemental Child* before finishing with *The Wizard.* The latter song was almost 10-minutes long but it really showcased Bolan's star quality.

Small in stature but big in personality, Marc Bolan had entered the world as Mark Feld. A story had done the rounds that his stage name was a play on the surname of one his friends, the actor James Bolam. It seemed feasible, though Tommy wasn't sure what the point was. Mark Feld was an okay name. There weren't any other Mark Feld's... it wasn't like David Bowie who'd started out life as plain old David Jones. He didn't want to be mistaken for Davy Jones the lead singer of The Monkees. The Bowie name was inspired by the character Jim Bowie, played by Richard Widmark, in the film *The Alamo*.

Rick reckoned that if Bolan, with his distinctive voice, pretty-boy looks, made-up eyes and corkscrew hair went full on electric with a proper band behind him he could really be on to something. Tommy agreed. Bolan as a solo artist hadn't really worked out nor had his stint in the group John's Children whose manager Simon Napier-Bell had at first thought about parachuting the singer into one of his other bands, The Yardbirds. That would have been interesting. In 1965, Yardbirds guitarist Jimmy Page had played on Bolan's first single *The Wizard.* By 1968, Page had evolved The Yardbirds into the New Yardbirds and then Led Zeppelin. Zeppelin were already enjoying huge commercial success with Robert Plant as lead vocalist... but had things worked out differently, it could easily have been Bolan!

Tyrannosaurus Rex, T-Rex, Marc Bolan... whatever. Despite all the mystical hippie messages in the songs, Tommy was blown away. Sophia would have loved it! Shame her powers of recovery had not matched his. After the party, they'd gone back to his workplace and the room at the back of Ted's office... it was passionate, it was dirty. Even now, 12 hours later he could still smell her on his skin... but then he hadn't had a wash... there hadn't been time. Earlier in the afternoon, he'd driven her home in the company van and then headed straight to the gig. Tommy never gave it a second thought that Rick, and in this instance more importantly Margaret, might not be there. Rule one in the un-written code of practice they abided by was that if you said you were going to be at a certain place on a certain date at a certain time... you'd be there. It worked for football matches, gigs and meeting at pubs... everything.

Lateness was accepted, but nobody had ever broken the rule which was astonishing... that's how friendships worked.

Tommy had said he'd be there, Rick had said he'd be there and Keith had said he definitely wasn't going to be there and that he'd next see his two friends on The Shed terrace at Stamford Bridge on Saturday for Chelsea's FA Cup tie with Birmingham City.

*****

'There's something about him that gives me the creeps,' said Keith, pulling the collar up on the navy-coloured Aquascutum rain mac he was wearing and putting his fingers in his ears. *Two Little Boys*, an old American Civil War song, had been a popular request on *Pre-match Spin* at Stamford Bridge for a few weeks. The interpretation being played, recorded by Australian entertainer Rolf Harris who'd made a name for himself his own BBC TV show, had hogged the No.1 spot in the singles charts.

'Yeah. I know what you mean,' replied Rick, looking up at the guttering sections of The Shed's corrugated steel roof and watching the rainwater drop through the myriad holes along their length. He'd come down with a cold and was glad, they'd had the presence of mind to go into the ground a little earlier today to make sure they were able to get a decent vantage point on the terrace that afforded shelter from the elements.

George and Fred weren't standing with them today. Someone Fred knew had got them tickets to sit in the rickety-looking North Stand at the north east end of the ground. Like The Shed, the North Stand didn't cover the whole terrace. George reckoned it had been constructed with the greyhound racing fraternity in mind rather than football spectators. Maybe it would get knocked down now that going to the dogs was no longer an entertainment option at the Bridge. The track had been closed in 1968 because it couldn't compete with White City, the home of the Greyhound Derby, in nearby Shepherds Bush.

Tommy wasn't interested in the weather or Rolf Harris. He lit a cigarette and contemplated Chelsea's chances in the FA Cup. After Chelsea had thrashed Crystal Palace 5-1 at Selhurst Park to move up to third in the table, (27 December, Peter Osgood x4, Peter Houseman), his father and Fred had placed bets with Nick Hill at the Nell Gwynne on the Blues to win the FA Cup at odds of 8/1. Fred said this was a better price than what the high street bookies were offering.

Tommy checked it out. 6/1. Fred was right and he'd been tempted, but he wasn't sure he wanted to get involved in gambling... even if was potentially just going to be just a one off bet.

Leeds United, six points better of than Chelsea in the First Division table, were 5/1 favourites to win the cup with current league leaders Everton priced at 13/2. All 32 Third Round ties were scheduled for a 3 p.m. kick-off with Leeds at home to Fourth Division Swansea City and Everton away at Second Division Sheffield United.

FA Cup Third Round
Chelsea 3 Birmingham City 0
Stamford Bridge
Attendance: 45,088
Referee: Gordon Hill

Chelsea: Peter Bonetti, David Webb, Eddie McCreadie, John Hollins, John Dempsey, Ron Harris, Charlie Cooke, Alan Hudson, Peter Osgood, Ian Hutchinson, Peter Houseman.
Scorers: Osgood 42, Hutchinson 78, 89.

Birmingham City: Herriot, Martin, Thomson, Page, Robinson, Beard, Murray, Hockey, Hateley, Vowden, Vincent.

The rain had eased off as the Chelsea and Birmingham players ran out onto a heavy Stamford Bridge pitch that looked like it would cut up easily and might lend itself to some spectacular sliding tackles.

'Why are we playing in yellow shirts when we're at home?' asked Rick, struggling with the concept of not being able to shout *Come On You Blues* at the Bridge.

'Says in here it's because Birmingham and Chelsea are both nicknamed the Blues,' replied Keith, looking up from his match programme. 'Today's teams will turn out in alternative colours.'

Rick shook his head in mock disgust. 'Doesn't really make sense that. I mean, if Birmingham are in their change strip of all white, why can't we wear all blue?'

Keith laughed. 'Well if you can't sing *Come On You Blues* and don't fancy *Come On You Yellows*... there's a new song here in the letters page being suggested.

Rick, who'd downed a couple of large brandies for medicinal purposes in the pub beforehand, and always liked a singsong anyway seemed keen. 'Go on then you sing it... and we'll join in if it's any good. What's the tune?'

'*Over There* The US military song that's in the Dickie Attenborough flick *Oh, What A Lovely War!*'

'Go on... sing it then.'

Roll the ball, roll the ball. We can win, put it in... roll the ball.
It's a crucial game, now, so take good aim now...
And you will see the City fall...

Tommy reached across and snatched the programme away from Keith whose attempt to get the song going ended right there with a protesting 'Oi!'

Supporters near them laughed and then someone at the back of The Shed shouted at the top of their voice, *Why don't you give me a C* and the whole terrace, Keith, Rick and Tommy included, responded *Cee-ee* and so it continued until *C H E L S E A* had been spelled out and chanted repeatedly accompanied by three claps each time.

'The old ones are the best ones,' said Tommy, lighting up a cigarette and blowing several large smoke rings which seemed to hang in the damp air before dissipating.

Birmingham, geed-up perhaps by the two ex-Chelsea players, Bert Murray and Tony Hateley, in their ranks, and cheered on by a decent-sized travelling contingent of at least 5,000, made their opponents look pedestrian for the opening 30 minutes of the game and the atmosphere became a little heavy as scuffles broke out on the North Stand terrace where the majority of the visiting fans were stood.

'Garrison and his mob getting some practice in for Leeds next Saturday,' said Keith, laughing. 'Must be fucking mad.'

'That's what they sing isn't it,' replied Rick.

We are mad in the head, we're the North Stand not The Shed
la la la la, la la la, la la la.

'That's a U.S military ditty as well isn't it... *The Army Goes Rolling Along,*' said Keith looking puzzled.

'It's all US military-based,' said Tommy. 'Garrison isn't really called Garrison. It's a nickname pinched from *Garrison's Gorillas* that TV series set in World War II. First Lt. Craig Garrison (portrayed by Ron Harper) leads a group of commandos recruited from U.S. jails on near-suicidal military missions against the Krauts.'

The conversation halted when Alan Hudson, who slowly but surely had begun to get a grip of midfield, was picked out by a neat first-time pass from Charlie Cooke. Hudson rinsed the Birmingham defence down the right flank and clipped a lovely ball across the box for Peter Osgood to head home at the far post.

After the break Chelsea got the bit between their teeth and took the game to the visitors. Ian Hutchinson's recent progress as a Blues player was as pleasing as Hudson's. In the 77th minute, Hutch, whose long throws had increasingly troubled Birmingham's defence, showed his prowess as a poaching striker when he doubled his side's lead firing home a flicked pass from Osgood.

We're gonna win the Cup, we're gonna win the Cup...
And now you're gonna believe us...
and now you're gonna believe us...
and now you're gonna be-lieve us...
We're gonna win the Cup.

The song, sung with great conviction by thousands of Chelsea supporters, reverberated off The Shed roof and carried across the pitch to the players. Presumptious perhaps, but it was a tradition followed by all clubs to sing it whether their was a chance of it actually happening or not.

Buoyed by the racket, a couple of minutes from time, Chelsea wrapped up what in the end was a comfortable victory when Hutchinson was in the right place once again to make the most of a speculative lob forward from John Hollins and drill the ball past City keeper Jim Herriot.

The Wembley dream was alive and kicking in London SW6. The crowd of 45,088 at Stamford Bridge was the largest by quite some margin for any of the Third Round cup ties played that day. The next highest attendance was at Highbury where 32,216 had turned up to watch Arsenal draw 1-1 with Blackpool.

Elsewhere, cup favourites Leeds United had to come from behind to beat Swansea City 2-1 at Elland Road but there was no such luck for table-topping Everton who came unstuck at Bramall Lane where the reverse happened and they surrendered an early lead to lose 2-1.

"We don't mind who we draw in the next round as long as it's at Stamford Bridge," Dave Sexton was reported to have said by the Sunday press, and the following day Chelsea were handed a home tie with Burnley who were hovering just above the First Division relegation places.

Tommy had listened to the draw on a transistor radio in Ted's office at work.

"Number 13 – Chelsea, will play Number seven – Burnley".

'That'll do,' said Ted. Tommy agreed. The tie of the Fourth Round paired Manchester United with Manchester City at Old Trafford while Leeds were drawn away against non-league opposition. Hillingdon Borough or Sutton United would host Don Revie's side once they managed to complete their fixture which had been postponed because of a waterlogged pitch.

DIRTY LEEDS
Saturday 10 January 1970

First Division
Chelsea 2 Leeds United 5
Stamford Bridge
Attendance: 57,221
Referee: Bill Gow

Chelsea: Tommy Hughes, David Webb, Eddie McCreadie, John Hollins, John Dempsey, Ron Harris, Charlie Cooke, Alan Hudson, Peter Osgood, Ian Hutchinson, Peter Houseman.
Scorers: Hollins 36, Osgood 41.

Leeds United: Sprake, Reaney, Cooper, Bremner, Charlton, Hunter, Lorimer, Clarke (Bates 36), Jones, Giles, Madeley.
Scorers: Clarke 16, Cooper 47, Giles 57 (pen), Lorimer 60, Jones 64.

> *We all hate Leeds and Leeds and Leeds,*
> *Leeds and Leeds and Leeds and Leeds...*
> *and Leeds and Leeds and Leeds... we all fucking hate Leeds!*

George Walker and Fred Evans didn't sing much at the football. You might hear them give it a *Come On Chelsea! Come On Chelsea!* now and again, although Fred, curiously, would always join in singing *We'll see you all outside*, but most of the songs they left to the younger generation... apart from one in particular... *We all hate Leeds...* basically because they did.

Tommy reckoned it was the tune that hooked them in. Eric Coates' iconic soundtrack for epic World War II film *The Dam Busters* was an evocative and patriotic instrumental piece that since the picture's release in 1955 had conjured up images of RAF 617 Squadron Lancaster bombers flying to Germany. This was still true, although now the younger generation of football supporters associated it with hating Leeds and antipathy towards the reigning First Division champions had become a nationwide thing.

As far as Chelsea were concerned, enmity towards Leeds hadn't originated on the terraces but on the pitch. Fred said it went back to 1962 and a Second Division game (15 September) between the sides at

Elland Road. Leeds won 2-0 but their right-half Eric Smith suffered a double-leg fracture challenging Chelsea midfielder Graham Moore for the ball. The injury ended Smith's career. The Blues won promotion at the end of that season, the Whites had to wait another year. With both teams in the top-flight, the fixture developed an edge to it which intensified in 1965 when Leeds finished runners up to champions Manchester United and Chelsea finished third.

According to Fred, in 1967 there were two matches that really stoked the rivalry between the clubs and saw it spread to the terraces in violent fashion. An FA Cup semi-final meeting at Villa Park (29 April) resulted in a 1-0 victory for the Chelsea (Tony Hateley) and a First Division game at Elland Road less than six months later (7 October) in which Leeds crucified the Blues 7-0.

The cup game had been marred by controversy. Referee Ken Burns disallowed a late Peter Lorimer equaliser for Leeds. Burns adjudged the Chelsea wall had not retreated 10-yards when Johnny Giles teed up Lorimer. The free-kick was retaken and came to nothing and the ref, who'd already ruled out a Terry Cooper 'goal' as offside, blew for full-time moments later. Blues boss Tommy Docherty celebrated on the touchline like he'd won the football pools. That was funny. Whites manager Don Revie was incandescent with rage and his team and their fans vexed at the perceived injustice of it all. That was even funnier.

There was nothing funny about losing 7-0 in that league game though. The hammering was attributed to Docherty having resigned the previous day and Chelsea, who were a lowly 19th in the table, being in disarray.

'Familiarity breeds contempt.' Fred was in full flow and he had a point. Stamford Bridge was packed for the latest instalment of the Chelsea / Leeds soap opera. This would be the fourth time the sides had met so far this season. The reverse league fixture at Elland Road played on 20 September the previous year had seen the Yorkshire outfit win 2-0 and four days later at the same ground the sides had played out a 1-1 draw in the Third Round of the League Cup. On that occasion, a last-gasp Paul Madeley equaliser for Leeds had cancelled out Alan Birchenall's low skidding drive which looked to have set Chelsea on their way to victory in the 71st minute. Because of Leeds participation in the European Cup, the replay was eventually played on Monday 6 October and the Blues ran out 2-0 winners at Stamford Bridge with Charlie Cooke and Alan Birchenall getting on the score sheet.

'What are they singing?' asked Keith as the game got underway. The Leeds fans gathered on the North Stand terrace had concocted a riposte to Chelsea's *We all hate Leeds* ditty that borrowed the melody from Doris Day's chart-topper from 1956, *Que Sera, Sera (Whatever Will Be, Will Be)*.

Rick had worked it out.

When I was just a little boy I asked my mother "What should I be?"
"Should I be Chelsea? Should I be Leeds?"
Here's what she said to me;
"Wash you mouth out son, And go get your fathers gun...
And shoot the Chelsea scum... Shoot the Chelsea scum!"

'Ha ha! Wankers!' said Keith.

'Forget them, what about our team,' said Tommy, tapping out a cigarette. 'No Bonetti!'

George shook his head. 'He's got the flu. Must be bad. Rick's had it for a couple of weeks and he's still here.'

With Peter Bonetti sidelined, Chelsea manager Dave Sexton selected reserve keeper Tommy Hughes to face Leeds. Hughes, a Scotland Under-23 international who'd been Bonetti's understudy since arriving at Stamford Bridge in 1965, had also been laid low by the same bug but was desperate for the opportunity to play and make an impression as he'd only made five first team appearances and as a result of his frustration at the lack of opportunities had handed in a transfer request.

Inside the opening five minutes it was clear that Hughes wasn't fit as he made a couple of blundering attempts at dives slithering across the six-yard box which resembled an icy sandpit and missing the ball on both occasions. The Shed drew its collective breath.

'Why haven't we got a decent reserve goalie?' asked Keith, shaking his head. 'We've got loads of top class talent that can't get in the side and yet no proper cover for Catty. Even the kid Alan Dovey would have been a better shout than Hughes today... he's making me nervous.'

'I know what you mean,' replied Rick, pausing to take a sip of Bovril from the cup he'd bought mainly to keep his gloveless hands warm. 'Thing is Dovey's only 17-years old and this is a big game to make your debut in.'

Tommy felt sorry for his namesake. 'Can't blame Hughesy for wanting to play. I'd want to... wouldn't you?'

The trio agreed, got nods from the elders George and Fred, and everyone forgot about the concern over Hughes for the next ten minutes or so immersing themselves in the cracking atmosphere being generated by both sets of fans. This lasted until the 16th minute when Bonetti's deputy dropped his first serious clanger of the afternoon and gifted Leeds the opening goal.

Billy Bremner pinged a forward ball from midfield to striker Mick Jones who shot squarely at the net. Hughes, who should have been better positioned, committed himself too early and went to ground deflecting the ball with his legs into the path of the always lurking Allan 'Sniffer' Clarke who toed it over the line from a tight angle off Blues defender John Dempsey.

The Shed cursed, the travelling Leeds fans cheered. Bitter rivalry simmering on the terraces was matched by skullduggery on the pitch. Jackie Charlton went through the back of Peter Osgood while Norman Hunter snapped at the legs of Ian Hutchinson like a rabid dog and Mick Bates had to replace Clarke who got injured in a goalmouth scramble.

Chelsea's swashbuckling style play wasn't going to be compromised by goalkeeping problems provided they could boss possession and John Hollins was at the hub of the action. It was Holly's driving run from midfield at the Leeds defence that brought the Blues an equaliser in the 37th minute.

'Give it to Huddy,' shouted Keith.

'Give it back! Give it back!' screamed Tommy.

'Go on Holly!' The Shed bellowed in unison as Hollins weaved his way into the Leeds penalty area evading tackle after tackle and crashed the ball past Gary Sprake and into the roof of the net.

Five minutes before the break Chelsea took the lead. The ball went out of play midway into the Leeds half. Hollins picked it up but changed his mind about taking the throw-in and handed it to Ian Hutchinson.

'Here we go. A Hutch long throw. As good as a free-kick that,' said Rick as Hutchinson picked up the muddied ball and used his shirt sleeves to rub it dry before taking a four-step run up and launching it high into the air, his arms windmilling on the follow through. The ball looped high and dropped into the middle of the Leeds penalty area where it was nodded on first by David Webb and then John Dempsey who found Peter Osgood inside the six-yard box. Boom! Ossie volleyed it past Sprake and the dregs of Rick's Bovril went flying into the air as The Shed celebrated and surged down the terrace taking anyone who wasn't in front of a crush barrier with them.

Chelsea led 2-1 at half-time and concerns about Tommy Hughes capabilities as a goalie ebbed and besides there was a major distraction on the North Stand terrace where a pitched battle was being waged and the police were struggling to restore order.

'Garrison's Gorrillas,' said Keith, rubbing his hands together. 'That's one way to keep warm. Good luck to them.'

'Funny how the North Stand mob thing started last season,' said Tommy. 'It was that Monday night game with the Gunners (24 April 1969: Chelsea 2 Arsenal 1, David Webb, Tommy Baldwin) when they had half The Shed and there was a row with their fans from start to finish. Garrison's mate Lenny decided he'd had enough and said he was going down the other end. He wasn't bothered that it was packed with Arsenal. The two of them, and a couple more lads Angus and Jim, went round there and gave a good account of themselves and decided to do their own thing after that rather than following Eccles' orders.'

'How do you know all that?' asked Keith.

'My boss Ted told me.'

'How does he know? I thought he was a square.'

'Well he is… but he's very well informed.'

The conversation concluded as the second-half kicked off and Chelsea picked up where they had left off before the break, taking the game to Leeds... but when Hutch fluffed a chance created for him by Ossie, the world caved in for the Blues and poor Tommy Hughes suddenly had thousands of angry prodding fingers pointing the blame at him.

Leeds full-back Terry Cooper fired a speculative right-footer from 20-yards out which Hughes dived across and should have palmed away, but he failed to make contact with the ball which fizzed into the back of the net.

'Fucking hell!' exclaimed Rick. 'If Hughes has got any sense he'll cancel his newspapers tomorrow and go on holiday to Cambodia. What a ricket.'

Keith shook his head, while Tommy thought about what his father had said before they'd left the house earlier. "Every Chelsea player will need to stand up and be counted today. Leeds are that good."

George was right and he nudged his son to remind him. The Blues looked a man down with Hughes in goal. Don Revie's side sensed more blood and ten minutes later they got it when John Dempsey brushed the ball with his arm under pressure from Leeds centre-forward Mick Jones. *Penalty!* Johnny Giles stepped up and zipped the ball to the right of Hughes who remained static.

Leeds taking the lead was the cue for more skirmishes on the terraces. On the pitch, it was only going to get worse... very quickly. A shanked David Webb clearance dropped invitingly in front of Peter Lorimer who chipped the ball over the advancing Hughes. Dempsey, whose contribution to the game was not far off matching Hughes in the calamity stakes, scrambled after it with Billy Bremner in close attendance. The ball bounced off the post and then off Dempsey and appeared to bobble over the line. The Chelsea centre-back prodded it out but the ball stuck in the mud and Lorimer, following up on his shot, raced in to stab it into the net.

There was still half-an-hour of the game left, and panic set in at the prospect of what further damage Leeds could do while the Blues were in disarray at the back. Panic turned to anger when five minutes later Giles sent over a cross which was flicked on by Bremner who caught Hughes square in the process of heading it into the path of Jones. Despite Dempsey being in close attendance, the Leeds striker found the time to sweep the ball into an empty net.

George and Fred had laid down a major rule when Tommy, Keith and Rick were still kids... never leave games early... but plenty of Chelsea supporters had seen enough and many were cursing loudly as they made for the exits with the sound of Leeds fans chanting *Easy, Easy, Easy* and *We want six* accompanying them on the way out of Stamford Bridge.

At the final whistle, George made the observation that Chelsea would have been soundly beaten even if Bonetti had been in goal. Fred shook his head and reminded him of their wager on the Blues to win the FA Cup.

'You might get even better odds now after that display,' said Keith. 'Right then. Where are we going to drown our sorrows?'

BURNLEY
Saturday 24 January 1970

Chelsea responded in the best possible way to the Leeds disaster by beating Arsenal 3-0 at Highbury a week later (17 January). Peter Bonetti returned in goal and Tommy Baldwin, who'd been fit and raring to go for several weeks, took Charlie Cooke's place in Dave Sexton's starting XI.

Cooke, absent with dental problems, wasn't missed as John Hollins, Ian Hutchinson and Baldwin scored in a comfortable Blues romp. The margin of victory could have been double had it not been for the inspirational form displayed by Gunners keeper Bob Wilson.

Sexton retained the same line-up for the FA Cup tie with Burnley and expectations were high given the Clarets were a lowly 17th in the First Division table... though as Rick pointed out, they had beaten fifth-place Wolves 3-0 at home in the previous round.

FA Cup Fourth Round
Chelsea 2 Burnley 2
Stamford Bridge
Attendance: 42,282
Referee: Jack Taylor

Chelsea: Peter Bonetti, David Webb, Eddie McCreadie, John Hollins, John Dempsey, Ron Harris, Tommy Baldwin, Alan Hudson, Peter Osgood, Ian Hutchinson, Peter Houseman.
Scorers: Hollins 67, Osgood 69.

Burnley: Mellor, Angus, Thomson, O'Neil, Dobson, Merrington, Casper, Coates, Wilson, Bellamy, Kindon.
Scorer: Dobson 80, 88.

'Quite smart their away kit,' mused Keith, pulling up the collar of the navy-coloured Aquascutum rain mac he'd worn to the Birmingham cup tie which he'd decided was his lucky coat.

'You can always tell when the match is shit,' replied Tommy, lighting a cigarette as he spoke. 'He starts talking about the players strips.'

Chelsea and Burnley were labouring on a heavy divot-riddled pitch that made decent football impossible to play.

'I agree with him though,' added Rick, smiling. 'It's nice and simple. White shirt, claret shorts, light blue socks. I like the way it relates to their home kit.'

'Fuck me. Not you as well?' said Tommy, exhaling smoke from his mouth as he spoke.

'Oh hello look, Puff the Magic Dragon's outnumbered on this one RIck,' said Keith, clapping his hands to applaud Alan Hudson as he made a fleeting run with the ball from midfield.

Tommy shrugged his shoulders. 'It's not as good as our away kit. I love the yellow shirt, blue shorts and yellow socks.'

Keith and Rick nodded their approval and refocused on the game but it was turgid fare and with the score locked at 0-0 at half-time, the trio chatted about the possibility of a replay and whether they would be prepared to make the near 500-mile round-trip to Turf Moor on Tuesday night. The answer was a no from Keith and Rick however Tommy had to make some deliveries for work in the north of England early in week with Manchester, just 30 miles from Burnley, being the final drop-off destination on Tuesday. It wasn't far. He'd definitely consider it.

George and Fred had opted to watch the Burnley cup tie from the North Stand though they'd paid their own way this time. Their decision had been swayed partly by Fred being superstitious and believing that it brought good fortune against Birmingham in the last round, but mainly by George who hadn't enjoyed being on the terraces at Highbury the previous weekend. The ground had been packed with 51,338 spectators and as with the Leeds game that preceded it there had been a significant amount of disorder particularly before kick-off.

Hindsight is a wonderful thing, and having advance knowledge that Chelsea were going to try and 'take' Arsenal's North Bank terrace should have been enough to persuade Tommy, Keith and Rick, given they had George and Fred in tow, to watch the match from the South Stand terrace (Clock End) where the majority of Blues supporters were housed but the queues had been off-putting and so they'd gone on the North Bank.

The funny thing was though, as Danny 'Eccles' Harkins led his cohorts into battle, George and Fred, realising what was going on and not wanting to be a part of it, marched through the scuffles and down to the front of the terrace. Calmly climbing over the low wall in front of them they walked all the way around the pitch without once being challenged by the police. Maybe they looked like a couple of middle-aged officials. The Chelsea supporters on the south terrace who'd been cheering on the efforts of Eccles and his troops, thinking George and Fred had been a part of the action, applauded them as they arrived and sang a new version of *Tennessee Wig-Walk,* the old Bonnie Lou number.

I'm a bow-legged chicken, I'm a knock-kneed hen…
Ain't lost a fight since I don't know when.
I walk with a wiggle and a waggle and a waggle and a squawk,
Doing the Chelsea boot walk!

Was changed to…

Bertie Mee said to Bill Shankly…
"Have you heard of the North Bank Highbury?"
Shanks said, "No, I don't think so…
But I've heard of the Chelsea agro!"

This had made it to The Shed terrace and been sung a couple of times during the first-half against Burnley.

'I reckon, that will stand the test of time,' said Rick, as it was briefly sung again just before the players ran out for the second half.

'I prefer that song that was being sung in the pub earlier,' replied Keith. 'The one that nicks that Royal Guardsmen tune *Snoopy vs. The Red Baron*.'

'Can you two remember the words?' asked Tommy, getting two nods by way of a reply. 'Come on then… now's our chance while no one's singing.'

10, 20, 30, 40, 50 or more…
The Chelsea North Stand were running up the score.
80 Arsenal died in that spree, when Chelsea ran riot at Highbury.
And out from the corner a hero arose…
A funny looking geezer with a big red nose.
His name is Harkins, they say he's insane…
And the North Bank Highbury was taken again.

The song was definitely more entertaining than the football, however Tommy, Keith and Rick failed to get the rest of The Shed to join in and were drowned out by a repeated chant of *Chelsea! Chelsea! Chelsea!*

'Wonder what Eccles makes of that song,' said Rick. 'I mean he's not really a *funny looking geezer with a big red nose* is he?'

'Needs a goal this game,' said Tommy, changing the subject. 'Do you reckon there's much nightlife in Burnley on a Tuesday night?'

Rick and Keith shrugged their shoulders and laughed. As the trio contemplated the possibility of a replay, John Hollins, who'd netted in Chelsea's last two games made a rampaging run into the Burnley penalty area. With time to pick his spot, Hollins, still 20-yards out, looked up and fired a speculative shot at goal which Clarets keeper Peter Mellor should have judged better.

'Yes! Get in there!'

Holly put the Blues 1-0 up and immediately Tommy forgot about going to Turf Moor. As the celebrations calmed down, he joined in with the rest of The Shed singing *You'll Never Walk Alone*… He never wore a scarf, neither did Keith but Rick did and the hundreds or maybe it was thousands like him that also did had them stretched above their heads as they swayed and chanted.

Today it's hard to imagine a Chelsea crowd or indeed any other crowd in English football apart from Liverpool singing *You'll Never Walk Alone,* but it was commonplace back then. The Kop, thanks to Mersey Beat group Gerry and the Pacemakers having a No.1 hit single in November 1963 with their version of the Rodgers and Hammerstein classic, had impressively sung along when the disc jockey at Anfield played the track before games and its popularity as a terrace anthem spread however the Scousers didn't originate what had become a week-in-week-out standard.

You'll Never Walk Alone, another song from the musical *Carousel* which had also provided *Blow High, Blow Low,* reworked as *Shoot High, Shoot Low* by the Chelsea crowd in the early 1950s, had also been heard at Stamford Bridge at that time and Fred was adamant this was the first place he'd heard it sung at a football game.

Tommy recalled it being a little slower in its phrasing and *Chelsea, Chelsea* being sung instead of *walk on, walk on...* and he was singing it that way now as John Hollins took a thow midway inside the Burnley half and picked out Alan Hudson. *You'll Never Walk Alone* ended as Hudson weaved his prodigious magic, smuggling the ball into the Clarets penalty area.

'Go on Chelsea!'

Hudson chipped the ball across the six-yard box to the far post where Peter Osgood had run in behind the Burnley defence to head home past Peter Mellor. Ossie ran behind the goal to salute the adoring Shed and Tommy, Keith and Rick got swept down the terrace in the midst of the celebrations.

2-0 up, with 20 minutes left, it didn't seem too presumptious for Blues supporters to sing *we're going to win the cup...* but maybe it was! If you're going to go down, you may as well go down fighting. Burnley manager Harry Potts decided to throw the metaphorical kitchen sink at Chelsea which in this case involved getting a message to his centre-half Martin Dobson advising him to play as a striker.

10 minutes from time, Dobson pulled a goal back for the visitors when Chelsea's defence ignored his presence in their penalty area and he fired an angled-ball low past Peter Bonetti.

'It's only a consolation goal,' remarked Rick.

Famous last words. With barely a couple of minutes remaining, Dobson scored again! Burnley winger Ralph Coates, who'd been causing Chelsea's backline increasing problems with his pace as the game wore on, latched onto the ball on the halfway line and put his head down and ran... and Dobson kept pace with him receiving a neat pass from his teammate and beating Bonetti with ease. 2-2. The Shed cursed loudly. Tommy cursed louder still. He'd only ever been to Turf Moor once... but that was about to change.

BURNLEY AWAY
Tuesday 27 January 1970

The FA Cup draw was always broadcast on the wireless by BBC Radio 2 on a Monday lunchtime following Saturday's preceding round. If your team was still in the competition it was essential listening.

The Fourth Round had seen Manchester United thrash Manchester City 3-0, Liverpool beat Wrexham 3-1 and Leeds United put six past non-league Sutton United without reply while Tottenham Hotspur had been surprisingly held at home to a 0-0 by Crystal Palace. Derby County, who had a very decent side, had easily beaten Sheffield United, Third Round conquerors of First Division leaders Everton, 3-0.

'Spurs or Palace away.' Ted rolled his eyes at the portable transistor radio he was holding as the draw was made. 'Not going to be easy that.'

'Got to get past Burnley yet,' replied Tommy, laughing. 'Easy draws for the other big teams eh. Leeds at home to Mansfield, Liverpool at home to Leicester and Man U away at Northampton.'

Ted nodded. 'Derby as well away at QPR, not exactly testing for the Rams is it.'

Tommy wasn't contemplating Chelsea reaching the FA Cup Final at all now... it looked a hard road. His father and Fred had moaned about the draw with Burnley when they'd met up in the Ifield Tavern after the game. Nick Hill was apparently now pricing the Blues at 9/1 to win the trophy. Those odds would shorten if the Blues won at Burnley. They laughed about it being a gamble... because that's what it was.

Tommy had only stayed for a couple of pints as he'd promised Sophia he'd go an watch Hawkwind with her again. The band were playing at the Temple Club which was located in Soho at 33-37 Wardour Street (now O'Neills, an Irish-themed pub) not far from his favoured live music haunt the Marquee.

Obviously Tommy wanted to see Sophia, he could take or leave Hawkwind... though it would be interesting to hear how they were developing as a group. He was actually more curious to see how he felt being in the venue again. When he'd first started going to clubs and getting into the Mod scene, what was now a progressive rock and hippie hang out, putting on bands to match, had been called The Flamingo, a Mecca for fans of Jazz and R&B and a meeting place for musicians... and gangsters.

It felt strange to Tommy. He was only 20-years old and yet he was nostalgic for the past. When it came to the bricks and mortar aspects, nothing had changed. The Temple, like The Flamingo before it, was a basement club with a low ceiling. It was poorly ventilated and dimly lit with toilets that represented a hazard to health and safety... like a lot of clubs in London... except he'd never thought about that when it was the Flamingo because he was too busy having a good time learning about life with like-minded souls.

As Hawkwind took to the stage, he closed his eyes and imagined Georgie Fame and the Blue Flames capturing his ears and his imagination when he was a 15-year old. At the beginning of 1965, the band, regular performers at the venue, had scored a No.1 hit with the foot-tapper *Yeh, Yeh*. Simple, sweaty, smoky, scenic music to dance to with a girl that had caught your eye. The Who had started out that way, and now they were performing a rock opera! It was strange the way bands evolved.

Looking at Hawkwind though, he couldn't see the band cutting their hair let alone changing their style. Maybe they'd start adding words to more of their free-form tunes which had got a lot tighter since that gig at the Pheasantry. The Temple was packed though. At least 300 people, a growing audience, was a sign that their was interest in what was going down and it was clearly tied into the thick, wall-to-wall, fug of reefer smoke which created an atmospheric, trippy vibe enhanced by an imaginative, psychedelic, light show that played with the senses especially during the intense 10-minute, kaleidoscopic, instrumental *Seeing It As You Really Are*. If a soundtrack was needed for those eerie silent images from last summer of man walking on the moon for the first time, Hawkwind's unique brand of beat-driven electronica could provide it. It was space rock for an increasingly spaced-out generation.

The band finished their set just after midnight, but The Temple was just getting going. In its previous incarnations, the club had stayed open until 6 a.m. and it was the same now which was just as well for those in the crowd who'd dropped acid... they would need those extra hours and be grateful for them. Fuck that! Tommy was glad Sophia hadn't suggested they experiment with LSD. The friends she'd met up with again who'd been at the Pheasantry and the Isle of Wight Festival were on it and they were at that freaking-out stage which made conversation both hopeless and pointless... now was a good time to leave.

Sophia said her parents didn't mind if Tommy stayed over with her at their house. He'd felt nervous about it and wondered what her father really thought about the idea. Enrico was capable of a look which didn't need words to accompany it. His eyes spelt out what he wanted to say... *You fuck with my daughter and I'll fuck with you.* It was only to be expected and he knew if it were him faced with the same situation he'd probably feel exactly the same way.

He couldn't bring himself to do anything. Lying in a single bed next to Sophia fearful that Enrico might burst through the door at any second with a meat cleaver in his hand wasn't the greatest aphrodisiac in the world. Sophia thought it was funny, she tugged at his cock and tried to get him hard but it was never going to happen. They had to get their own place... that would put an end to the frustration... and fear!

*****

FA Cup Fourth Round Replay
Burnley 1 Chelsea 3 (after extra-time)
Turf Moor
Attendance: 32,000
Referee: Ken Burns

Chelsea: Peter Bonetti, David Webb, Eddie McCreadie, John Hollins, John Dempsey, Ron Harris, Charlie Cooke, Alan Hudson, Tommy Baldwin, Ian Hutchinson, Peter Houseman.
Scorers: Houseman 72, 116, Baldwin 92.
Booked: Harris, McCreadie.

Burnley: Mellor, Angus, Thomson, O'Neil, Dobson, Merrington, Casper, Coates, Wilson (Latcham 105), Bellamy, Kindon.
Scorer: Coates 35.

The only change to the Chelsea side from Saturday's frustrating draw with Burnley at Stamford Bridge saw Tommy Baldwin shift to centre-forward in place of Peter Osgood who hadn't recovered from an ankle injury he'd sustained towards the end of the game. Charlie Cooke was the beneficiary of Ossie's absence, returning to Dave Sexton's starting XI with a clean bill of health from his dentist!

It was a bitterly cold, foggy evening in Lancashire and gags were being cracked that Burnley had left the floodlights on for a couple of days to help keep the heavily-sanded pitch thawed out to ensure the replay would go ahead. The damp, clinging mist that filled the air for much of the day was a different matter though, however referee Ken Burns had carried out an inspection an hour or so before kick-off and could see both goals from the centre-spot. That was enough. The match was definitely going ahead which was just as well for the thousands of Chelsea supporters who'd gone absent without leave from their places of work earlier in the day to make the long trek north.

Tommy laughed as he queued in a chip shop in Parliament Street not far from where he'd parked the company van. The place was packed with locals with claret and blue scarves tied around their necks all saying the same two things. The shandy-drinking southern softies wouldn't like it up them tonight and Ralph Coates was going to skin Chopper and Eddie Mac alive.

The 'southern softies' assumption was naïve. Chelsea were more than capable of handling the rough stuff and dishing it out as Coates would probably find out. Retribution was due. The England Under-23 international had traumatised the Blues defence at the Bridge on

Saturday. Tonight, Ron Harris would we all over him like a rash. Joking aside, Coates and Co. would need to be stopped if Dave Sexton's team were going to stay in the competition... however confidence abounded that the gaffer had a plan, it seemed like he really wanted to go all out to try and win the FA Cup this season.

Tommy's empty stomach rumbled as the distinct odours of salt and vinegar sprinkled on fish and chips and the cooking fat they'd been deep-fried in mingled and permeated his olfactory system. Part of the attraction of going to games in this part of the country were the 'chippys'. As the queue advanced, he was able to see what was in the heated glass display cabinet above the friers... a dozen battered cod, several nice pieces of rock, some hake, and beside them... fish cakes, saveloys, spam fritters, scallops, meat and potato pies, minced beef and onion pies, cheese and onion pasties, steamed steak puddings... fucking handsome!

Suddenly, Tommy yearned for his childhood. Before the redevelopers got to work in the neighbourhood, the unimaginatively named Fish 'n' Chip shop on Dartrey Terrace, a five-minute walk from Slaidburn Street, had been a gateway to food heaven... especially on Friday's when they did skate in a crispy beer batter. He'd tasted nothing finer for years until the first time he'd travelled to Turf Moor with Keith and Rick on a supporters club coach to watch Chelsea play Burnley (25 February 1967, Burnley 1 Chelsea 2, Jim Thomson, Tommy Baldwin).

The journey had taken almost seven hours and hunger had seen the trio pile into the first chippy they'd seen after arriving in the town. A couple of older Blues supporters on the coach had been talking enthusiastically about steamed steak puddings and a type of beer called 'mild'... both seemed like a great idea. The steamed pudding exceeded expectations... unlike the 'mild' which tasted and looked like very dirty dishwater.

The woman behind the counter had smiled at Tommy when he'd asked for steamed pudding and chips.

'First time love?' she'd enquired.

He'd smiled and nodded. She reminded him of Aida, a dinner lady at school... all hairnet, bingo wings and fag-ash-Lil cockney croakiness. The chip shop lady though, well her gravelly northern accent was brilliant. Better than anything the brassy women on the TV soap opera *Coronation Street* could muster.

'We've got a virgin 'ere,' she'd continued, cackling as she fluttered her mascara-laden eyelashes at him. 'Holland's steak, chips and gravy. I'll give you extra gravy love. All the northern boys love gravy.'

That was it. Tommy was hooked, even if he didn't get the line about northern boys loving gravy... everyone loved gravy!

Back in London, he'd done his best to persuade the chippy in Dartrey Terrace to stock steamed steak puddings, but the owners Jimmy and Elsa had more serious matters to consider. Shortly after, Dartrey

Terrace, which faced onto Dartrey Road, was bulldozed along with Seaton Street, where Keith lived, Luna Street, Vicat Street, Bifron Street and Raasay Street where Rick lived. Construction of the monolithic hi-rise World's End Estate got underway and the residents affected moved out... among them, Keith to Hackford Road in Brixton, and Rick to Vibart Gardens in Tulse Hill. Not far away, but they both felt they'd lost the sense of community they had in Chelsea. It was worse for their parents... Fred was forever complaining.

Among these dark Satanic mills in England's green and pleasant land lies Turf Moor, the home of Burnley Football Club. Tommy made a point of welding a couple of random lines from William Blake's fabled poem *And did these feet in ancient time,* which later spawned the hymn *Jerusalem,* into the yarn he told his father about the trip. Burnley was the northern version of their World's End!

The really funny thing about all this *dark Satanic mills* stuff though had been pointed out to Tommy by Ted as they'd discussed the Burnley replay at work. Ted shook his head and explained the mills Blake had written about were flour mills in London not cotton mills in Lancashire... but everyone thought the mills must be up north, because everyone down south was of the opinion that it was grim up north! Geographical bleakness was a state of mind perhaps... maybe it was the weather then that always made the north feel gloomy.

Finally, Tommy reached the front of the queue and was greeted by the same woman who'd served him the first and last time he'd visited the chippy.

'Yes love, what would you like?' asked 'Fag Ash Lil', licking her fleshy lips lewdly and winking at him.

'Hollands steak, chips and extra gravy please.'

'D'yer want scraps with that love?'

'Scraps?'

'Fag Ash Lil' brandished the stainless steel chip shovel she was holding before thrusting it into a container in front of her which was brim-full with small pieces of left-over batter that had been scooped out of the friers.

'Scraps love,' she said, showing the appetising contents of the shovel to Tommy. 'All the northern boys love scraps.'

Tommy nodded and looked nervously along the queue to his immediate right... a row of ruddy-cheeked, stern faces stared back at him. 'I bet they do. Go on then treacle, pile them on and plenty of salt and vinegar too.'

*****

It was a 10-minute walk from the chippy to the Turf Moor. Burnley was a small, compact town and despite the nearby temptations of Manchester football powerhouses United and City, it was obvious to Tommy that the local folk were fiercely loyal to the Clarets. The team was steeped in history and had enjoyed great success a decade previously winning the

First Division title in 1960 and being runners-up in both the league and FA Cup two years later.

The tight, terraced streets he ambled along while eating his dinner were packed with excitedly chattering adults and kids all heading in the same direction... claret and blue-winged moths being drawn to their stadium by the ethereal glow of its floodlights whose wattage was powerful enough to penetrate the mist that was still hanging in the air and enveloping the smokey chimneys that made up the skyline.

Tommy bought a match programme for a shilling and put it in his coat pocket. Something to read later when he returned to the bed and breakfast in Manchester that he'd stayed in the previous evening. They'd only wanted £2 for the extra night with a cooked breakfast thrown in as well. He'd made his final delivery of secure banking stationery earlier in the day to city centre department store Lewis's, located in Market Street (now a Primark).

Yesterday, he'd delivered to other branches of the chain in Birmingham, Leicester and Hanley. Ted was growing this line of his printing business impressively, building on the success he'd had with Swan & Edgar. He'd worked out the delivery route for Tommy and told him he didn't need to be back in work until Thursday, he'd even said he'd chalk an extra £10 off the balance he owed for loan on Sophia's engagement ring. They say you make your own luck, but meeting Ted completely by chance in the West Stand at Chelsea felt more like an undeserved blessing from the man upstairs whom he hadn't shown any gratitude to whatsoever. He'd change that now. 'Thank you God!'

Zigger Zagger, Zigger Zagger. Oi, Oi, Oi.

Distracted by the sound a familiar Chelsea chant, Tommy turned a corner by the football ground and caught sight of a large group of Blues supporters gathered around a man near the away entrance turnstiles who was clearly stood on a crate of some sort such was the height advantage he had.

Zigger Zagger, Zigger Zagger. Oi, Oi, Oi.

Recognisable immediately by his trademark yellow Harrington jacket, Mick Greenaway was a rallying target at away grounds for Chelsea fans wanting to ensure they were in the right place.

Zigger Zagger, Zigger Zagger. Oi, Oi, Oi.

This was the right place. Greenaway, like Danny 'Eccles' Harkins, was one of the faces of The Shed who went everywhere following the team. He'd assumed a role in life to orchestrate the Blues travelling support...

Zigger... Oi... Zagger... Oi.

... and did an impressive job... although he sometimes attracted the attention of opposition gangs which is when having an accomplice like 'Eccles' came in handy!

Zigger Zagger, Zigger Zagger. Oi, Oi, Oi.

The chant, as far as its use by Chelsea supporters and Greenaway in particular was concerned, had it's origins not much more than 10 miles away from where Tommy was stood right now. Ewood Park, the home of Blackburn Rovers. A while back (28 December 1964), a group of Blues fans had trekked north to nearby Blackpool hoping to watch the team take on the Seasiders, but the game was postponed because of snow.

Having travelled all that way, they decided to take in a game and went to watch Blackburn play Leeds United. Dirty Leeds won 2-0, but the highlight of the afternoon was hearing an early version of *Zigger Zagger*. Mick Greenaway wasn't at Ewood Park that day, but he always asked his friends to pay attention to what was being chanted on terraces up and down the country to help him improve and expand Chelsea's repertoire and that's how he found out about *Zigger Zagger* which he then stamped his own personality on.

Apart from Greenaway, Tommy recognised plenty of Chelsea supporters who were either milling around or queuing. He wasn't going to waste time chatting outside the ground though as he'd overheard a conversation in the chip shop that Turf Moor would be packed out and there was a chance the gates would be locked early.

Considering it was only the Fourth Round of the FA Cup, the level of interest the replay generated was extraordinary. It might have been down to history. The last time Burnley and Chelsea met in the competition was at the same stage back in 1956. On that occasion, it took five matches for a winner to emerge!

28 January, Burnley 1 Chelsea 1, Eric Parsons; 1 February, Chelsea 1 Burnley 1 after extra-time, Frank Blunstone; 6 February, Chelsea 2 Burnley 2 after extra-time – match played at St. Andrews, Peter Sillett, Roy Bentley; 13 February, Chelsea 0 Burnley 0 after extra-time – match played at Highbury; 15 February, Chelsea 2 Burnley 0, match played at White Hart Lane, Ron Tindall, Jim Lewis.

Chelsea emerged victorious! But the joy at winning this club-record-breaking marathon was short-lived. Three days later, the Blues were knocked out of the competition losing 1-0 to Everton at Goodison Park. With this in mind, Tommy wondered how things would pan out this time around against Burnley.

Chelsea! Chelsea! Chelsea!

Blues supporters never hid their lights under any bushels and they were everywhere tonight. There was no point travelling all this way from London and then not watching the game. 'Home End', 'Away End'... it made no difference.

Chelsea! Chelsea! Chelsea!

Tommy was stood on the Longside terrace which ran down one side of Turf Moor. Burnley supporters occupied half of it, the rest was packed with Chelsea. Sporadic scuffles breaking out on the Bee Hole terrace behind one goal and in the new Cricket Field End stand at the other end of the ground highlighted the presence of Blues fans where they shouldn't be. The atmosphere was feisty.

Chelsea! Chelsea! Chelsea!

The chanting intensified as the players of both sides took to the pitch, Chelsea looking smart under the floodlights in their change strip of yellow shirts, blue shorts and yellow socks. As the game got under way, the prediction that Burnley fans had made in the chippy earlier about their livewire winger Coates roasting Chelsea's defence was coming worryingly true. The Clarets speed and distribution was as eye-catching as it was frustrating, particularly for Ron Harris and Eddie McCreadie who resorted to increasingly physical challenges on Coates as they tried to break up the home side's high-tempo style of play. Referee Ken Burns eventually lost patience with the duo and booked McCreadie for a rash tackle on the Burnley player and Harris for diving to palm the ball away from his feet!

Despite hogging possession early on, with Chelsea goalkeeper Peter Bonetti in imperious form as the last line of defence, Burnley couldn't find a way through.

Catty for England, chanted Tommy as Bonetti denied Frank Casper a goal with a breath-taking fingertip save. More was to follow as he boosted his claims for inclusion in Alf Ramsey's squad for the coming summer's World Cup tournament in Mexico with further acrobatics denying both Martin Dobson and Brian O'Neill.

Tommy's love of Bonetti was on a par with his adoration of Peter Osgood and admiration of young neighbour Alan Hudson. Oh and how Chelsea would have benefited from the presence of Ossie in the 20th minute. With Burnley threatening to run riot... but failing to do so, all of a sudden a chance presented itself for the 'Yellows'.

Hudson, once again playing with verve and intelligence that belied his tender years, gave the Burnley defence the slip, just as he had done when teeing up Osgood's goal on Saturday. He got a shot away which beat Clarets keeper Peter Mellor all ends up but the ball struck the post and bobbled slowly in the goalmouth. A predatory Ossie would have pounced and rattled the ball into the net, but for some reason Tommy Baldwin stood momentarily transfixed, like a rabbit caught in the headlights, and by the time he tried to take order, the danger was cleared.

Motivated by this let-off, Burnley seized the initiative and in the 35th minute Coates, whose hair was yet to look like a wig about to detach itself from his head everytime he ran at pace, switched flanks and charged fully 40-yards with the ball before unleashing a left-footer so powerful it would have beaten two Peter Bonetti's keeping goal simultaneously.

Undeterred by going 1-0 down, Chelsea supporters continued to chant the name of their team repeatedly. Joining in, Tommy thought it was magnificent

Chelsea! Chelsea! Chelsea!

Half-time came and went, and although Dave Sexton's battlers were now coming more into the game and appeared to be the fitter of the two sides it was Burnley who continued to hold the advantage right up until the 72nd minute when Peter Houseman mirrored Coates' achievement and scored a goal of pearlescent beauty. Hudson played a short pass to Houseman who ran fully 50-yards before curling a low shot inside Mellor's near post. What a goal! 1-1

We've got tiger, tiger, tiger Houseman on the wing on the wing.
We've got tiger, tiger, tiger Houseman on the wing on the wing.
Tiger, tiger Houseman, tiger Houseman on the wing.
Tiger, tiger Houseman, tiger Houseman on the wing.

Tommy loved the song which borrowed the melody from *Ging Gang Goolie* a weird ditty much-loved by Boy Scouts and Girl Guides. Last year, The Scaffold had recorded a version they called *Gin Gan Goolie* which had dented the charts and of course it had spread to the terraces.

There was another set of words Chelsea supporters had which were less praiseworthy of Houseman... *tiger* was replaced with *Mary*... which seemed harsh on the winger particularly when he was capable of turning a game in the way he just had and the way he would do in the first period of extra-time.

Ordinarily, when the ref had blown for full-time at the end of 90-minutes Tommy might have been wondering how he was going to get back to London but he didn't have that problem tonight. He lit a cigarette and relaxed a little. He sensed that Chelsea were going to prevail. At least the next round would be played in London even if it was away from Stamford Bridge.

'Go on Tigerrrrrr!'

Just three minutes into extra-time, Peter Houseman went on a mazy run with the ball to the left corner flag and fizzed over a cross which bamboozled the Burnley defence so-much-so that Peter Mellor and Dave Merrington collided with each other. Making amends for his hesitancy early on in the game... and ensuring he was perfectly positioned this time, Tommy Baldwin headed the ball over the Clarets duo and into the net. 2-1 to Chelsea!

Houseman came in for an unfair amount of stick at the Bridge, but tonight... away from home... he'd pulled his team up by their yellow socks and set them back on the road to Wembley... and the winger wasn't done yet. With a few minutes of time remaining, he cut into the Burnley penalty area, held off a couple of challenges that Chopper Harris and Eddie Mac would have been proud of, and curled another left-footer past Mellor in the net. 3-1, game over.

Tommy wondered if he'd ever seen a more complete performance from a Chelsea player. He probably had... but right now what he'd just seen was at the forefront of his mind.

Tiger Houseman on the wing had done his side proud and hopefully, with so many Blues supporters in the crowd, the word would get around that he wasn't as brittle as many thought.

CRYSTAL PALACE AWAY
Saturday 7 February 1970

Given the high probability that arch-rivals Tottenham Hotspur would be Chelsea's next opponents in the FA Cup, there was great interest in their Fourth Round replay with Crystal Palace and Tommy had mixed feelings about the outcome of the game which Palace surprisingly won 1-0 thanks to a 57th minute header from Gerry Queen.

Blues supporters would head over to South London in large numbers to cheer on the their team, another sell-out crowd would be guaranteed. Spurs away though, that would have represented a first meeting of the sides in cup competition since the 1967 FA Cup Final... revenge and all that. Still, their was some consolation to be had... the Lilywhites, mid-table in the league and out of both cups, were now stranded in a desert of despair.

Palace away turned out to be a cracking day for a number of reasons. This was the Glaziers debut season in the First Division and there was no historical rivalry with Chelsea despite respective grounds being less than 10 miles apart. Tommy had missed the league game a month ago between the sides at Selhurst Park. While getting increasingly drunk in the Ifield after the Southampton game, he'd decided to use the pub's payphone to call Sophia and asked her to meet him at work so they could spend the night together on their own. It was another case of his little head ruling his big head and the over-indulgence that followed rendered him totally useless the following day.

'Football... it's just a game isn't it Tommy,' Sophia had said as she'd cradled his hungover head in her arms.

'Just a game... ha ha. Maybe. But I'll never hear the end of it for not going, especially as we'd made arrangements in the pub yesterday.'

'But you watched Chelsea yesterday. It doesn't matter if you don't see them today... they'll still be there tomorrow and the day after that and next week and next month and next year.'

'Yeah but you don't get it do you? And besides something might happen and I'll never hear the end of it.'

Of course, as is so often the way when you miss a game for what would be considered by your mates as a feeble excuse, something did happen. Chelsea went nap at Palace and thrashed them 5-1 and Ossie, of course it had to be him, scored four of the Blues goals. It was the first time he'd scored more than two goals in a league match and Keith and Rick had scarcely been able to contain their glee at the prospect of ribbing Tommy with you've changed-style patter for swerving the game to be with his fiancée. Of course he had to take it.

'Chelsea's fixtures are like a box of Black Magic chocolates to you Tommy Walker,' Keith had said as loudly as he could while they were stood on The Shed before the cup game with Birmingham which followed the Palace game. 'You just pick out the best ones. Almond crunch, raspberry heaven, dreamy fudge, whole hazlenut praline, orange sensation or caramel caress...'

'You ain't interested in the plainer chocolates,' said Rick interrupting. 'Pick and bloody mix, that's what we'll call you from now on.'

Tommy laughed along with Keith and Rick and everyone else around them who'd been listening in. Deep down he was gutted though and it was part of the reason he'd been so keen to go to the replay with Burnley at Turf Moor. He'd got his own back on his friends with interest before the home game with Sunderland that followed at the weekend (31 January, Chelsea 3 Sunderland 1, Peter Osgood x3).

An elaborate description of Chelsea's rugged fightback against the Clarets and the atmosphere generated by the Blues travelling support that night put an end to the pick and mix jibes. Now it was his turn to have the attention of those around him on The Shed.

'Yeah, I'm with your old man now Rick, and mine for that matter. I'm betting we're going all the way to Wembley and we're going to win the FA Cup for the first time in our history. In years to come, I'll tell a story about how I went to every game of that glorious cup run. In fact I'll write a book about it and call it *Que se fucking ra!!*

'That could be a best-seller in 50 years time,' said Keith. 'Write it then. Not sure about that title though. Why not call it *Liquidator?*'

Rick nodded his approval as the opening bars of the by now familiar tune pounded out of the Stamford Bridge Tannoy system. The conversation ended at the point where the resounding *(clap, clap, clap, clap) Chelsea!* refrain was dropped into the tune by the crowd. Everyone stopped what they were doing to do that, in a few short months it had become standard practice.

*****

Tommy, Keith and Rick agreed they should have a night out on their own on the Friday evening before the cup tie with Crystal Palace. Having checked with his father first, Rick said Tommy and Keith could stay at their house in Tulse Hill. It was just over 10 minutes by train from there to Thornton Heath and then a short walk of less than a mile to get to Selhurst Park. Perfect! If Tommy was going to have a hangover the day of a Palace game again, at least he'd be virtually on their manor and wouldn't have Sophia whispering in his ear talking him out of going.

He was right about the hangover! They spent the evening at the nearby Bali-Hai nightclub on Streatham High Road (Now Streatham Ice and Leisure Centre). This was a great venue with a friendly atmosphere. The entrance to the club was adjacent to the Silver Blades ice skating rink which was an odd match at face value but it actually gave the place a unique character especially once inside when you climbed the stairs and found you could look out on the rink down below and see skaters practising into the small hours.

The Bali-Hai's artificial palm trees and tropical decor were a bit on the garish side but dropped off the radar after a few drinks as everyone's attention tended to be drawn to what was going on on the club's two smallish dance floors. It was obvious people came here to dance and listen to the music, an even mix of Motown, Soul and R&B, rather than to preen and pose although everyone was dressed sharp.

Since he'd moved from World's End to Vibart Gardens, and before he met Margaret, Rick was a regular at the Bali-Hai on a Friday night and had got to know a couple of local faces who were holding court in a roped-off VIP area near the main bar.

'Who are they?' asked Tommy, as Rick gave a thumbs up to a beckoned invitation from Rod 'Slim' Miles, the Bali-Hai's chief bouncer, to join the duo.

'Gorgeous George' Skevington and Paul 'Headcase' Hicks. Rick looked pleased with himself as he reeled off their gangster-style names in a matter of fact fashion.

Dressed in matching double-breasted navy herringbone Lord John suits with their shiny, youthful, angular faces framed by Brylcreem-laden dyed black hair, at first glance Keith thought they were a pop group, a theory he backed up with by pointing out the half-dozen or so dolly birds in hot pants and knee-high, fuck-me boots who were in their company and looked like Pan's People, the dance troupe who featured weekly on the television show *Top of the Pops.*

'Nah, keep guessing,' replied Rick as they walked over. 'But keep it sensible,' he added, in a cautionary tone of voice. 'Get on the wrong side of them and we'll have 'Slim' on our case. He made his name as a bare-knuckle boxer on the fairground circuit. Never lost a fight.'

After brief introductions had been made, Tommy noted the way the men spoke out of the corner of their mouths in exaggerated Cockney accents and whispered to Rick that rather than pop stars they looked and sounded like they could be South London's equivalent of Ronnie and Reggie Kray the notorious gangster twins who'd emerged from the East End in the 1950s and achieved celebrity status before both getting banged up for a 30 stretch last year when their luck finally ran out.

Rick shook his head and told Tommy he should keep that notion to himself if he spoke to them further during the course of the evening. It was sound advice because as it turned out the the two men were totally above board... well as above board as it was possible for car dealers to be he joked.

Between them, 'Gorgeous George' and 'Headcase' owned ten garages with forecourts right across London and Tommy was soon chatting Mark 2 Jags with 'Headcase' and secure banking stationery with

'Gorgeous George'. Rick and Keith were more interested in chatting up the dolly birds who were in fact part of a prim and proper promotional team down from the Midlands helping out the car dealers with the launch of a new family saloon, the Hillman Avenger.

It was a boozy evening but nobody disgraced themselves and the following morning after a decent black pudding, double egg, double sausage, bacon and baked beans fry-up expertly prepared by Rick's mother they decided to head to Selhurst Park early for a hair of the dog.

Tommy was buzzing at the prospect of going to a new ground. Prior to the league game there over Christmas which he'd famously missed, the last time Chelsea had faced Palace away from home was in 1926 (30 January, FA Cup Fourth Round, Crystal Palace 2 Chelsea 1, Albert Thain) which pre-dated his support by three decades.

Unlike the league fixture which had pulled in a crowd of 49,498, the FA Cup tie was all-ticket. Fred and George had paid £1 each for the privilege of sitting in the brand new Arthur Wait Stand which had been built to coincide with Palace's rise from football's lower divisions to the top-flight, while Tommy, Keith and Rick parted with the regulation five shillings to stand on the open terrace at the Whitehorse Lane end of the ground.

The Railway Telegraph on Brigstock Road right by Thornton Heath railway station was the agreed meeting point. Fred had all the tickets and his was the most welcome face to see when they'd arrived just before midday. The pub was packed with Chelsea supporters who worked their way through a full repertoire of chants and songs ensuring alcohol-lubricated tonsils were in full working order ready to cheer on the Blues.

All the latest songs were tried out in pubs before games and today there was a new one which was catching on quickly. Sandpaper-voiced, American tough-guy actor Lee Marvin had released a single version of *Wand'rin' Star* which was a part of the soundtrack for the film *Paint Your Wagon* that also starred Clint Eastwood.

Wand'rin' Star was creeping up the charts and so the melody was already familiar with plenty of people. From the corner of the pub, a handful of supporters who'd reworked the lyrics were determined to get the whole place joining in with what they'd come up with. To help them, Mick Greenway clambered onto a table and hollered out to everyone to shut-up and pay attention.

I was born under a Chelsea Shed.
I was born under a Chelsea Shed.
Knives are made for stabbing, guns are made to shoot…
If you come under the Chelsea Shed, we'll all stick in the boot.
I was born under a Chelsea Shed.

It was brilliant. It was infectious. It was definitely going to catch on because even George and Fred couldn't stop themselves from joining in.

By 2 p.m. when they left to go to the ground, the whole pub was singing it and it would go from there to Selhurst Park and then Stamford Bridge.

Wand'rin' Star ended up being a massive hit for Lee Marvin, eventually reaching No.1 in March 1970 and staying there for three weeks... in the process preventing *Let It Be* by the Beatles from reaching the top slot!

Chelsea supporters seemed to outnumber their Crystal Palace counterparts inside Selhurst Park. There were plenty of blue and white scarves to be seen in the opposite end of the ground to were they were stood, but even so the home crowd were in good voice particularly just before kick-off when they joined in with the chorus of the Dave Clark Five hit *Glad All Over* which was being played over the Tannoy.

Keith made a point of saying, 'well obviously Tommy, you weren't here, but they played it before the league game... the one in which Ossie scored four goals.'

'How many goals did Ossie score in that game against Palace that Tommy missed?' asked Rick.

Tommy winced before replying. 'Fuck off the pair of you or I'll remind you both about Burnley away.'

An old boy stood next to them who'd been eavesdropping their conversation chipped in with some insight about the *Glad All Over* / Crystal Palace link telling them that the Dave Clark Five had played the song live at the ground before a home game a couple of years previously and it had caught on from there. The old boy added that it was pretty funny because Dave Clark himself was a keen Tottenham Hotspur fan and was devastated that Spurs fans hadn't adopted *Glad All Over* first especially given the fact it had topped the charts years ago (January 1964).

'Chelsea should get Harry J. All Stars to play *Liquidator* live at Stamford Bridge,' said Rick rubbing his hands and blowing on them as the players came out onto the pitch.

Keith nodded and pulled up the collar of his navy-coloured Aquascutum rain mac which of course by now was designated as lucky FA Cup attire... until it wasn't lucky anymore.

Tommy laughed as the sight of match referee Ray Tinkler standing in the centre circle on the pitch down in front of him made him remember the previous evening and Paul 'Headcase' Hicks proudly explaining why he was nicknamed 'Headcase'.

'People think it's because I'm mad,' he'd said. 'But actually it's because I can name every referee that's officiated an FA Cup Final since the first final between Wanderers and the Royal Engineers in 1872... that was Alfred Stair.'

Tommy hadn't asked why 'Headcase' would want to have such information stored in his brain or indeed what use it might be... he simply concluded that actually 'people' were right in their assumption. He was mad. Bloody nice bloke though.

'Look at that state of that!' exclaimed Keith, pointing at the pitch which in places looked like a swamp. 'It's a mud bath.'

Tommy and Rick shrugged their shoulders.

'What did you expect?' asked Rick. 'Perfect green grass, mowed at just the right height for the ball to stick to Huddy's boot as he glides through the Palace defence and delicately rolls it to Ossie to score?'

Keith laughed. The Stamford Bridge pitch looked like a sandpit at this time of the year, but this was something else. Quite how the referee had decided it was playable was beyond belief... but he was glad he had. This was going to be a proper game of winter football. A slugfest in the mud. It was brilliant to watch this Chelsea side play with the swift fluency which had become their trademark under Dave Sexton, but the mark of a great side was adaptability. How would the Blues cope with these conditions?

Come On Chelsea! Come On Chelsea! Come On Chelsea!

FA Cup Fifth Round
Crystal Palace 1 Chelsea 4
Selhurst Park
Attendance: 48,479
Referee: Ray Tinkler

Chelsea: Peter Bonetti, David Webb, Eddie McCreadie, John Hollins, John Dempsey, Ron Harris, Tommy Baldwin, Alan Hudson, Peter Osgood, Ian Hutchinson, Peter Houseman.
Scorers: Osgood 37, Dempsey 64, Houseman 73, Hutchinson 86.
Booked: Hutchinson.

Crystal Palace: Jackson, Sewell, Loughlan, Payne, McCormick, Blyth, Taylor, Hoadley, Hynd, Queen, Hoy.
Scorer: Hoy 52.
Booked: Hynd, Loughlan.

As the game got underway, Tommy looked puzzled.

'I wonder why, we're playing in blue today when Palace are playing in claret and blue shirts? Their kit isn't much different to Burnley's home kit and yet we wore yellow shirts for that replay... THAT I WENT TO.'

Rick shook his head at both the question and the barb that went with it. 'Maybe, the yellow kit isn't back from the launderette yet.'

Keith nodded. 'It's a fair point. I wonder how they decide? I mean, look. You can easily tell the two teams apart in the kits they're wearing.'

'Maybe it's to do with them showing games on television,' Tommy concluded. 'A lot of kits probably look the same on a black and white set.'

Palace took the game to Chelsea early on and Peter Bonetti's emerald green goalkeeping jersey was soon muddied when Roger Hynd and David Payne tested his cat-like reflexes. On a decent pitch, Hynd, despite his height, would have been easy to deal with. He was cumbersome and slow for a striker. But it seemed he'd been practising slithering and slide-tackling in advance of the match and he was causing the Chelsea defence, and John Dempsey in particular, all kinds of problems.

'Webby needs to get tighter on their centre-forward. Chopper and Dempsey need help,' advised Rick to no one in particular.

Tommy meanwhile was unconcerned. He lit a cigarette and smoked in a patient, methodical manner. It was clear to him that Blues midfield duo John Hollins and Alan Hudson had the talent to wrestle back control of the game once Palace had run out of ideas and the initial enthusiasm that an underdog home side always had in any cup game.

Midway through the first half, it was Chelsea's turn to lay siege to Palace keeper John Jackson's goal. Tommy Baldwin saw a tight-angled shot blocked and Ian Hutchinson following up on the loose ball also had a shot hoofed clear.

Chelsea! Chelsea!

The loud and constant encouragement from the massive contingent of Blues supporters in the ground was impressive and it clearly motivated Dave Sexton's side to try and break down the stubborn resistance they were facing. It looked as though they had the lead when Peter Houseman lobbed a cross which Tommy Baldwin met with his head.

Yes… ohh…

A unified cheer turned to palpable frustration in an instant as Baldwin's goalbound header looped over a flailing Jackson but was headed off the line by John Loughlan.

Time marched on and with barely ten minutes left of the first-half, the game was still goalless.

'We're gonna score now.' Keith sounded supremely confident as he pointed at Houseman walking across to the right-hand side to take a corner-kick. 'This is our sixth corner. Enough practice. This one's going to count.'

Not for the first time, Keith's uncanny perception proved well-founded although there was an element of foul-play about Chelsea's opening goal. This time, Houseman executed the perfect corner. Well over 48,000 pairs of eyes watched the projectile-like flight of the ball following its parabolic path through the air and into the Palace penalty area where it was met by the head of Peter Osgood who rose highest of all from a standing position to nod the ball powerfully so it angled past Jackson into the back of the net.

Ossie! Yesss!

It didn't matter to the jubilant away support that their imperious striker had invoked the dark-arts to push Palace winger Mel Blyth, who had taken up a defensive position in front of him, out of the way.

It didn't matter to the Chelsea players who were celebrating like they didn't have a care in the world... which in truth they didn't.

The referee's a wanker!

The home crowd jeered at Mr Tinkler while Glaziers manager Bert Head looked incandescent with rage on the touchline as he danced a jig of indignant frustration.

Que Sera, Sera, whatever will be, will be...
We're going to Wembley... Que Sera, Sera.

Chelsea supporters serenaded their team off the pitch at half-time and during the break most of them, as far as Tommy could hear, seemed to be chatting about one man... Sir Alf Ramsey had been spotted at Selhurst Park. Many Blues fans had developed an increasingly jaundiced view of the England manager mainly because he appeared to have little in the way of serious time for their idol Peter Osgood who right now was just a couple of weeks shy of his 23rd birthday and scoring for fun.

Whether it was a foul or not, Osgood's latest goal had brought his tally for the season to 21 and it was only the beginning of February. It didn't feel right that he had yet to win a full England cap and Tommy, Keith and Rick weren't alone on the terraces in airing the opinion that it was because he was just like them... too much like them maybe.

Os was one of the lads who liked a drink and a laugh and staying out late carousing. That was Chelsea for you. Dave Sexton didn't like it and Tommy Docherty before him had major problems with the 'go hard or go home' drinking culture in the Blues dressing room. So what though? The problem, if that's what it was, wasn't confined to Stamford Bridge, it was prevalent elsewhere. Footballers were like pop stars now. Manchester United had George Best, QPR had Rodney Marsh, Arsenal had Charlie George, Manchester City had Stan Bowles.

As far as Osgood's England chances were concerned they were still being limited by Best's Man U teammate Bobby Charlton even though at 32-years of age his best seasons were behind him. Charlton was the safe option. It rankled.

'There's an England friendly with Belgium coming up,' said Rick. 'Why not pick Os for that game?'

Tommy and Keith nodded.

'And look at Huddy,' continued Rick, 'He's in a class of his own and still only 18-years old.'

'Yeah, too young for Ramsey and he's already being seen out and about,' added Tommy, punching the air as Chelsea's players re-emerged for the second-half. 'Anyway, it's club before country any day of the week for me,' he shouted, before braying *Come On Chelsea! Come On Chelsea!*

The whole terrace followed his lead. When the chant had died down, he winked at his friends, clenched his right fist, blew on the fingers and rubbed his chest. It always felt special when you got a chant going.

Tommy hadn't done it intentionally, it just happened... but it was decent and he got a nod from Mick Greenaway who was stood further down the terrace and had turned round to give him a thumbs-up appreciative acknowledgement before launching into *Why don't you give me a C ee ee... Ai-aitch... Eee-eee... Llll... Sss... Eee-eee... Aa-aaa.....*

There was a cockiness and swagger to Chelsea's play not too dissimilar to the Burnley game in the previous round of the cup at the Bridge. On that occasion the Clarets had stunned the Blues fighting back from 2-0 to level the tie and Palace were now having a go at their opponents in a similar fashion. Throwing caution to the wind and pressing forward, Loughlan and Hynd in particular were now making ploughing though the mud with the ball look like a balletic art form and it was this duo who combined to set up the Glaziers equaliser in the 52nd minute.

Ron Harris and John Dempsey failed to contain the Palace pair as they broke from defence and exchanged passes in a move which culminated with Hynd zipping the ball into the Chelsea penalty area for Roger Hoy to head powerfully past Peter Bonetti. 1-1.

Fortunately, the goal jolted the Blues back to life and ten minutes later they retook the lead. Dempsey who had toiled in defence had a useful knack of adding value to his team when joining the attack and he was in an advanced position when John Hollins fired over a 40-yard free-kick from the right into the Palace box. With the Glaziers backline monitoring Peter Osgood and Ian Hutchinson, goalie John Jackson might have made a better fist of the situation which saw unmarked Dempsey rise to nod home a simple header... but he didn't. 2-1 Chelsea!

The Wembley chants started again and continued as the Blues took control of the game. Osgood flashed a shot off the post, but it was centre-back Dempsey who stole the striker's thunder. Having just scored, he was also involved in Chelsea's third goal which ended Palace's resistance, heading down a ball from David Webb into the path of Peter Houseman who smashed it past a bemused Jackson. 3-1.

Houseman for England, Houseman for England, bellowed Keith.

'Have you been drinking?' asked the old boy nearby who'd told them about the Dave Clark Five.

'Houseman for England,' continued Keith, undeterred and now clapping his hands above his head. Tommy, Rick and a couple of others joined in before their efforts were drowned out by a continuous chant of

Chelsea! Chelsea! It didn't take long for the trio to forget championing Houseman and fall in line.

Chelsea! Chelsea! Chelsea! was beautiful. It made the hairs on the back of your neck stand on end. The difference in class between the teams was now manifesting itself all over the pitch. Compact in defence, menacing in midfield, and razor sharp in attack, Sexton's side were now bossing the game and it was also being noted by their fans that in a physical contest littered with X-rated tackles they were giving as good if not better than they got.

With four minutes left, Chelsea scored again. There was an inevitability about what was going to happen as Peter Houseman stepped up to take yet another corner. Throughout the match, Palace goalie John Jackson had displayed an irrational fear of coming off his line to try and claim the ball and once again it would prove his undoing.

Houseman clipped the ball over and Ian Hutchinson hustled and bustled his way into the box to ensure he was unopposed when heading home. As with Osgood's opener, it looked as if a foul had been committed but referee Tinkler waved the resultant Palace protests away. 4-1 to Chelsea, it was time to sing *You'll Never Walk Alone...* the Blues had coasted through to the FA Cup quarterfinals.

All eight Fifth Round ties had kicked off at 3 p.m. and as they walked out of the ground, Tommy, Keith and Rick paused to join a group of people gathered around a man who was holding a portable transistor radio in his hand. It was the 'Dave Clark' old boy. Everyone was keen to hear the results and get a sense of who the Blues might draw in the next round.

'It's five o'clock. Time for *Sports Report*,' announced BBC presenter Peter Jones. The programme's orchestral theme music *Out of the Blue* followed. It seemed appropriate... 'and now today's classified football results read by John Webster.'

A hush descended nearby as everyone listened.

'FA Cup Fifth Round... Carlisle United 1 Middlesbrough 2... Crystal Palace 1 Chelsea 4... Leeds United 2 Mansfield 0... Liverpool 0 Leicester City 0... Northampton Town 2 Manchester United 8... Queens Park Rangers 1 Derby County 0... Swindon Town 3 Scunthorpe United 1... Watford 2 Gillingham 1'.

Tommy, Keith and Rick walked away at that point and headed back to the Railway Telegraph to meet George and Fred. When they got there they learned that George Best had scored a phenomenal six goals in the Red Devils rout of the Cobblers. Man U along with Leeds were the teams they agreed Chelsea needed to avoid when the quarterfinal draw was made on Monday.

QUEENS PARK RANGERS AWAY
Saturday 21 February 1970

Football supporters often spoke about the 'magic of the cup' and it wasn't lost on Tommy that the four sides drawn at home in the quarterfinals of the competition that Chelsea had yet to win all plied their trade in Division Two.

Middlesbrough v Manchester United
Queens Park Rangers v Chelsea
Swindon Town v Leeds United
Watford v Liverpool

Was a giant killing on the cards? QPR at Loftus Road would be interesting... a West London derby. Tommy's father George always joked that QPR actually stood for Quarter Pound of Rubbish and with good reason in his book. Apart from last season, the Rs had spent their entire history in the lower divisions although they had managed to win the League Cup in 1967 becoming the first Third Division club to do so when beating West Bromwich Albion 3-2 in the first final to be contested over a single game at Wembley.

QPRs' fleeting glimpse of life in the top-flight hadn't ended well, they'd finished bottom of the table with a meagre 18 points... that said, on home turf they shouldn't be underestimated as Derby County had found out in the last round. Chelsea were overwhelming favourites to win the tie at the first attempt though. A combination of thrashing Palace and being paired with QPR had Tommy buzzing about the possibilities.

The Blues next opponents in the league were Derby who were smarting from the QPR defeat. It was a midweek game (11 February) and unlike the Burnley cup replay a couple of weeks previously it was never going to be practical to get to the Baseball Ground. Tommy's work schedule required him to be in London and he'd been honest with himself as well. Basically it boiled down to one thing... he didn't fancy it.

Pick and mix ha ha. Sometimes you just had to let go of things and get on with real life, and besides he had other things on his mind like taking Sophia out to dinner on Saturday as it was St. Valentine's Day. He'd also booked a room at the Cumberland Hotel near Marble Arch, a louche establishment at that time and a favoured haunt of rock musicians, groupies and nocturnal London's flotsam and jetsam. It would be worth the expenditure to have some comfort and privacy. He planned to head straight there after Chelsea's home game with Liverpool and have a nice, relaxing hot bath... a luxury that didn't come his way too often. The weather was turning colder, thawing out in a tub of hot water with a beer at his side after watching the Blues beat the Reds while waiting for his girlfriend to arrive was something to look forward to.

The Derby game read like a thriller on the back pages of the newspapers. Chelsea contrived to squander a two-goal lead afforded them by Peter Osgood and Alan Hudson as the Rams pegged them back to a 2-2 draw. Ossie's strike was his 22nd of the season and Huddy's, a peachy volley by all accounts, his first for the club. That was the good news. The flip-side was letting a 2-0 lead slip with just 14 minutes to go and Osgood picking up his third booking of the season.

Tommy's cosy plans for Valentine's Day got cosier still when the country was gripped by a wintry blast of snow and ice that led to the postponement of 33 matches in England and Scotland including Chelsea's home fixture with Liverpool. Maybe this was a blessing in disguise, a weekend off for Blues players whose ankles wouldn't be tested by a glacially-hard pitch further wrecked by the deep freeze.

Sexton's side would be raring to go against QPR whose game away at Hull City at Boothferry Park had gone ahead. Better still, the Rs had also played a midweek game against prior to the Chelsea cup tie. Yes, Les Allen's men would be buzzing having won both those matches (2-1 and 4-0) but their exertions in doing so in trying conditions would hopefully prove detrimental to their cause in the cup.

As with Selhurst Park and Crystal Palace in the previous round, Tommy had never been to Loftus Road as he'd missed the first ever competitive meeting between Chelsea and QPR the previous season (14 September 1968, QPR 0 Chelsea 4, Tommy Baldwin x2, Peter Osgood, Alan Birchenall), nevertheless, he was very well acquainted with the Shepherds Bush area of West London that was home to QPR.

Tommy had first seen The Who performing live at The Goldhawk Social Club on Goldhawk Road, less than a mile from Loftus Road, on 31 July 1964. Along with Keith and Rick, three wannabe teenage ace faces, he'd caught the number 49 bus from Sydney Street, Chelsea, to Shepherds Bush Green and kept quiet about the fact. Tommy reckoned that Mods didn't use public transport as it wasn't cool so at the club door he lied about his age and the Vespa GS 150 scooter he didn't own that wasn't parked-up 'round the back'.

It would have been brilliant if the The Who supported Chelsea. Imagine that. But it wasn't to be despite the quartet being born and bred West London boys. Roger Daltrey from Acton, Keith Moon from Alperton and Pete Townshend and John Entwistle from Chiswick. Geographically, Queens Park Rangers was at the centre of their early world, but the Rs were Third Division fodder then which might explain a lack of interest or maybe music was the band's all-consuming passion. Yeah that was definitely it. Even back then, The Who played like they practised their instruments 24 hours a day. Over the next 18 months, Tommy, Keith and Rick went to as many of their gigs as they could.

Towards the end of '64, with interest in the band building, they were given a Tuesday night residency at the Marquee and as their reputation spread across London, the venue became a sweaty, heaving, 700-capacity sell-out. The Marquee was like a football ground in this respect. When it was packed, it felt like there were a lot more than 700 people in there... a thousand maybe. False accounting again!

Tommy had bought The Who's first single *Zoot Suit* which was released by the band at the beginning of July that year under the short-lived monicker The High Numbers. He'd first heard the track on pirate station Radio Caroline which had begun transmitting in March and that's what snagged his interest in going to see them play live at the Goldhawk. Other than actually going to gigs or hanging out in record shops, listening to Caroline was the main way to hear new music at that time. BBC Radio 1 would change the listening habits of the nation, but that didn't start broadcasting until September 1967.

Tommy thought that early on The Who had sounded a bit like the Kinks but with that little bit extra... a secret ingredient that had proven to be addictive down the years. Lighting a cigarette, his reminiscences of the band were suddenly turbo-charged by the opening chords of *I Can't Explain* blasting from the Loftus Road Tannoy speakers. This was the second single The Who released, the first under the name The Who, and as if to underline what he'd previously thought, The Kinks influence was stamped all over it. Keith knew what Tommy was thinking and started singing the words to the Kinks track *All Day And All Of The Night*. Rick meanwhile did a passable impression of drummer Keith Moon's manic sticksmanship.

Poor Moony thought Tommy. A tragedy had enveloped the musician. It wasn't 100% clear what had happened, but on 4 January, along with his wife Kim, some friends and his chauffeur Neil Boland, he'd attended the opening of a disco at The Cranbourne Rooms adjacent to the Red Lion pub in Hatfield and made a short speech. The venue had attracted a large number of skinheads who clearly had a problem with the rockstar and his entourage who they perhaps saw as having cast off their working class roots for a life of excess.

At the end of the evening, things got heavy. As the Moon party bundled themselves into his status symbol Bentley to make a sharp exit, the skinheads attacked the car pelting it with coins. Instead of flooring the accelerator to get them out of the car park and away from the scene, Boland, who was behind the wheel, got out to have a go at their assailants. It proved to be a fatal mistake. Keith Moon slid across the front seat and attempted to drive, initially jolting the car forward and at some point in the process running over Boland who was pinned underneath the car and killed outright as it moved away.

An inquest, initially opened on 9 January, had been adjourned until yesterday, 20 February. Tommy had refamiliarised himself with the harshly sensationalised 'drunken rockstar kills chauffeur' story in the morning paper before heading out to QPR game. Moon, who'd been breathalysed and found to be well over the drink-drive limit and also confessed to driving without a license or insurance, was cleared of culpability and a verdict of accidental death was returned. He would have to return to court on 23 March to answer the charges related to drink-driving and not having a license or insurance.

Tommy tried to process the guilt that Moon must be carrying. The whole idea of having a chauffeur was so he had someone to take care of things when he got inebreiated… what an absolute shocker that his friend had died in such awful circumstances. He vowed alcohol would never cross his lips from this point on if he was intending to drive and wondered how Moon would be affected in the long run. Poor Boland's life had ended early though, for him there would be no long run and his family faced a future grieving his loss. It was sobering. The cup tie which was about to kick-off was a welcome distraction.

FA Cup Sixth Round
Queens Park Rangers 2 Chelsea 4
Loftus Road
Attendance: 33,572
Referee: Kevin Howley

Chelsea: Peter Bonetti, David Webb, Eddie McCreadie, John Hollins, John Dempsey, Ron Harris, Charlie Cooke, Alan Hudson, Peter Osgood, Ian Hutchinson, Peter Houseman.
Scorers: Webb 7, Osgood 8, 43, 58.
Booked: Osgood.

Queens Park Rangers: Kelly, Clement, Gillard, Watson, Mobley, Hazell, Bridges, Venables, Leach, Marsh, Ferguson.
Scorers: Venables 27 (pen), Bridges .

The *Oi,Oi,Oi* riposte to Mick Greenaway's barnstorming *Zigger Zagger* was remarkable.

> *Oh when the Blues go steaming in…*
> *Oh when the Blues go steaming in.*
> *I wanna be in that number… Oh when the Blues go steaming in.*

It didn't matter to Chelsea supporters, who seemed to be in every part of the ground and present in far greater numbers than the Club's 8,000 combined stand, enclosure and ground ticket allocation suggested, that their team was once again wearing its yellow change strip… Tommy by now thought it was lucky anyway… as lucky as the blue Aquascutum raincoat Keith was wearing once again especially for the cup tie.

QPR, with familiar Chelsea old boys Terry Venables and Barry Bridges in their ranks, started brightly with their flair player Rodney Marsh catching the eye.

'I honestly can't believe Marsh ain't playing for a bigger club,' said Keith, as the Rs number 10 gave Ron Harris an early defensive workout. Chopper was up to the task though and after five minutes he had Marsh in his pocket from where he rarely emerged... a combination of dynamic tackling and perceptive positional play neutralising his effectiveness.

Ron Harris, Ron Harris to the tune of *Three Blind Mice* was given an early airing by appreciative Chelsea supporters, however it was Chopper's defensive partner football crime David Webb who soon stole the limelight.

Approaching the seventh minute of the game, John Hollins squared the ball wide from midfield to Charlie Cooke who picked out Webb advancing from the back in what by now was customary fashion. With a piece of skill that Cooke himself would have been proud of, Webby stylishly flicked the ball out to Hollins overlapping on the flank and continued his buccaneering run into the QPR box where he found himself perfectly positioned to powerfully volley Hollins' deflected cross through the hands of Rs keeper Mike Kelly and into the net.

Tommy, Keith and Rick were still celebrating Webb's goal and commenting it was as good any that star striker Peter Osgood might score, when Os himself got in on the act and doubled Chelsea's lead.

Webb was a rumbustious presence yet again. Making good use of the muddy Loftus Road pitch with a perfectly executed sliding tackle to dispossess Mike Ferguson, he passed to Cooke who progressed a few yards, looked up and saw Osgood had sprinted into an unmarked position on the edge of QPRs penalty area.

An inch-perfect pass saw the ball leave Cooke's right boot and drop perfectly on the sodden ground in front of Ossie who controlled it deftly as he moved in on Kelly's goal and slipped it past the keeper into the net. 2-0 to Chelsea inside 10 minutes!

Que sera sera, whatever will be will be...
We're going to Wembley, que sera sera.

Rick, who'd gone to relieve the pressure on his bladder created by over-celebrating Osgood's goal and one bottle of light ale too many in the pub before kick-off, returned with news that England manager Sir Alf Ramsey was once again in attendance.

'Alf's gotta pick Ossie for the Belgium / England friendly international this week surely,' he said. 'Can't believe that game's on the same night as Chelsea are playing Newcastle in the league. Whose idea was that? I mean, I know we were meant to be playing them today and obviously we are playing in the cup, but it seems ridiculous.'

Tommy and Keith shrugged their shoulders. George and Fred would know, but they were watching the game from the dilapidated, tin-roofed grandstand that skirted Ellerslie Road while they were stood on the Loft terrace which was meant to be the home end.

QPRs response to going two goals behind was to address the reason for it... shocking marking... and as a result they came back into the game. Just before the half-hour mark, former Chelsea favourite Barry Bridges got the better of his ex teammate Eddie McCreadie skipping into the visitors penalty area ahead of McCreadie who attempted a tackle which only succeeded in sending Bridges to ground.

Referee Kevin Howley pointed at the spot and although plenty Chelsea fans cursed, it was the players who were really complaining... led of course by Eddie Mac with his hands raised in the air.

'Hate to say it, but that was a pen all day long,' said Tommy shaking his head as Terry Venables stepped up to try his luck against Peter Bonetti. The Cat was equal to Venables' low shot though diving to his left to catch it. Chelsea supporters cheered as Bonetti released the ball to get play moving again but one of the linesmen was flagging maniacally. The Cat was adjudged to have moved before Venables struck the ball.

Always a tricky one to ref... but Mr Howley whistled for play to stop and the penalty to be retaken. Peter Osgood and Ron Harris aggrieved at the perceived injustice remonstrated with Howley without luck. Bonetti might have second-guessed his old teammate the first time but Venables made no mistake the second time around firing the ball into the net with Catty virtually motionless.

Chelsea players continued to argue with Howley but he waved them away and was treated to a voluble rendition of *Who's the wanker in the black?*

The goal naturally gave QPR renewed impetus and Bonetti had to be at his agile best to deny Vic Mobley. Barry Bridges, once again outwitting Eddie Mac, also went close to equalising for the home side losing his marker and getting goal-side of him to meet a great cross from Ian Watson with his head. With Bonetti beaten, the ball flashed off the woodwork to safety.

It was a let off for Chelsea who stepped up their game as the first-half drew to a pulsating close. Gliding gracefully but with great purpose through the mud to intercept a Venables throw-in that had been directed at Bridges, Eddie Mac punted the ball forward into the path of Ian Hutchinson who laid it off to John Hollins.

Fancying his chances from 35-yards, Hollins thumped a screaming volley at the QPR goal. Mike Kelly saved well but calamitously spilled the ball into the path of Peter Osgood whose predatory instinct had sensed an opportunity. Ossie got his right boot to the ball and prodded it through the mud into the back of the net.

3-1 to Chelsea at half-time and the chatter at the break was about two topics. Firstly, possible semi-final opponents. As expected, Leeds

United were winning at Swindon, but Manchester United and Liverpool were being held by Middlesbrough and Watford respectively. Maybe there would be a giant-killing and a favourable draw to ease the Blues path to Wembley. Secondly, there was a potential problem looming on the horizon for two-goal Peter Osgood. Ossie had been booked for an innocuous-looking foul on Dave Clement, his fourth caution of the campaign.

'He's already waiting to appear before the FA for getting booked three times,' said Keith in a worried tone of voice. 'He could get a ban and miss the semi or the final if we get there.'

Rick shook his head. 'Surely, if he gets suspended it would be before then?'

Tommy lit a cigarette and pointed at the Ellerslie Road Stand. 'Another thing to ask our fathers later eh.'

After the break, Chelsea were back in the groove with Alan Hudson's youthful stamina benefiting him on a pitch that was getting heavier with every passing minute.

'Be great to see Huddy playing on a decent surface,' said Rick, applauding another darting run by the 18-year old from midfield. 'Wonder who the next kid will be from the manor to play for Chelsea?'

Tommy drew heavily on the cigarette he was smoking. 'At the rate they are pulling the manor down, there won't be any houses round the ground for local kids to grow up in,' he said, frowning as he spoke.

Concerned chatter about the manor ended abruptly just before the hour mark when Chelsea scored again. Hudson exchanged passes with Osgood inside his own half before looping a probing ball down the left flank which fell kindly for Peter Houseman following a miskick by Dave Clement.

The winger jinked his way into the QPR penalty area and fired a shot which Kelly did well to parry. The loose ball was eventually recycled by Houseman to Hudson who clipped it back into the box where Ian Watson fluffed an attempted clearance... inadvisable with Ossie lurking and chasing his third hat-trick of the season.

Os lapped up the invitation to score firing a left-footer past Kelly into the corner of the net. The linesman had been flagging for an off-the-ball kerfuffle between Ian Hutchinson and Ian Gillard but the ref wasn't interested and signaled a goal. 4-1 to Chelsea.

Osgood for England! Osgood for England! Osgood for England!

Watching from the stands, if England manager Alf Ramsey had any doubt about selecting Ossie based on pure football reasons they had to have been allayed by now. You never knew with Ramsey though, why had he waited so long? Osgood had celebrated his 23rd birthday the previous day. He was young, but he wasn't a kid as young as Alan Hudson who must have also caught his eye.

Having saluted their hat-trick hero, Chelsea supporters then sang *Que sera* once again... but QPR weren't ready to give up just yet and within a matter of minutes they pulled a goal back through Barry Bridges who played throughout the game like he had a point to prove to his former employers.

Rodney Marsh finally broke the shackles Ron Harris had placed on him and sent a measured ball through to Bridges. Despite Peter Bonetti diving bravely at his feet, the Rs forward was able to smartly find the net. With almost 30 minutes still to play, another quick QPR goal might have unsettled Chelsea, but Dave Sexton had his backline well-drilled.

John Dempsey lacked the maverick-style of many of his teammates, but he more than made up for it with his no-nonsense, tough-tackling approach to the game and he covered all the bases in the final half-hour to keep the home side at bay.

We're gonna win the cup, we're gonna win the cup...
And now you're gonna believe us...
And now you're gonna believe us...
And now you're gonna be-lie-ve us... we're gonna win the cup!

Shortly after the final whistle, news filtered through that Watford had beaten Liverpool 1-0. A huge cheer went up. Middlesbrough had also done well holding Manchester United to a 1-1 draw, but with the replay at Old Trafford the Red Devils would be hot favourites to progress. Leeds United, currently heading the First Division table by two points from Everton who had a couple of games in hand, prevailed against Swindon Town winning 2-0.

WATFORD AT WHITE HART LANE
Saturday 14 March 1970

The FA Cup draw was indeed kind to Chelsea. The Blues semi-final opponents were Watford. Dave Sexton's flamboyant high fliers, securely third in the First Division, were overwhelming favourites to beat Ken Furphy's dour, relegation-threatened Second Division stragglers. Mind you, the Hornets beating supposedly mighty Liverpool in the quarterfinals in front of just over 34,000 fans at Vicarage Road had been no mean feat.

That result was the major shock of the tournament so far eclipsing second-tier Blackpool's feat of knocking out top-flight Arsenal after a replay in the Third Round. It had also been pointed out that Watford had also beaten another First Division side, Stoke City, in the Fourth Round.

Sexton then needed to be sure that complacency did not creep into the Chelsea dressing room. Surely though, the desire to win through to Wembley would override everything?

Tommy laughed when the semi-final venue had been named. White Hart Lane, the home of Tottenham Hotspur... the club they'd all thought the Blues would be playing in the Fifth Round instead of Crystal Palace. His father had queued for their semi tickets which had gone on sale on Sunday 8 March.

'I queue, you pay,' he'd said. It was fair enough. 10 shillings for a ground ticket was reasonable. George had gone down there with Fred who was getting Rick's ticket with the same arrangement applying. Two tickets per person were the rules and they'd had to ask if anyone was buying a single so Keith would be sorted out. It all worked out okay, but if Chelsea got to the final as was expected they'd need a better plan to accommodate the five of them.

Three frenetic weeks had passed since the quarterfinal win at QPR. Tommy enjoyed the way the pace of his life had stepped up as his new job had evolved. He was making more deliveries outside London now for Ted as the business expanded and between that, having a fiancée, watching Chelsea, going to gigs and eating, drinking and sleeping days were blurring into each other.

Working overtime, which he'd previously agreed to do, meant missing out on Chelsea's rearranged First Division game at Stamford Bridge with Newcastle United (25 February, 0-0) and he hadn't seen any television highlights of England's 3-1 win over Belgium in Brussels, the international friendly played the same night in which Peter Osgood was handed a deserved first cap by Alf Ramsey.

Rick and Keith had gone to the Bridge and said the Blues clearly missed Ossie's bite up front though they were full of praise for stand-in goalie Tommy Hughes whose clean sheet was a vast improvement on the five goals he'd conceded against Leeds United in his last first team outing. Osgood's England debut meanwhile was described in the papers as 'quietly satisfactory'. Oh well. It would have been nice had he scored, especially for his father who'd bet £5 on the possibility.

Ossie was back in Chelsea's starting XI for the next game against Coventry City at Highfield Road, but he he didn't find the net in a comfortable 3-0 win (28 February, Tommy Baldwin, David Webb, Alan Hudson).

Four days later, Osgood and Hudson lined up for the England Under-23 side against Scotland at Roker Park. Ossie netted twice and could conceivably have scored a hattrick or more... but the match was abandoned after 62 minutes because of heavy snow on Wearside.

Tommy was back at Stamford Bridge for Chelsea's home game with Nottingham Forest (7 March, 1-1, Tommy Baldwin). Minus Eddie McCreadie and John Dempey, absent through injury, the Blues looked brittle at the back, while up front, fit again Ian Hutchinson was overlooked by Dave Sexton. Hopefully the trio would be back in the frame for the cup semi-final.

The most memorable part of the day for Tommy, Rick and Keith came at the end of a sparkling rendition by The Shed of the often sung song *We hate Nottingham Forest, we hate Arsenal too. We hate West Ham United, but Chelsea we love you.*

'Why do we hate Nottingham Forest?' Rick had asked at half-time. 'I mean, I understand hating Arsenal and West Ham... but Forest?'

Fred put his hand up, 'Blame King Edward VII, Edward Elgar, Arthur Benson and Blackpool Football Club,' he said, smirking as he spoke and continuing before he could be interrupted. 'The King told Elgar that *Pomp and Circumstance March No.1* would make a great song and so he fiddled around with the tune and came up with *Coronation Ode* and got his mate Arthur Benson to write some words that included the refrain *Land of Hope and Glory, Mother of the free. How shall we extoll thee, who are born of thee?*'

Tommy lit a cigarette and shrugged his shoulders. 'Yeah. Well thank you for explaining that, but what about Nottingham Forest and what have Blackpool got to do with it?'

Fred was enjoying his moment. It felt to him perhaps that it was a story he should have saved for the pub after the game, but it was too late for that now. 'Blackpool started it. They finished bottom of the First Division in 1967 and when they were losing 2-0 to Forest at the City Ground a few of their fans started singing *We hate Nottingham Forest, we hate Tottenham too. We hate Man United, but Blackpool we love you.*'

United won the league that season, with Forest finishing second and Spurs third... the Seasiders ended up bottom. Other teams playing Blackpool heard it and changed it to suit their rivalries like Chelsea have, but the *We hate Nottingham Forest* bit at the beginning remained as it fits with the melody.'

'What about the *and Leicester* bit that we sometimes sing after *we hate Arsenal too* then?' asked Rick.

Fred shrugged his shoulders. 'There's a potty story that did the rounds about Garrison and his North Stand mob going up to Leicester for a row at a reserve game (18 March 1968, Leicester City 1 Chelsea 1, Roy Summers) a couple of days after our first team played the Foxes here at the Bridge (16 March, Chelsea 4 Leicester City 1, Tommy Baldwin, Bobby Tambling x2, Peter Osgood). There'd been bad blood between the mobs of both clubs ever since the 1965 League Cup Final second leg at Filbert Street (5 April, Leicester City 0 Chelsea 0). We won the trophy obviously having won the first leg here (15 March, 3-2, Bobby Tambling, Terry Venables, Eddie McCreadie) and their lot weren't happy about it and it kicked off and it's kicked off at every game since... even the reserve games.'

George, who'd been silently listening up to this point, chipped in with his tuppence worth of wisdom. 'I blame the end of National Service for this lack of discipline. Fighting at football games is ridiculous. If you're going to fight, fight for Queen and Country. These hooligans would all shit themselves if they were patrolling the streets of Northern Ireland. If they had real bottle, they'd join the British Army and do something worthwhile like fight the IRA.'

Tommy laughed. His father had used the National Service line when there'd been trouble between Mods and Rockers and also when hippies had first started appearing on the scene. Maybe he was just getting old. He thought about the song *My Generation* by The Who and remembered when he'd met Sophia on the Isle of Wight. Nobody really hopes they die before they get old. He didn't, not now, even though he sang it. There was too much to live for starting with watching Chelsea hopefully beat Watford to reach the FA Cup Final.

*****

There was nothing good about White Hart Lane. Absolutely nothing. As far as Tommy was concerned, that line *All hope, abandon ye who enter here*, which Sophia's father Enrico had told him originated in Dante's *Divine Comedy* and was said to have been inscribed on the gates to hell, should have been graffitied above the turnstile entrances for away fans at the Lane. They should also have a version of the line at Seven Sisters underground station... *All hope, abandon ye who exit here.* What a shit-hole... all of it, a fucking great big shit-hole.

Walking from Seven Sisters up Tottenham High Road to the Lane had never been something to write postcards home about... ever. Not that you would, but that figure of speech was appropriate. It was a 30-minute ramble that always felt arduous and after dark it was intimidating.

No matter how self-assured or hard you thought you were, putting safety first made good sense. Small mobs lurked on every dimly lit street corner sizing-up passersby looking for opportunities. *It's a long walk to Seven Sisters*, Spurs fans always sang... and they were right.

'If I live in the World's End, what the fuck is this place then?' joked Tommy as they neared the ground. Forget about the 17th-century and King Charles II in his carriage heading out of town to Chelsea for a bit of entertainment... imagine it's now and Her Majesty The Queen is heading to Tottenham, what would she call it?'

'Tottenham,' replied Keith, starting to laugh.

'Rottenham,' added Rick.

'I've never seen us win a game here,' said Tommy. 'First time I came was in 1964 and we drew 1-1 (24 October, George Graham). The following year we lost 4-2 (11 December, George Graham, Barry Bridges). Then it was 1-1 again (18 March 1967, Chico Hamilton). 2-0 (18 November 1967) and 1-0 (22 March 1969) followed that and finally 1-1 again at the start of this season.' (27 August 1969, David Webb)

'There's always a first time for everything,' said George, cupping his hands and blowing on them. 'Just be grateful Palace beat Spurs in that replay otherwise we'd have been playing them here.'

'And if we'd lost that game, we wouldn't be here listening to your boy moan would we,' interjected Fred. 'Although I expect he would have been complaining next season if we came.'

Unwanted, negative memories dissipated as they reached the turnstiles. The here and now reality was that Watford were today's opponents and Chelsea were not only favourites to win the game, but the FA Cup itself.

His name is Tommy Baldwin he's the leader of the team
(What team?)
The finest football team that the world has ever seen.
We're the Fulham Road supporters and we're louder than The Kop
(What Kop?)
If anyone wants to argue, we'll kill the fucking lot.
La la la la.

Mick Greenaway, arms aloft encouraging everyone passing him to join in the Tommy Baldwin song, sung to the melody of *McNamara's Band*, was the first recognisable face they saw as they clicked through the turnstiles.

Baldwin was an immensely popular player with Chelsea supporters and had been pretty much since he'd signed for the Club from Arsenal (29 September 1966) in a part-exchange deal that saw George Graham move the other way.

The morning newspapers reported that he'd asked for a transfer the previous day. It was frustrating, though it was understandable. The emergence of Alan Hudson from the youth ranks and the signing 18 months previously of striker Ian Hutchinson from Burton Albion meant Baldwin was no longer an automatic pick for manager Dave Sexton especially now Peter Osgood was back in the form of his life having fully recovered from that leg break he'd sustained in 1966.

On his return, Ossie had briefly been deployed as a midfielder... but it was up front where the King reigned supreme. Everyone agreed though that Baldwin was needed, because in football anything could happen. To sell the 24-year old at this stage of the season would be madness.

FA Cup Semi-final
Watford 1 Chelsea 5
White Hart Lane
Attendance: 55,209
Referee: Gordon Hill

Chelsea: Peter Bonetti, David Webb, Eddie McCreadie, John Hollins, John Dempsey, Ron Harris, Charlie Cooke, Alan Hudson, Peter Osgood, Ian Hutchinson, Peter Houseman.
Scorers: Webb 3, Osgood 58, Houseman 73, 79, Hutchinson 75.

Watford: Walker, Welbourne, Williams, Lugg, Lees, Walley, Scullion, Garbett, Endean, Packer, Owen (Garvey 65).
Scorer: Garbett 12.

The Paxton Road End was absolutely heaving. Blue and white-scarved human sardines packed in a steel and concrete can cheering for their team. It felt to Tommy like there were too many people in the end. It was claustrophobic... but that was normal. If an end didn't feel confining and oppressive then something was wrong. Football was about packed crowds, everyone was here for the Chelsea.

Come on Chelsea! Come on Chelsea! Come On Chelsea!

The pitch, as expected, was an uneven blend of mud and sand with little in the way of decent stretches of grass. It had been the same everywhere for months as a combination of hard frosts, rain and snow made the jobs of groundsmen up and down the country challenging to say the least. Still it was dry. That was the main thing. Watching football in the rain was a miserable experience. You couldn't even smoke properly as cigarettes quickly bloated with water and the taste of the nicotine in the tobacco became bitter beyond belief.

This was the first time Chelsea had ever played Watford and nobody really knew anything about them... apart from the fact they'd beaten Liverpool in the last round of the cup so they shouldn't be underestimated. Complacency was definitely ill-advised and this was apparent in the opening minutes as Second Division side took the game to their more illustrious opponents.

Fortunately, Chelsea got an early grip on the semi-final when Hornets goalkeeper Mike Walker's poor goal-kick failed to make distance and the loose ball eventually fell at the feet of Alan Hudson.

Go on Huddy!

Thousands of Blue-biased voices shouted the same encouragement to the youngster. Right from the start, Hudson was out to show what he could do. The lad was amazing, and Tommy, Keith and Rick were still at an age themselves when they found it hard to cope with the reality that they were older than him.

Tommy remembered his father saying that you could measure your football-following life by stages related to age. When you're a kid, well everyone is older than you. Then you're the same age as the youngest player... then suddenly you're older than all the players... then you're older than all the players and the referee and linesmen... and finally the managers as well. Ha... that's life.

Hudson may only have been 18-years old, but he played the game with purposeful poise and maturity and he was bang up for this game... keen to impress... keen to get Chelsea to the final. '

Go on Huddy!

Hudson used his pace to evade tackles while charging through the White Hart Lane mud to the Watford penalty area where he exchanged passes with Peter Houseman before being well tackled by Duncan Welbourne. *Corner!*

Tommy's father had insisted they stood at the top side of the terrace because his knees couldn't take it if he got caught up in the crowd surge when the front of the end 'fell' as it just had with that Chelsea chance.

Huddy flicked over a beautiful corner-ball which was nodded on by John Dempsey, always a menacing presence at set pieces. Lurking at the far post was fellow defender David Webb who was equally effective at causing problems in opposing penalty areas.

Webb, who'd scored Chelsea's opening goal against Queens Park Rangers, repeated the feat against Watford, prodding the ball past Walker. Easy! 1-0 to the Blues! As the crowd surged rapturously down the terrace, Tommy grabbed at the lapels of Keith's lucky mac pulling him with him. Only the sheer weight of numbers in front of them prevented a fall to the floor.

Chelsea! (clap, clap, clap) Chelsea! (clap, clap, clap)

Despite the dreadful surface, the game was being played end-to-end at a frenetic pace with both sides squandering possession all too frequently.

'Maybe it's the ground, but Eddie Mac doesn't look fully fit,' said George, as Watford keeper Walker punted a clearance downfield.

'I don't know how you can tell,' replied Keith, as Hornets midfielder Terry Garbett nodded the ball on as far as McCreadie who headed it awkwardly back towards the half-way line. There was insufficient power however in the Chelsea defender's header for it to carry more than a few yards and the ball fell at the feet of Garbett who ran unopposed at the Blues penalty area before trying his luck with a shot just before he reached the box.

Peter Bonetti maybe should have done better. Garbett's strike took a bounce off the surface in front of the diving Cat and fizzed into the back of the net. 1-1. It was a poor goal to concede and now, with just 12 minutes gone, Watford were right back in the cup tie... something that hadn't felt possible when Webb had scored early on.

The Watford fans crammed in the Park Lane end raised their yellow and black scarves aloft and sang *Que Sera, Sera, whatever will be, will be... We're going to Wembley...* It was unnerving, Chelsea look rattled.

Stewart Scullion and Brian Owen harried the Blues backline, traumatising poor Eddie Mac who was clearly being targeted as a weak link. Was another giant-killing going to happen? The thought did occur to Rick, but he was immediately shouted down by Keith for then voicing his concern.

Referee Gordon Hill, who at the time was reckoned by many to be one of the fairest in the game, made a couple of big calls. First, he waved away a Watford penalty appeal when Scullion took a tumble with McCreadie in close order, and then he allowed Peter Osgood to get away with a retaliatory kick on Walter Lees after the Hornets central defender had gone through him. Osgood was subsequently jeered everytime he touched the ball by unforgiving Watford fans who also suggested Mr Hill was born out of wedlock... repeatedly chanting *the referee's a bastard.*

'God bless Gordon Hill,' said Keith, proffering a masturbation-orientated hand signal at the Watford fans.

'School headmaster during the week isn't he,' replied George. 'The kids in his class will be asking him who he supports after they've watched the highlights of this game on *The Big Match.*'

As the first-half progressed it was clear that Watford had the wind in their sails and it was just as well for Chelsea that Ron Harris and John Dempsey were standing tall to quell their attacking endeavours or the Blues might have run into problems.

Watford! (clap, clap, clap) Watford! (clap, clap, clap)

'Go on Chopper, let him have it,' hollered Tommy, as Harris put his feet through Garbett to let the Hornets goalscorer know he was being man-marked now and would no longer have the freedom to pose the same threat he had earlier in the game.

The Second Division side drew strength from the vocal support they were getting and continued to create problems for Chelsea.

'I'll be glad when it's half-time,' said Keith, as Barry Endean tested Peter Bonetti's reflexes.

'Me too,' replied George. 'I'm desperate for a piss!'

You couldn't take your eye off the game for a minute. The queues for the toilets were going to be long, because nobody was moving for fear of missing anything as Hudson bringing a good save out of Walker proved. Moments later, to prove this point, Peter Houseman sent a long-range volley zipping just over the bar.

Chelsea! Chelsea! Chelsea!

Blues supporters found their voices again and drowned out their counterparts. Allowed too much freedom to advance from midfield, Houseman was soon at it again. A swashbuckling run was followed by a deeper shot, but Walker was equal to it. Relief for many in the crowd came when Mr Hill blew his whistle to signal half-time. 1-1. It was a game worthy of a semi-final and Watford clearly weren't at the Lane just to make up the numbers.

The other semi-final which was being played at Hillsborough between Leeds United and Manchester United who'd beaten Middlesbrough 2-1 in their quarterfinal replay at Old Trafford had kicked off 15 minutes earlier and was still goalless. Chelsea v Leeds or Man U at Wembley... either opponent was a mouthwatering prospect... but there was still work to be done by the Blues at White Hart Lane if the dream of playing in another final was to become a reality.

'Come On Chelsea!' Tommy hollered, as Hutchinson, Osgood and Hudson stood over the ball in the centre circle waiting for the referee to blow his whistle and get the second-half underway.

It was a scrappy start with neither side dominating possession. Atmosphere-wise, both sets of fans were urging their teams on and an entertaining exchange of *Watford! Chelsea! Watford! Chelsea!* was eventually won by Blue's fans who persisted with a continual, shouted version of *Chelsea! Chelsea! Chelsea!*

With just under an hour played, Dave Sexton's side made the vital breakthrough. Charlie Cooke finally got some joy down the right flank and crossed a decent ball over which Hutchinson headed down towards goal but Walker was equal to it.

Chelsea! Chelsea! Chelsea!... the chanting seemed to grow louder.

Hollins played a loose ball forward which was laid off for Hutchinson by Osgood, both players using skills picked up in training to get their bodies between the ball and the oppostition.

'Give it to Huddy!' roared Keith.

Of course Hutch couldn't hear Keith or everyone else in the Paxton clamouring for Hudson to be played in… but he did just that. With an uncanny sixth sense, Huddy sensed that Houseman had tracked forward down the left flank so he slipped the ball wide to the winger, who picked his moment and clipped an inch-perfect cross into the Watford six-yard box where Ossie had stolen in unmarked. A simple header and the Chelsea striker maintained his record of having scored in every round of the cup this season.

Osgood's momentum carried him into the back of the net and he grabbed at it hanging for a brief second before dropping to the floor and punching his right arm in the air in celebration. Suddenly, there were plenty of blue and white scarves aloft in the Park Lane End behind Walker's goal.

Chelsea! Chelsea! Chelsea!… the chant was incessant now… even George and Fred joined in.

Watford's resistance was weakening as Chelsea, clearly now the fitter of the two sides, sensed the opportunity to kill off the tie with another goal and continually pressed forward.

'I like that it's Houseman giving them the runaround,' said George. 'I know I've said it before, but I don't like the amount of stick he gets at the Bridge and I don't like all that Mary and Tiger nonsense either… or Nobby for that matter! He's a local kid from the other side of Battersea Bridge. Deserves more respect.'

'Every Chelsea player deserves respect,' added Fred. 'I'd love to see all these critics bring their boots and have a go at playing the game themselves. I bet they wouldn't like the crowd getting on their back.'

The tempo of the game had changed since the Blues took the lead, Sexton's side sensed the opportunity to put the tie beyond doubt. Alan Hudson, full of youthful running, surged at the Watford defence and picked out Peter Houseman with a chipped pass. The Chelsea winger volleyed the ball goalward but Mike Walker thwarted him with a smart save.

Undeterred, Houseman continued to be a thorn in the side of the Hornet's defence, and in the 73rd minute his tenacity was rewarded with a goal that has stood the test of time in respect of it's sheer brilliance and beauty.

Editor's note: *Tommy Walker's eyes misted over as he recalled it almost half a century later.*

"*When Eden Hazard scored that fantastic solo effort at the Bridge against Arsenal (4 February 2017, Chelsea 3 Arsenal 1, Marcos Alonso, Eden Hazard, Cesc Fabregas). The first thing I thought of when someone said "that's the best goal I've ever seen a Chelsea player score" was Peter Houseman's goal against Watford in the FA Cup semi-*

final. Hazard was playing on a perfect pitch when he bamboozled the Gunners' defence and slotted the ball past former teammate Petr Cech into the net. Yeah, it was genius... but how would Hazard have fared trying the same moves on the quagmire of a pitch Houseman had to contend with?"

Latching onto a lofted David Webb clearance, Houseman, who'd switched flanks with Cooke again and was now operating on the left, picked up the ball midway in the Watford half. Jinking past two Hornets defenders, he cut inside and advanced to the penalty area evading desperate challenges from Tom Walley and Mick Packer and switching the ball between his feet before volleying the ball low past Walker into the bottom right hand corner of the net. 3-1 to Chelsea!

The brilliance of Peter Houseman's strike sapped Waford's morale and within a couple of minutes they fell further behind. Scarves were aloft in the Paxton as *You'll Never Walk Alone* was being sung when Alan Hudson, probing down the right side, exchanged passes with Charlie Cooke and went skipping through the mud with the ball seemingly welded to his feet.

After nutmegging Mike Packer, Huddy flicked it out to Peter Osgood who one-touched it to Ian Hutchinson in an advanced position in the Watford penalty area. Hutch turned on a sixpence and sent a rising volley crashing into the Hornets net. Wallop! 4-1 to Chelsea. If Houseman's goal had been down to individual brilliance... this was a team effort to match.

Easy, Easy, Easy chanted Chelsea's jubilant supporters. Of course it hadn't been that simple... but the Blues were now threatening to run riot and, sure enough, another goal soon followed.

With a little over 10 minutes left, Houseman back on the left side, played a double one-two with Hutchinson picking up the final pass at the edge of the Watford six-yard box and angling the ball over Walker into the roof of the net. 5-1.

We want six, we want six, we want six.

It was all Chelsea now, on the pitch and on the terraces and a sixth Blues goal almost became a reality. Following neat interplay between Ian Hutchinson and Peter Osgood, John Hollins chipped a ball from the edge of the Watford box which landed squarely at the feet of Ossie who volleyed it into the net. 6-1... No! The goal was disallowed for offside and shortly after Mr Hill blew the final whistle.

We shall not, we shall not be moved,
We shall not, we shall not be moved.
Just like a team that's gonna win the FA Cup...
We shall not be moved.

The belief was there. Reworking a song borrowed from the Civil Rights Movement in the USA that had recently found popularity on The Seekers *Best Of* compilation album, a version of which Manchester United fans had sung during the 1968 European Cup Final, Blues supporters were in no doubt at that moment what destiny awaited their team. What they didn't know was who Chelsea's opponents at Wembley were going to be as the other semi-final between Leeds and Man U had ended in a goalless stalemate.

*****

After the game, Tommy, Keith and Rick got a taxi to Dagenham which although not too far away from Tottenham, wasn't an obvious choice of location for a Saturday night out. By now, Rick was regularly dating Margaret, the girl from the BBC, and she'd got them all on the guestlist at the Village Blues Club (Dagenham Roundhouse) which in a short space of time had built up a really good reputation as a live music venue. It was decent of Margaret to organise it and it would be great for the boys and their girls to be out together.

Fairport Convention, a folk-rock band that Sophia was a massive fan of, were playing that night. Every time Tommy went to her house, she would play their album *Unhalfbricking* which had been released in July last year just before they'd met. On first listen he'd thought it was a bit airy-fairy, but there was an Englishness to the tunes and the lyrics which appealed to him in the same way the music of The Who did. Richard Thompson the lead guitarist was pushing sonic boundaries just like Pete Townshend had been doing for a few years but in a different direction which made Fairport's sound innovative and interesting.

What made the album really shimmer though for Tommy as it grew on him was the poignant and haunting voice of singer-songwriter Sandy Denny. A former trainee nurse at the Royal Brompton Hospital in Chelsea, Denny's sublime vocals and elegiac lyrics anchored Thompson's virtuoso guitar work and came to the fore on the track *Who Knows Where the Time Goes?* a melancholy and mesmerising ballad that Denny had written when she was just 19-years old. Thompson himself was only 20; it was truly extraordinary how gifted young people could express their talents in different ways... Alan Hudson doing remarkable things with a football was another good example.

Sophia always cried when *Who Knows Where the Time Goes?* played out, and this made Tommy cry as well, something which had never happened before and something he didn't share with anyone and swore her to secrecy about. Part of the reflective sadness of love and loss that the song drew out of them both was knowledge of the tragedy that had struck Fairport Convention a couple of months before *Unhalfbricking* was released.

In the small hours of the morning of 12 May, the band had been travelling back to London from a gig at legendary Birmingham rock venue Mothers (now a supermarket called Extra plus) when driver and roadie Harvey Bramham, who had previously complained of feeling unwell, fell asleep at the wheel and the Transit van they were in veered off the M1 close to Scratchwood Services and plunged 15-yards down an embankment. 19-year old drummer Martin Lamble was killed along with Richard Thompson's girlfriend, fashion designer Jeannie Franklyn.

Thompson, who'd grabbed at the steering-wheel in a bid to prevent the van crashing, sustained a broken shoulder while two other Fairport members Ashley Hutchings and Simon Nicol were also injured along with Bramham who would subsequently be charged with causing death by dangerous driving and jailed for six months. Sandy Denny had opted to get a lift back to London with boyfriend and fellow musician Trevor Lucas and wasn't involved in the accident.

Tommy imagined how the crash would have played, and was still playing, on the minds not only of the survivors but also Denny who must have had a few 'their but for the grace of God' moments. He and Sophia had chatted often about this and again earlier this year after Who drummer Keith Moon accidentally killed his friend, driver and bodyguard Neil Boland while under the influence and consequently escaped a custodial sentence. Psychologically, it must be a burden. People talked about their lives getting 'heavy'... having a conscience in such circumstances had to make things 'heavier' still.

The Fairport's gig at Dagenham was good and everyone had a great night out, however the fact Sandy Denny had recently left the group and wasn't performing with them was disappointing for Tommy and Sophia and he often wondered how they would have reacted had Denny been there to sing *Who Knows Where the Time Goes?*

TOTTENHAM HOTSPUR
Saturday 4 April 1970

The following Friday, Tommy and George had debated at some length over a few pints in the Wetherby who Chelsea would be better suited to play against in the FA Cup Final. Tommy was going for Manchester United because the Blues had bossed them at Old Trafford. George reckoned Leeds United would be a better bet because they might be fatigued given that as well as challenging for the First Division title, Don Revie's side were in second place just above Chelsea and just behind Everton, they were also in the semi-finals of the European Cup.

Billed as the 'Battle of Britain', Leeds, the reigning champions of England, had been paired with Celtic the champions of Scotland. The first leg of the semi was scheduled for 1 April. Before that, there would be the Man U replay and of course there were league games to be factored in. By the end of the drinking session, George had won Tommy over principally by persuading him that it would feel a whole lot better to beat 'dirty' treble-chasing Leeds than the Red Devils.

It was that whole familiarity breeds contempt thing again. The Peacocks had beaten the Blues home and away in the league. That 5-2 home thrashing in January still rankled. Tommy bloody Hughes, poor sod. It wasn't really his fault was it? Although Chelsea had prevailed after a replay in the Third Round League Cup tie the sides had contested... that was largely academic because they'd been knocked out in the next round by Carlisle United. That was so often the way. Like the marathon five-match FA Cup tie with Burnley in 1956... all that drama just to lose to Everton in the next round.

The FA Cup semi-final replay between Leeds and Man U was played at Villa Park on 23 March... the game once again finished 0-0 but this time it had gone to extra-time! George's point about fatigue was now increasing in validity. Three days later, the sides tried again at Burnden Park, the original home of Bolton Wanderers. On this occasion, matters were settled as early as the eighth minute when Leeds tigerish midfielder Billy Bremner beat United keeper Alex Stepney with a blistering long-range shot. 'Dirty' Leeds v Chelsea it was then. Tommy laughed when he'd read Bremner's comments in the paper the next day.

"You have to be there in that large bowl at Wembley to appreciate the tremendous kick it gives a player when he trots out of the tunnel and into that arena," said the flame-haired, chain-smoking Scotsman. "So today I'm on top of the world. That Wembley feeling is in the air again. I could do a dozen somersaults if I didn't have such a five-star hangover at the moment! The champers popped last night, I can tell you and now we're gunning for Chelsea."

Bremner's enthusiasm shone through his words. Leeds might be gunning for Chelsea, but Blues skipper Ron Harris wasn't bothered and that made Tommy laugh even more.

"I don't think it mattered who got through from the other semi-final to meet us," said Harris in an indirect response to Bremner. "We have been warning everyone that we could win something this season. It gets a bit annoying reading that only Leeds, Manchester United, Everton or Liverpool are in the running for honours."

It was the self-entitlement halo that Leeds wore which infuriated Tommy… they needed a comeuppance… and they got a double-dose of it on 1 April… 'fools day'… when Celtic turned them over 1-0 at Elland Road in the first leg of the European Cup semi-final. Unlucky ha ha! On the same night, Everton confirmed their status as FIrst Divison champions beating West Bromwich Albion 2-0 at Goodison Park. Poor Leeds. From treble-dreams, to double-hopes being potentially dashed, to maybe just having the FA Cup to play for with a bunch of knackered players.

Somewhat insanely, because of a fixture pile-up, the day after the Celtic defeat Leeds were obliged to fulfill an away league fixture with West Ham United and manager Don Revie picked a strong side. This is incomprehensible in the context of the modern game. Can you imagine the tantrums that the likes of Jose Mourinho and Pep Guardiola would throw if they were ever confronted with such a situation?

In Revie's starting XI to face the Hammers was gifted right-back Paul Reaney who not only played a starring role for Leeds but was also a part of Alf Ramsey's plans as England prepared to defend the World Cup in Mexico. Unfortunately, Reaney broke his leg in the game at Upton Park and the injury meant he wouldn't play football again until the following season.

George's notion that Leeds were a better bet for Chelsea to play against in the FA Cup Final looked sounder with each day that passed as the big day, 11 April, approached… but the problems the Yorkshire club were experiencing were a mirror of what was happening in London where the Blues had significant problems of their own to contend with.

*****

'There was no one near Huddy when it happened,' said Keith to Tommy and Rick as they approached The Shed turnstiles early doors ahead of Chelsea's game with Tottenham Hotspur. 'Well apart from Baggies midfielder Asa Hartford. He went down like he'd been shot. Turned his left ankle badly and apparently tore his ligaments.'

Tommy shook his head. 'Bloody awful thing to happen to any Chelsea player, well any player really. Hudson's been brilliant for us this season. He's not much younger than us, I bet he's been dreaming about playing in the final just like we've been dreaming of watching it.'

'Do you reckon the doctors actually know what they're doing?' asked Rick. 'I mean the X-ray showed he hadn't broken his ankle, so why put a plaster cast on him and give him a pair of crutches to hobble around on?'

'I know what you mean,' replied Tommy. 'Casing it up like that's just going to make his ankle stiff especially if it's swollen up.'

'They've taken the cast off now though haven't they,' said Keith. 'Maybe they decided it was a bad idea after all. Even so, I reckon it's going to take a miracle for him to be fit for next week.'

First Division
Chelsea 1 Tottenham Hotspur 0
Stamford Bridge
Attendance: 44,925
Referee: Kevin Howley

Chelsea: Peter Bonetti, David Webb, Eddie McCreadie, John Hollins, John Dempsey, Marvin Hinton, Tommy Baldwin, Peter Houseman, Peter Osgood, Alan Birchenall, Charlie Cooke.
Scorer: Baldwin 4.

Tottenham Hotspur: Jennings, Kinnear, Knowles, Mullery, England, Beal, Gilzean, Perryman, Chivers, Peters, Morgan.

Chelsea's line-up for the visit of Spurs reflected the injury problems the Blues were currently facing. A fixture pile-up of their own which had seen Dave Sexton having to cope with selecting teams to play five matches in 13 days following the Watford semi-final hadn't helped matters and had to be a contributory factor.

Hudson's ankle injury, sustained against West Bromwich Albion the Monday preceding the Spurs game (30 March, West Brom 3 Chelsea 1, Ian Hutchinson) grabbed the headlines because he was a prodigious talent widely talked about, but in that same game at the Hawthorns, the less fashionable but equally important Ian Hutchinson bruised his hip and kidneys and Bobby Tambling hobbled off the pitch with a season-ending hamstring injury. Hutchinson, had underlined his importance to the team when scoring both goals for Chelsea in a 2-1 victory over Manchester United at Stamford Bridge (21 March).

George, Fred, Tommy, Keith and Rick had made a schoolboy error that afternoon. Having spent longer than usual in the Nell Gwynne sorting out more bets for the cup final, they'd arrived at Stamford Bridge too late to gain admission and were among 15,000 supporters locked out! The gate for the visit of Man U, 61,479, was the largest of the season and more than double that of the home games with Stoke City and Sheffield Wednesday it was sandwiched inbetween.

On the Tuesday following the Watford game (17 March), 28,996 were at the Bridge to see Chelsea beat Stoke 1-0. A very late Charlie Cooke goal had seen off The Potters in what was understandably a lacklustre display by the new FA Cup finalists. The Man U game followed on the Saturday and then the Blues hosted Wednesday on Wednesday! (25 March) 29,590 turned up and were treated to a wonderful individual goal by Alan Hudson who'd just been notified he'd made the reserve list for the England World Cup squad in which his teammates Peter Bonetti and Peter Osgood had been included as expected.

Hudson's strike rounded off a comprehensive 3-1 victory over the relegation-threatened Owls with Ian Hutchinson and Osgood from the penalty spot also finding the net. It wasn't all good news though, skipper Ron Harris injured his left hamstring and was stretchered off after 60 minutes.

'Chopper will be okay because he's Chopper, but I really don't think Huddy's going to make the final,' said Tommy, heaving a desperate-sounding sigh as he spoke. 'That goal he scored against Wednesday was bloody genius. I can still see him down there now, latching onto a loose ball in our half and skinning half their team before teasing the goalie out of position and burying it in the back of the net.'

Keith nodded. 'Yeah. That's what we've got with Huddy. A player with the talent to take on anyone. He's better than George Best I reckon.'

Rick laughed. 'He's got a way to go yet before you can say that about him. But I tell you what, in Huddy, Ossie, Hutch we haven't half got some players to believe in. Lads our age who are doing what we could only ever dream of.

'What about Holly?' asked Tommy, waving his match programme in the air. 'He's only 23 same as Ossie and he's on Ramsey's reserve list for the World Cup... and it says in here he's our Player of the Year... beating Os into second and Huddy into third.'

'I believe in all our players,' said Keith. 'Especially Peter Houseman, because he's proved me wrong about him.'

Those three consecutive home victories after the Watford semi had buoyed the mood of Chelsea supporters for Wembley and saw plenty take advantage of the 11/10 odds high street bookmakers were offering on Dave Sexton's side winning the cup (Leeds were favourites at 8/11), however two away defeats had followed and coupled with the injury to Alan Hudson and concerns about the fitness of other key players it was fair to say that exuberant optimism in its many guises had been reined in a little.

Last weekend (28 March), the Blues had been hammered 5-2 at Goodison Park by First Division champions-elect Everton. Minus Peter Bonetti (ankle), Ron Harris (hamstring) and Eddie McCreadie (groin), Chelsea's defence wilted. Deputy goalie Tommy Hughes, who'd stood in for Bonetti against Sheffield Wednesday and done okay, had a shocker on a par with the Leeds debacle back in January... except illness wasn't a factor in a dithering performance which contributed greatly to Chelsea being 5-0 down inside an hour! It could have got worse, but instead it got marginally better as John Dempsey and Peter Osgood reduced the arrears. Then just two days later, on Easter Bank Holiday Monday, Chelsea had lost that game to West Brom... and possibly Alan Hudson for the FA Cup Final.

We're going to Wembley, We're going to Wembley, you're not, you're not sang a swelling mob of Chelsea supporters gathered at the bottom of The Shed terrace to the tune of *Camptown Races.* The taunting of visiting Tottenham fans gathering in numbers at the opposite end of the ground was starting early. Spurs seemed to be a team in decline, mid-table laggards who'd lost all sense of purpose since Crystal Palace had embarrassed them in the FA Cup. Good!

Keen to avoid a repeat of the Manchester United game they'd ended up missing, and thinking they might be locked out of the day's big London derby if they were late arriving at the Bridge, this time George, Fred, under protest because he saw it as a waste of valuable drinking time, Tommy, Keith and Rick made a point of clicking through the turnstiles almost 90 minutes before the scheduled 3 p.m. kick off.

One of the quirky aspects of attending football matches in the mid-to-late 1960s and early 1970s was what had now become a bizarre tradition of the away club's hooligan element (if they had one) 'taking' or trying to 'take' the main end of the opposition by pitching up at grounds early while the home supporters were still in the clubs, pubs and bars that surrounded it. This had happened at Stamford Bridge on a number of occasions... with Manchester United, given the vast numbers that followed them on their travels, masters of art. Chelsea's mobs of course engaged in this activity away from home as well. It was somewhat of a false economy, but it was interesting to watch... if of course you could be bothered to enter a ground such a long period of time before kick-off.

As it transpired, concerns about getting locked out of the Tottenham game were unfounded as the attendance of just under 45,000, although the First Division's highest that day, was well shy of the 60,000 plus who had packed the ground for the Man U game.

'State of that lot,' said Tommy, pointing across the pitch as a section of Tottenham's mob stood on the North Stand terrace suddenly moved down to the low wall at the front and clambered over it readying themselves to run towards The Shed. The lilting sound of current chart-topping Simon and Garfunkel hit *Bridge Over Troubled Water* boomed through the stadium Tannoy providing a surreal accompaniment to the ensuing madness.

George shrugged his shoulders and pointed first at a group of police officers stood by the half-way line and then at the Chelsea mob at the bottom of The Shed. 'This would look good in slow motion on the silver screen,' he said in a relaxed manner. 'Like one of those Sergio Leone Spaghetti Westerns.'

Tommy laughed. 'Yeah. Be handy if it was slow motion because they'd take longer to get here and our lot would have time to ready themselves to deal with them because those five Old Bill over there won't.'

As the front runners of the Spurs mob, numbering around 100, began running across the pitch. Keith pointed at the top of The Shed at a group of skinheads who had emerged onto the terrace and were moving swiftly down it. 'Looks like Eccles!' he exclaimed. 'Here to save the day.'

Rick clapped his hands. 'Also looks like they'll need some help.

'Come on then,' replied Tommy, beckoning his friends.

'Idiots!' said George, shaking his head.

'*Bridge Over Troubled Water* ha ha.' Fred patted George on the back. 'I told you we should have stayed in the pub.'

By the time Tommy, Rick and Keith had made their way down the terrace to the perimeter wall, the Tottenham horde had reached the penalty area... however a much larger Chelsea mob had already vaulted the wall and were ready to confront them. There was a stand-off. It looked like a game of Army in the school playground. It felt like it needed someone to say 'charge'... but nobody did. There was a comedy caper aspect to what happened next as the Tottenham mob, realising they were not going to progress further and conscious now of a growing police presence, turned and ran back to the North Stand chased by the Chelsea skinhead gang.

Everyone standing further up The Shed began humming the *Laurel and Hardy* theme tune *Dance of the Cuckoos* as the police moved onto the pitch to take control of the situation.

Tommy, Rick and Keith stayed down by the perimeter wall for a few minutes watching as order was restored before walking slowly back up the terrace to where George and Fred were waiting to greet them with wanker hand signs.

The Shed looked up and they saw a great star,
Scoring goals past Pat Jennings from near and from far.
And Chelsea won, as we all knew they would.
And the star of that great team was Peter Osgood.
Osgood, Osgood, Osgood, Osgood...
Born is the King of Stamford Bridge.

There was no more crowd trouble before kick-off, and as the game got underway The Shed unified to sing one of Tommy's favourite songs, *The First Noël,* Christmas Carol-themed tribute to Peter Osgood.

At its conclusion, George laboured the point that although Ossie had racked-up an impressive 28 goals so far this season to add to the 49 he already had to his name so far as a Chelsea player, he had in fact only beaten Pat Jennings twice to date (8 January 1966, Chelsea 2 Tottenham Hotspur 1, George Graham, Peter Osgood. 31 August 1968,

Chelsea 2 Tottenham Hotpsur 2, Alan Birchenall, Peter Osgood (pen).

Editor's note: Ossie would only score one more goal past Pat Jennings, 22 December 1971, the opening goal in a dramatic 3-2 (Peter Osgood, Chris Garland, John Hollins) League Cup semi-final first leg win over Spurs at Stamford Bridge... but it never detracted from the beauty the song composed in his honour.

Fred told George to shut up and stop being boring and as Tommy, Keith and Rick laughed, transfer-seeking Tommy Baldwin, ironically back in the side because of the injury to Alan Hudson, scored what turned out to be the only goal of the game.

Peter Osgood and Alan Birchenall, engaging in what looked like a training exercise for headers, nodded the ball between themselves into and across the Tottenham penalty area where it fell invitingly for Baldwin who picked his spot and leathered it past Jennings.

There were more chances in the match, notably to the visitors, but Peter Bonetti, back under the bar for the Chelsea, was at his cat-like best. Spurs did ripple Bonetti's net with 10 minutes left, but Alan Gilzean's effort was ruled offside by referee Kevin Howley. That was decent, Howley had been a pain in the arse when he'd reffed the cup game with QPR.

Baldwin's fourth minute strike might have been the highlight of the afternoon for the vast majority of Blues supporters gathered at the Bridge, but for some there was further excitement related to winning to be had. As the match was taking place, the Grand National was being run at Aintree and George wasn't the only Chelsea supporter who liked a punt that had brought a portable transistor radio to listen to the commentary of the iconic horse race which started at 3.20 p.m.

From time-to-time, George made a point of saying he'd had inside information about a certain race from a 'connection' and his success rate was surprisingly good... so-much-so that his friends in the Wetherby and Fred would invariably regret not following his tips for fear of missing out.

George never disclosed who his 'connection' was and so Tommy suspected he was a figment of his imagination, a belief he held right up until his father's funeral almost 30 years later when an elderly gentleman who attended introduced himself as a former school friend and advised during the short conversation they'd had that he'd once worked with former champion jockey and trainer Fred Rimell.

One of Rimell's horses, a small bay gelding named Gay Trip which had won the Mackeson Gold Cup at Cheltenham the previous year, was George's tip. Tommy, Keith and Rick knew nothing about racing but they'd been caught both ways with his advice in the past.

'Win some, lose some,' George would always say.

'Win some, lose more,' was his wife Helen's standard reply.

Fred, who loved a bet anyway, always followed George's tips and the Grand National was no exception. To make the punt worth while they'd all agreed to put £10 each into a mini-syndicate and backed Gay Trip at odds of 20/1 with Nick Hill in the Nell Gwynne. These were better odds than the best price of 15/1 available with 'regular' bookies. George joined them in the syndicate, though he'd also backed Gay Trip on his own at antepost odds of 25/1.

George was so confident, he'd insisted that the bet was placed on the nose rather than each-way. 'It's going to win. It's that simple, so don't reduce your winnings by bottling the bet and covering the minor places.'

Tommy could afford to lose £10, they all could, but it didn't stop Rick moaning as they huddled around George and his transistor radio and listened to the commentary when the race got underway.

'What a waste of money,' he said, as Gay Trip, being ridden by Pat Taaffe, failed to get a mention in the early stages of the race.

'Plenty of time yet,' replied George without a hint of defensiveness, but Rick shook his head, swore, and departed to the toilets.

28 horses started the race, and as it progressed each fence seemed to claim one or more fallers. Tommy was also in desperate need of relieve himself, but he stayed with his father, Keith and Fred.

'Gay Trip,' shouted Fred enthusiastically as the horse finally got name checked by the commentator. 'Go on my son!'

A couple of minutes later, and the excitement was mounting as Gay Trip took up closer order to the race leaders Miss Hunter and Vulture who was out in front.

'Only seven horses still running in the National,' said George, quoting the commentator verbatim and widening his eyes as he stared at the radio in his hands and shook it slightly.

'Go on Gay Trip!' shouted Tommy, Fred and Keith in unison.

By the second-last fence Gay Trip had taken the lead.

GO ON GAY TRIP!

Nine minutes, four miles, 856-yards and 30 formidable jumps after setting out... Gay Trip was first past the winning post... the horse's margin of victory was a phenomenal 20 lengths.

Tommy and Keith hoisted George up in the air. If Chelsea were going to score a winning goal in the FA Cup Final... this is what it was going to feel like.

'You beauty! What a result!' shouted Fred, clenching his fists and punching the air. The football was now a sideshow and fans stood nearby who'd been drawn to the commotion and realised what had happened offered envious congratulations.

'Told you,' said George winking smugly. 'Shame Rick wasn't here, I'd have offered him his stake back while the race was still unfolding.'

Tommy bumped into Rick on the steps down to the toilets. The Grand National was the last thing on his friend's mind.

'I've just heard Bill Shankly's here. He wants to sign Baldwin for Liverpool,' he said with a vexed look on his face

Tommy laughed. 'I reckon my old man's just won enough to buy Baldwin himself and pay him to carry on playing for Chelsea.'

Rick looked shocked. 'Are you winding me up?'

Tommy's swollen bladder prevented him from continuing with the conversation and he continued on his way to the toilets. As he turned the corner at the bottom of the steps, he looked back up and caught sight of his friend bounding up them two-at-a-time. Rick loved a pound note and he was clearly keen to find out if it was true that Gay Trip had just won the National.

LEEDS UNITED AT WEMBLEY
Saturday 11 April 1970

Tommy sat on the living room sofa at his parents house smoking a cigarette and briefly contemplated the merits and demerits of having knocked back the opportunity to share a bed with Sophia last night. Realising that his thoughts were motivated mainly by the fact he'd woken up feeling horny, he ditched them as he didn't want to feel guilty and then he was distracted as he reached across to the ashtray on the adjacent coffee table.

Next to the ashtray was a copy of yesterday's *Daily Mirror* newspaper. Tommy grimaced as he caught sight of the headline which read, *Paul Quits The Beatles*. What a knee to the bollocks that was. "I have no future plans to record or appear with the Beatles again. Or to write any more music with John," proclaimed McCartney in the attendant article.

It had been coming. The previous September rumours had surfaced that John Lennon had told the rest of the band he was leaving. The Beatles hadn't toured since 1966. Brian Epstein who'd been largely responsible for their commercial success and keeping them together as fame took hold had died of a drug overdose the following year and then of course John had got Yoko Ono wrapped around him.

So that was that. *Let It Be...* Tommy wondered if it was just a coincidence that the announcement came with the band in the charts with that song. He hadn't tried to interpret the lyrics. 'Mother Mary' coming to McCartney sounded a bit biblical, but he could have been talking about his own mother who'd passed away when he was only 14. So it was just down to the three words in the title that formed the chorus then... a simple resonance... *LET IT BE*. Yeah, that was it, just leave it there and *Let it Be.*

Great rockstars or bands, like great footballers, had to have a beginning a middle and an end to their careers. Once you reached the pinnacle of success, it was difficult to surpass it but very easy to underwhelm. Who knew what the future held for John, Paul, George and Ringo, the four members of The Beatles? The future was unwritten, but the band's legacy as a unit was intact, a complete body of work that Tommy, as he stubbed out his cigarette in the ashtray, was sure he would still be enjoying in years to come.

He'd worked late last night and hadn't planned on having a drink as he wanted to be fresh for the cup final to make the most of the day and start with a clear head, but on his way home he'd seen his mother and father walking hand-in-hand into the blue and white streamer-bedecked Wetherby. His father winning a small fortune on the Grand National had clearly worked wonders for his parents relationship, he hadn't heard them argue once this week. A swift one wouldn't do any harm and it would be nice for them to be together.

The Wetherby's landlord Bob Weems and his wife Anne had put a decent spread of food on; pork pies, cheese, pickles, and Shippams sardine and tomato paste sandwiches which Tommy, who'd forgotten to eat as he'd been driving around London making deliveries during the day, tucked into gratefully as he ended up having more than a 'swift one' and traded pints of Watney's Red Barrel with his father while his mother tested her liver function with an endless supply of brandy and Babycham.

'You have to be careful with the Red Barrel,' said George to Tommy as he placed another two pints on the table they were sitting at. 'It can be a bit of a trouser-browner. Don't want to get caught short at Wembley tomorrow do we.'

The pub had been as busy as it ever got on the Eve's of Christmas and New Year... in fact the decorations and the happy buzz in the place did gave it a festive feel. All the chatter was understandably about Chelsea's chances of winning the FA Cup for the first time. Confidence was high and seemed higher than it had been three years previously ahead of the disastrous final with Spurs.

Maybe this time fortune was going to favour the Blues who had been a music-hall joke for decades when it came to the FA Cup thanks largely to the efforts of BBC radio comic Norman 'a song a smile and a piano' Long who'd co-written and recorded a ditty entitled *On The Day That Chelsea Went And Won The Cup*. Bob Weems had a 10-inch, 78rpm, crackly shellac resin copy of the song which had been pressed in 1934... long before Chelsea won any kind of trophy and at 10.30 p.m. he rang the pub bell to get everyone's attention and played the record.

Everyone knew the words. It was a hand-me-down thing... the song had been as funny to Blues supporters as it was to fans of other clubs and the world in general. Long's verses advised of extraordinary occurrences that would happen *On The Day That Chelsea Went And Won The Cup*... the inference being it was pure hypotheses, bordering on fantasy, as Chelsea winning the FA Cup would never happen.

Tommy laughed at the memory and started singing...

Now a little while ago, I dreamed the most amazing dream...
It tickled me to death when I woke up.
Now you know just how impossible the things we dream of are...
But I dreamt that Chelsea went and won the cup.
Of course as a result of an astounding thing like this, a host of other strange events occurred.
All folks and things were opposite to what they really are and the

happenings were really most absurd.
On the day that Chelsea won the final, all the universe went off the
wheel.
Great Sir Harry Lauder used a five bob postal order to stop his shoe
from rubbing at the heel.
The sun came out in Manchester and funny things like that....

A loud insistent knocking at the front door distracted Tommy. Hopefully his mother or father would answer it. He looked at the clock on the wall. 7.30 a.m. He was disappointed about the interruption, and thought about singing the song from the start again, but instead he got up and belted out the last line at the top of his voice so everyone in the house and whoever was outside knocking on the door could hear him.

Doctors wrote prescriptions that we all could understand...
Toast got drunk and eels got stewed and lobsters all got canned...
And Gordon Richards wore Carnera's trousers in the Strand...
ON THE DAY THAT CHELSEA WENT AND WON THE CUP!

Tommy, already smartly dressed and ready for the day ahead, walked out into the hallway and bumped into his dishevelled-looking father who was still in his dressing gown, had shaving cream smeared across his cheeks and was brandishing a cut-throat razor.

'Who is that son? I'll cut their bleeding ears off making all that row at this time of the morning on a Saturday.'

George's eyes had menace in them, but the shaving cream on his face likened him to Santa Claus. Santa with a cut-throat razor might have been a scary proposition for a child, but it wasn't going to put the fear of God into Keith and Rick who'd taken Tommy at his word when he'd said to them they'd make a full day of it and start early with a proper breakfast. As far as they were concerned it was breakfast time now.

George opened the door...

Que sera sera, whatever will be will be, we're going to Wembley...
Que sera sera...

The dynamic but inharmonious singing duo were in full flow, arms outstretched like the hour and minute hands of a couple of giant novelty clocks displaying the time as ten-to-two.

Que sera sera...

George slammed the door in their shocked faces. 'Soppy wankers!' he bellowed before walking back down the hall to the bathroom.

Tommy laughed. The singing stopped and he waited for the knock at the door to come again (much, much quieter this time) before opening it and stepping out to greet his friends.

Looking sharp top-to-toe for Wembley, they walked with a swagger up Slaidburn Street. All three sported matching number #3 crops... 3/8 of an inch of hair showing cut to a fade.

Tommy was wearing his favourite navy Harrington over a matching button-down Oxford shirt, pristine shrink-to-fit Levi 501xx with ½ inch turn-ups and basket-weave, black tassel loafers.

Superstitious Keith felt a bit over-dressed, but was compelled to wear his 'lucky' Aquascutum raincoat and had stuck with the regulation 501s and Florsheim short-zipper ankle boots he'd donned to every game through the winter and into the spring.

Rick hadn't bothered with a jacket and was leaning towards the skinhead look garbed in a blue and white checked button-down Ben Sherman shirt with the pleat and loop at the back, white Sta-Prest trousers with ¼ inch turn-ups, ½ inch blue braces and wingtip brogues.

Keith was in the mood for singing again, and it was *Na Na Hey Hey Kiss Him Goodbye* by Steam which had nudged into the top 10 UK singles last month and had been regularly played during *Pre-match Spin* at Stamford Bridge that he gave a makeover too.

Na na na na, na na na na... hey, hey, hey... Chelsea Shed boys...

As they reached the end of Slaidburn, Tommy turned around and looked up. The sky was a patchwork quilt of puffy clouds and pure azure... it was still chilly and there was a stiffening breeze, but it felt like it was going to be a nice dry day.

Just like 1967 when Chelsea had reached the FA Cup final against Tottenham Hotspur, the entire street was festooned with blue and white bunting, balloons and banners that stretched high across the road and were secured from the upstairs windows of the houses.

1,2,3 CHELSEA FOR ME
WIN OR LOSE UP THE BLUES
GOOD LUCK CHELSEA YOUR THE GREATEST
(the spelling mistake didn't matter)
CHELSEA FOR THE CUP
SEXTON'S SIZZLERS
CHELSEA PRIDE OF THE SOUTH
CHELSEA FA CUP 1970

Even the kerb stones had been painted blue and white. Nobody was going to complain to the council because everyone in the street supported Chelsea, and a victory party had been planned that would start in earnest after the final whistle and last into Sunday.

It may still have been early, but some of Slaidburn's younger urchins were already out having a kick-about. Chelsea rosettes pinned to their chests, noisy arguments ongoing about who was allowed to be Peter Osgood.

'On my head son,' said Tommy, missing the ball completely as a perfectly-flighted cross from a toothless, Chelsea-kit-wearing seven-year old sailed past him and bounced off the roof of a Ford Cortina parked outside the Wetherby.

'Bloody useless,' said Rick, laughing as the kids poked fun at Tommy. 'Hope we don't miss chances like that today.'

'Who's going to create our chances though,' said Keith, pointing at some graffiti daubed on the wall at the end of the street as they turned the corner onto the King's Road. 'What a crying shame for the kid.'

HUDSON IS ACE

Having had the plaster removed from his leg the day before the Tottenham game, Alan Hudson had spent the early part of the week with Chelsea physiotherapist and trainer Harry Medhurst trying to regain full movement in his injured ankle. It hadn't worked and in the pub last night there'd been stories doing the rounds that poor Huddy had been to see a faith healer and then a clairvoyant as a last resort. Apparently, all the spiritualist was able to tell Hudson was that he wouldn't score in the final. What a prescient and sobering kick in the gonads that must have been.

There'd been the regulation late fitness test. Huddy had tried to run round the remnants of the old dog track that still skirted the Stamford Bridge pitch but it was hopeless, he was still lame. It was a grand tragedy not only for the player but all the Chelsea supporters who'd cheered him on especially those who were his World's End neighbours.

There was some better news on the fitness front though, Blues skipper Ron 'Chopper' Harris had recovered from his hamstring injury and was raring to go at Wembley. His leadership and battle-ready approach to the game of football would be needed in what was certain to be an uncompromising contest against Dirty Leeds.

Tommy, Keith and Rick discussed Chelsea's chances over an Eggs Purgatorio special breakfast at the Tea Rooms café on Museum Street in Holborn (Number 11 closed in 2004, property has been boarded-up ever since). Sophia's father Enrico had introduced Tommy to the dish and to Rina and Eugenio Corsini the owners and fellow Italians whom he'd known for years when he'd asked to meet him to chat about his prospects in a bit more detail after the surprise marriage proposal made to his daughter at Christmas.

'You have to see past the condensation-clad, floor-to-ceiling, carmine-red mosaic Formica and taste the food,' Tommy said to Keith and Rick, repeating what Enrico had told him when he'd first dined at the Tea Rooms.

'Forza Chelsea!' said Eugenio as he served up breakfast. Tommy was already on board when it came to Eggs Purgatorio and Keith and

Rick joined him. Sophia's father always says "Meraviglifuckingoso" when he has this nosebag. I think it means fucking marvellous in Italian.

'He ain't wrong,' replied Keith. 'It is meraviglifuckingoso.'

Between forkfuls of Eggs Purgatorio, the three friends talked tactics and considered what plan Dave Sexton might have for Tommy Baldwin who he'd confirmed was in Chelsea's cup final starting line-up as a replacement for Alan Hudson.

'Sponge will play on the right side of midfield,' said Rick in a knowledgeable tone of voice. 'He'll have to stop Terry Cooper going on those overlaps like he did against us at the Bridge when they spanked us 5-2 and he'll be having a dig at Eddie Gray.'

Keith nodded. 'Gray's their one player that really worries me.'

'Bremner and Giles will need dealing with,' added Rick.

'And what about Hunter?' asked Keith frowning.

'Sponge is going to be busy if he has sort that lot out and score a goal. Good job he's Superman then.' Tommy shrugged his shoulders, finished his breakfast, lit a cigarette and checked the time on the wall-clock. 'Talking of the Sponge, it's almost 10 a.m. Come on let's go to the Prince of Wales Feathers. It's only a 20-minute walk to Warren Street. I'm not using Tottenham Court Road tube station on principle because of the name.'

Keith laughed before standing up and patting Tommy and Rick on their heads. 'Fair enough. Both your Dad's will be at the bar by the time we get there.'

We're the famous Chelsea FC and we're going to Wembley…
Wembley… Wembley

*****

Tommy had seen some lame excuses for football pitches this season, but Wembley… well, far from being the expected hallowed turf, it resembled a field that had just been ploughed by a drunken farmer with severe learning difficulties.

For the past couple of years, the Horse of the Year showjumping event had been staged at the stadium around this time and he remembered watching highlights of last year's League Cup Final between Arsenal and Swindon on TV and laughing at the state of the playing surface which had been thoroughly trampled by the hooves of galloping and jumping horses.

The Robins, then of the Third Division, pulled off one of the funniest cup upsets of all time, beating the Gunners 3-1. Maybe they were better-suited to the playing conditions than their more illustrious opponents. Chelsea and Leeds were on a par though in terms of capabilities. Both teams had been playing on the same heavy pitches throughout the winter and early spring which quite frankly made it all the more ridiculous that the FA had persisted with allowing the home of English Football to be ruined by equestrian folk who had also erected a huge tent in the centre circle surrounded by fences. Obviously, the inclement weather hadn't assisted the Wembley groundsmen in their endeavours... their toils appeared to have been in vain.

Tommy hadn't seen any of the showjumping on television, but he'd watched a re-run of the Grand National on *Match of the Day* the night of the Tottenham game the previous week and could see the detrimental effect the horses had on the Aintree fields which had been churned into mud. That was a reminder, Gay Trip's win in the big race was paying for everyones day out at Wembley... or rather his father was indirectly as it had been his selection.

Getting terrace tickets for the final hadn't been as big a problem as they thought it might be given that Chelsea's allocation, like that of Leeds, was a paltry 16,000 of which 6,000 were seats. A right royal shit-show considering the attendance at the game would be the standard 100,000. Coupons cut out of the back page of match programmes for the 20 home games Chelsea had played this season up to and including Stoke City had been posted into the Club so no queuing had been required this time.

Fortunately, Fred was an avid programme collector and he always bought programmes when people missed games. It was something he had done for Tommy, Rick and Keith since they'd started going as kids. Sometimes they'd laughed at this whimsical tradition when they weren't in his company... not anymore.

The real stroke of luck was the fact the Manchester United game they'd all been locked out of and missed getting a programme for because they were sold out came after the cut-off... it was the first home game after Stoke! Now that would have ruined things and forced them to source tickets on the black market.

If matters weren't bad enough for those desperate to get to the game who missed out on the official allocation, there was news of ticketing scandal which affected both clubs. In the last couple of days leading up to the final, tickets stamped in the name of both Chelsea and Leeds were being sold on the black market by touts with £15 the going rate for a 25 shillings (£1.25) seat. FA Secretary Denis Follows had ordered an inquiry, but that wasn't going to help the many thousands of ardent supporters of both teams who weren't going to get to see the final from inside the Twin Towers despite having attended games regularly throughout the season and being in possession of the required number of precious programme coupons.

There had been a few scuffles along Wembley Way... not between rival supporters but between angry fans and greedy touts. The word was that a lot of spivs had been given a good hiding and relieved of the tickets they were holding. Plain-clothed police officers had also been deployed to feel their collars. A deserved double-whammy for the touts then, but there was no doubt that plenty of them still made a killing.

Talking of Old Bill, Fred pointed out how many uniformed officers there seemed to be on duty. He couldn't recall ever seeing so many at a football match. Rick quipped they might be needed on the pitch to arrest the players if the referee wasn't able to control them when things got feisty. He was convinced it was going to be a brutish spectacle.

George had wanted to get into the stadium reasonably early so they could find a decent vantage point with a crush barrier behind them. A 12 shillings and sixpence standing ticket (£0.63) got them a place in the upper tier behind the goal at the tunnel end of the ground which is where the vast majority of Chelsea supporters were gathered.

Tommy was pleased they'd followed his father's wishes. The view was fantastic and the atmosphere was building. Down on the pitch, the bandsmen of the Royal Marines conducted by Frank Rea were pumping out some old familiar tunes. It was traditional... 'community singing' they called it.

When You're Smiling
Underneath The Arches
Strolling

Supporters of both clubs... and the 68,000 neutrals ha ha... were meant to join in, but the funny thing was, as George and Fred were keen to tell Tommy, Keith and Rick, *Strolling* had been adapted and used by Chelsea supporters to voice their support for the Blues.

Maybe Frank Rea was a season ticket holder at Stamford Bridge. The original version of the song owed its popularity to fabled comedy duo (Bud) Flanagan and (Chesney) Allen who'd championed it during the war years of the early 1940s. As the band struck up the tune, George and thousands of other Chelsea supporters sang the words they were more familiar with.

Strolling, just strolling in the cool of the evening air.
I don't envy the rich, in their automobiles.
For a motor car is phoney, I'd rather shag a pony!
When I'm strolling, just strolling, in the light of the moon above.
Every night I go out strolling, and I know my luck is rolling, when I'm
strolling, with the one I love.
Chelsea! (clap, clap, clap) Chelsea! (clap, clap, clap)

George and Fred sang the Blues version of the whole song from memory as Tommy, Keith and Rick laughed before joining in with the *Chelsea!* (clap, clap, clap) refrain. The Leeds supporters at the other end of the stadium responded with an imaginative chant of *United! (clap, clap, clap) United!*

'That *United* chant I always associate with Man United,' said Rick. Keith nodded. 'Yeah, me too.'

Tommy lit a cigarette before making what turned out to be the most

profound statement of the day. 'There are lots of teams called United...
but there is only one team called Chelsea.'

Chelsea! (clap, clap, clap) Chelsea! (clap, clap, clap)

With about 15 minutes to go before kick-off, the band played the
first of two tunes that really did foster a sense of community among the
crowd no matter which team they bore allegiance to.

Abide With Me - sung at Wembley since the 1927 final when Cardiff
City beat Arsenal.

'You know I don't believe in God son,' said George, putting his arm
around Tommy's waist and pulling him close. 'But singing this gets me as
close to that feeling those who do believe in the man upstairs must get.'

Abide with me; fast falls the eventide;
The darkness deepens; Lord with me abide.
When other helpers fail and comforts flee,
Help of the helpless, O abide with me.
Swift to its close ebbs out life's little day;
Earth's joys grow dim; its glories pass away;
Change and decay in all around I see;
O Thou who changest not, abide with me.

Tommy knew why his father felt this way. The hymn made him think
about his own father Paul, Big Paul, the family hero who'd laid down his
life for Crown and Country.

The poem *Abide With Me* had been written in the mid 19th-century
by Henry Lyte, an Anglican vicar stricken with tuberculosis who would
pass away within months of completing it. The mournful tune, *Eventide*,
that came to be most mostly associated with the poem was composed a
few years later by William Henry Monk whose three-year old daughter
had recently passed away.

Big Paul had been killed in battle 5000 miles from home fighting an
enemy he never knew for a cause he believed in but probably didn't fully
understand. As he sang, Tommy tried to imagine being his father when
he'd received the news. Numbing shock, anguish and guilt perhaps that
he had chosen a different path to help the British war effort... one which
hadn't involved putting his life on the line in the same way as his father.

I fear no foe, with Thee at hand to bless;
Ills have no weight, and tears no bitterness.
Where is death's sting? Where, grave, thy victory?
I triumph still, if Thou abide with me.

For a brief moment, the unbridled tension and sense of bitter rivalry
between supporters of Chelsea and Leeds that blanketed Wembley was

lifted as intense private emotions were shared publically in what was a communal confrontation with death and the catharsis that comes with affirmation. Humanity as one... seeking hope in the darkest of times. The truce would not last... but while it did, it was thought-provoking and serene.

> *Hold Thou Thy cross before my closing eyes;*
> *Shine through the gloom and point me to the skies.*
> *Heaven's morning breaks, and earth's vain shadows flee;*
> *In life, in death, O Lord, abide with me.*

Yeah, humanity as one... hoping for life after death maybe a reunification with lost loved ones or just something to believe in... a brighter day? Was that it? Who knew? Rest In Peace Big Paul. Tommy bit his lips hard, but couldn't stem the flow of tears. George was weeping openly gazing at the heavens.

A large cheer from the crowd went up as the hymn ended and the ethereal sensation was gone along with the ghostly images of all those people whose memories had been invoked by relatives and friends present. Wiping away the tears from his face, Tommy had no doubt that death was the ultimate force in this world... but for now he was very much alive... they all were.

> *Chelsea! Chelsea! Chelsea!*
> *United! United! United!*

The players from both teams emerged from the tunnel below the stand they were in, Chelsea in bright red tracksuit tops, Leeds in light blue.

'Wonder what the red's all about?' asked Tommy.

'Dunno,' replied George. 'But you see Leeds are wearing red socks, that's from their away kit and Chelsea white socks from their home kit. We must have won the toss. Can't see the point of avoiding a clash of colours on socks.'

'I remember when we played Palace, Tommy reckoned it was to do with TV coverage,' interjected Keith, trying to be helpful. 'Most people still have black and white sets.'

Rick made a point which appealed to all their naturally superstitious natures. 'When we lost to Spurs here in '67, there was a sock clash and we wore blue socks and lost... and we wore all blue when we lost at Elland Road in the league last September.'

'Maybe it's just our turn to choose the socks then,' said Fred. 'Anyway, winning today isn't going to be down to what our lads are wearing... it's going to be down to the quality of football we play and not losing our bottle.'

Come On Chelsea! Come On Chelsea!

Supporters around them cheering the Blues on brought an end to their conversation and they joined in, applauding as the players of both sides as they walked, led by skippers Ron Harris and Billy Bremner and followed by managers Dave Sexton and Don Revie, single file round the side of the pitch towards the half-way line. There, they faced-up ten or so yards apart, like gunslingers at a duel, and waited to be introduced to Her Royal Highness Princess Margaret whom it was expected would be presenting the FA Cup to the victorious captain at the conclusion of the match.

When the formalities were concluded, there was one last tradition to uphold. George, Fred, Tommy, Keith and Rick stood adroitly as did every man, woman and child in the stadium and belted out the *National Anthem*.

As *Abide With Me* briefly unified the crowd spiritually, so did *God Save the Queen* patriotically. The cheering and applause of the crowd at the end of the anthem was rapturous. The Queen's subjects were loyal... 100,000 at Wembley all standing and singing a tribute to her, Tommy wondered briefly if that would ever change.

On the pitch, the players broke away and went through their final warm-up and stretching routines and then referee Eric Jennings, a 47-year old grandfather from Stourbridge in the West Midlands completing his last season on the football league list, whistled to signal it was time to assume formations and get the game under way.

FA Cup Final
Chelsea 2 Leeds United 2 (after extra-time)
Wembley
Attendance: 100,000
Referee: Eric Jennings

Chelsea: Peter Bonetti, David Webb, Eddie McCreadie, John Hollins, John Dempsey, Ron Harris (Marvin Hinton 90), Tommy Baldwin, Peter Houseman, Peter Osgood, Ian Hutchinson, Charlie Cooke.
Scorers: Houseman 41, Hutchinson 86.

Leeds United: Sprake, Madeley, Cooper, Bremner, Charlton, Hunter, Lorimer, Clarke, Jones, Giles, Gray.
Scorers: Charlton 20, Jones 84.

'The ref's gonna have his work cut out keeping order among that lot today, mused George, clapping his hands in anticipation as Leeds kicked off. As expected, Don Revie's side were snapping at Chelsea's heels from the outset. Inside the opening ten minutes they were first to the ball, first to the tackle, first in fact to everything... including testing Peter

Bonetti's reflexes.

Charlie Cooke lost the ball to Paul Madeley who played the ball into the path of Peter Lorimer on the edge of the Blues penalty area. Tommy grimaced as Lorimer, reputed to have one of the hardest shots in the game, unleashed a piledriver... but Bonetti was equal to it, tipping the ball over the bar with out-stretched fingertips for a corner.

Ay, Ay, Ay, Ay, Bonetti is better than Yashin...

George and Fred bellowed out the words at the top of their well-lubricated voices. *Cielito Lindo* aka the *Ay, Ay, Ay, Ay* song had first been heard courtesy of visiting Mexico fans during the 1966 World Cup tournament. England beat Mexico 2-0 at Wembley in the group stages of the competition (16 July, Bobby Charlton, Roger Hunt) but it didn't stop the Mexicans partying throughout the match and singing *Ay, Ay, Ay, Ay* at every opportunity.

Mexico didn't qualify from the group, but a couple of other countries, Portugal and Russia, who made it all the way to the semi-finals, each had a player in their ranks that in the fullness of time would become recognised as a true football icon. Portugal striker Eusebio won the 66 World Cup Golden Boot with nine goals while the agility of Russia goalie Lev Yashin was largely responsible for his country's progress in the competition.

Taking everything in, by October 1966, George and Fred who'd been at the England / Mexico game had come up with their own version of the *Ay, Ay, Ay, Ay* song, a tribute to Peter Bonetti and new striker Tommy Baldwin who'd signed from Arsenal the previous month.

On 1 October, Baldwin scored on his Chelsea debut in a 4-1 (Bobby Tambling, Tommy Baldwin, Joe Kirkup, Peter Osgood) rout of Manchester City at Maine Road, a game in which Bonetti pulled off a string of outstanding saves and towards the end of the month (26 October), Baldwin followed Bobby Tambling onto the scoresheet, netting twice in a 3-0 cuffing of Tottenham Hotspur at Stamford Bridge.

George and Fred, who always maintained they had originated the opening line of the Chelsea version of *Ay, Ay, Ay, Ay,* heard Mickey Greenaway belt out a second line on The Shed during the course of that victory over Spurs. Wherever the truth lay, it was one of their favourite football songs and they sang it whenever they saw fit... like right now.

Ay, Ay, Ay, Ay. Bonetti is better than Yashin.
Baldwin is better than Eusebio...
And Tottenham are in for a thrashing.

Eddie Gray zipped over the corner and Bonetti caught it cleanly which encouraged George and Fred to continue *Ay, Ay, Ay Ay*-ing their ode to the Cat who set Chelsea on a counter-attack with a smart throw which eventually brought about a corner of their own when Paul Madeley cleared a Peter Houseman near-post cross meant for Tommy Baldwin.

A wasteful kick saw the action swiftly move back into the Blues half where Leeds won another corner. This time Peter Lorimer sent a teasing cross into the Chelsea penalty area… fortunately, John Dempsey was on the money to head it away with Whites striker Mick Jones lurking.

Leeds! Leeds! Leeds!

The Yorkshire side, roared on by their followers who were becoming increasingly expectant, were in the driving seat.

'Oi Fred, How much cash have we left on the table in the Nell Gwynne?' asked George, contemplating his exposure to Nick Hill on the outcome of the game as Eddie Gray, easily Leeds best player in the opening 20 minutes, went across to take another corner.

As with the previous kick, Jackie Charlton had stationed himself on the Chelsea goal-line… this time Eddie McCreadie and Ron Harris were in close attendance. Charlton moved out as Gray's corner-kick floated over and in the melee that ensued the Leeds centre-half appeared to impede Peter Bonetti while managing to head the ball somewhat tamely towards the Blues goal.

'Too much,' replied Fred, looking on apprehensively as the ball landed and both McCreadie and Harris, deceived by the spongy quality of the mud-bound pitch which was preventing a natural bounce, aimed clearance kicks which connected with nothing but thin air. Eddie Mac fell onto his backside in the goal and the ball trickled across the line to join him. Harris protested to the referee that a foul had been committed but it was futile. 1-0 to Leeds United.

Leeds! Leeds! Leeds!

While George and Fred questioned Eric Jennings' parentage, Tommy and Rick complained once again about the state of the pitch and how it was affecting the game.

'It's just the same for Leeds though isn't it,' said Keith, shrugging his shoulders. 'I'm more worried about Gray giving Webby the runaround and the fact Ossie hasn't turned up yet.'

Tommy and Rick frowned at Keith's observations but they both knew he was right. Chelsea needed to find a way to get into the game or it would run away from them. What the Blues team needed was their supporters to back them vocally and that's exactly what happened with discussions about evolving problems temporarily forgotten as a glorious chorus of *Chelsea, Chelsea, Chelsea* swelled until it drowned out the sound of the Leeds fans.

Inspired perhaps, Peter Osgood, who noticeably had scarcely featured in the game, almost brought Chelsea level in the 39th minute when Ian Hutchison nodded down a John Hollins cross into the Blues striker's path. Ossie volleyed the ball first time beating Leeds keeper Gary Sprake, but Jack Charlton cleared off the line.

'Finally, we're in the game,' said George to Fred, resting his elbows against the crush barrier he was leaning against and laughing as the ranks stood in front of him, Tommy, Keith and Rick included, surged a good twenty feet down the terrace... *Yessss!* cheers morphed into *Ohhh!* and worse as the end fell.

Chelsea! (clap, clap, clap) Chelsea! (clap, clap, clap)

As Tommy, Keith and Rick were jostling their way back up the terrace, Charlie Cooke sent a left-footed dipping volley over Sprake's crossbar and sections of the Chelsea end fell again.

'We're back in this lads,' said Fred, as the dishevelled-looking trio eventually rocked-up in front of him.

Moments later, Jack Charlton clattered into Peter Osgood from behind... thuggery enough to see Eric Jennings award the Blues a free-kick just inside the Leeds half which was taken by Ron Harris. Harris played a short ball through to Eddie McCreadie who flicked it on to Ian Hutchinson who was stood on the edge of the Leeds penalty area. Hutch tried a back header but skied the ball and at the second attempt nodded it down to Peter Houseman...

Hit it Mary...
Hit it Tiger...
Hit it Nobby...
FUCKING HIT IT!

Every Chelsea supporter screamed a brief and obvious instruction to Houseman... but it wasn't needed, he knew exactly what to do. 25-yards out from goal he leathered the ball first-time and it squirmed past Sprake into the back of the net.

Mary...
Tiger...
Nobby...
You fucking beauty...

The Chelsea end fell once more as triumphant bedlam ensued. Sprake perhaps should have done better... or maybe the pitch was to blame for this goal as well as the first one of the afternoon. Right now, it didn't matter. The debate could be had in a few minutes at half-time. Chelsea were back on level terms and, not for the first time in this season's FA Cup journey, Peter Houseman was the Blues hero.

As he stood there, right arm raised in celebration being mobbed by his teammates George shouted out, 'well done Peter'... and laughed at his own joke.

The last piece of serious action in the first-half saw Johnny Hollins do what David Webb had failed to do so far in the contest and get close enough to Eddie Gray to kick a lump out of him.

'That'll learn the Yorkshire bastard,' quipped Tommy, as referee Jennings blew the whistle on an eventful opening 45 minutes.

'He's Scottish,' replied Keith. 'Just call him a Leeds bastard if you have to call him a bastard.'

There was plenty of chatter at the break about the pitch looking like the Thames Estuary at low tide and plenty of enthusiasm for Chelsea's chances of securing victory despite Leeds looking the better side overall. At 1-1 the Blues weren't chasing the game anymore and Dave Sexton would have renewed his instructions about keeping tabs on Eddie Gray.

Because Gary Sprake's mistake had come well after the Harris / McCreadie gaffe that led to Leeds opening the scoring, it was still fresh in the mind. As the players came out for the second-half, the Peacocks goalkeeper now found himself stationed in front of the Chelsea supporters and by way of a greeting for him a new song was given an airing for the first time.

To the tune of The Troggs 1967 chart hit *Give It To Me (All Your Love)*, *Give us a goal, give us a goal, Gary Sprake, Gary Sprake* was chanted. It was hilarious!

Poor Sprake was no stranger to errors and being teased mercilessly about them. A minute or so before half-time during a First Division game between Leeds and Liverpool at Anfield (9 December 1967), the Wales international keeper, defending the goal in front of The Kop, had readied himself to throw the ball out to his full-back Terry Cooper but changed his mind as Reds winger Ian Callaghan was bearing down swiftly to close down the angle.

Sprake's change of momentum, coupled with an unfortunate loss of grip on the ball, resulted in him throwing the ball into his own net! Moments later, the Anfield disc jockey played Des O'Connor's No.1 chart hit *Careless Hands*. A genuine football comedy gold moment. Fortunately, Sprake had a sense of humour and almost 40 years later he would publish his autobiography giving it the title... *Careless Hands*.

Ian Hutchinson kicked off the second-half for Chelsea and it wasn't too long before both sides were getting physical with each other again... John Dempsey going in hard on Mick Jones.

'Jones will have been glad of a couple of fags and a break from Dempsey kicking his arse,' quipped Tommy, sparking up himself and applauding the Blues centre-half's tackle. For all the joking about Sprake, the Leeds keeper then made a couple of brave saves from Hutchinson in the same passage of play which concluded with Peter Osgood seeing another shot cleared off the line, this time by Norman Hunter.

'Ossie, you ain't lost the magic,' shouted Rick, struggling to find his feet as the crowd jumped up as one and this time swayed sideways down the terrace.

Chelsea! Chelsea! Chelsea!

The encouragement from Chelsea supporters was raucous and deafening and the Blues players seemed to draw strength from it.

Once again, Peter Houseman tried his luck from distance, but this time Gary Sprake's last-minute snatch prevented the ball crossing the line.

'Shouldn't have taken the piss out of him as much as we did,' said Keith shaking his head in disbelief. 'Look at him now, he thinks he's Gordon bloody Banks.'

The sight soon after of Ron Harris in full-on Chopper mode and Billy Bremner, a recent recipient of the Football Writers Association Player of the Year Award, getting feisty with each other brought plenty of cheers and jeers from both ends of the ground. Referee Jennings left his notebook in his pocket... or maybe he'd forgotten it. What other explanation could there be for the fact he'd yet to take anyone's name. The ref's leniency and willingness to let things go served as a dare to the players to carry on tackling wildly and all the while Eddie Gray continued to torment David Webb.

'Why didn't Sexton change it at half-time... shift Chopper to right back and push Webby into the middle with Demps?' It sounded like a question from George, but it was in fact a lament.

Gray continued to roast Webb and was making a solid case for being named man-of-the-match. Time and again, Peter Bonetti's cat-like reflexes were being tested and the Chelsea keeper also had the crossbar to thank when the tricky winger bent his fingers back with a fiery shot having once again bamboozled Webb.

Come On Chelsea! Come On Chelsea!

Support wasn't waning, but the Blues were getting bogged down and with the clock ticking down to full-time there was a growing sense of unease about the level of dominance Leeds were now enjoying.

Leeds! Leeds! Leeds! Leeds!

The Yorkshire crowd bayed their allegiance to their team... and then Chelsea had a chance. Charlie Cooke who'd had a quiet game found some space on the right to work up a pin-point, cross-field pass to Peter Houseman.

This was going to be it thought Tommy. One of Mary, Tiger or Nobby was going to win the cup for Chelsea and he was never going to be called called Mary, Tiger or Nobby again... just Peter.

Hit it Mary…
Hit it Tiger…
Hit it Nobby…
FUCKING HIT IT!

The instructions from the crowd were simple… just as before. This time though, Houseman screwed his shot feebly wide of Sprake's far post.

'Should've passed it to Hutch,' shouted Rick loudly.

'Wanker!' Keith was more direct and added a couple of boos to underline his disappointment.

'You wouldn't have done any better,' said George, clipping Keith across the top of the head. Keith looked at him and grinned, but he soon realised George was vexed with him. 'Don't boo the Blue son. Do you understand?'

Tommy laughed, this was why he still loved going to games with his father. Distraction from Houseman's fluffed chance and Keith upsetting George came in the unwanted form of Leeds going in front.

With just seven minutes remaining, the Whites carved the Blues open. Billy Bremner caught Eddie McCreadie square with a floating pass which found Johnny Giles who one-touched the ball across the Chelsea penalty area into which Allan 'Sniffer' Clarke had stolen in. Clarke's powerful header beat Peter Bonetti but not the post… the rebound off the woodwork however fell kindly for Mick Jones who for once was far enough away from John Dempsey to size up a shot… BOOM! Jones crashed the ball into the net. 2-1 to Leeds United.

We're gonna win the cup, we're gonna win the cup…

Keith wanted to curse Peter Houseman for missing that chance moments earlier, but he looked across at George who was glowering at him and thought better of it. Down below, Sprake was celebrating on his own. Tommy wouldn't have been surprised if the Leeds keeper had turned around and stuck two fingers up at the Chelsea fans who'd been taunting him every time he'd touched the ball in the second-half. What a load of shit! Not again. Not another lost final.

'Come on Chelsea, straight back into them.' George's rallying call snapped Tommy's train of thought.

Chelsea! Chelsea! Chelsea!

With four minutes left, Eddie McCreadie cleared a loose ball out of defence to Charlie Cooke who slipped it on to John Hollins. Still inside the Blues half, Hollins picked out Ron Harris wide on the left and Chopper exchanged passes with Peter Osgood… the ball advanced into the Leeds half. It was a beautiful intricate move that took the breath away... especially given the condition of the pitch which had continued to deteriorate if that was at all possible. Jackie Charlton then did what he had successfully done for much of the game... impede Ossie. As a punishment, referee Jennings, still refusing to book repeat offenders like Charlton, awarded Chelsea a free-kick wide left of the Leeds penalty area.

'We scored last time this happened,' said Fred, nudging George and rubbing his hands together in anticipation. 'Big Jack clattered Ossie in the first half... and we ended up equalising from open play after the free-kick. It's gonna happen again now. Trust me!'

'Well if it happens I'm going to end up down there with my boy,' replied George, pointing down the terrace.

'Me too!'

Eric Jennings signalled for the kick to be taken and Ron Harris rolled the ball to Johnny Hollins who stepped up and clipped a cross towards the Leeds six-yard box. Jack Charlton and Ian Hutchinson leapt in the air... but it was Hutch won the aerial duel and headed the ball past Sprake.

GOAAAAAAAAAL!

True to their words, George and Fred launched themselves off the crush barrier and went down the terrace with Tommy, Keith, Rick and everyone else around them. A joyful, foaming congregation of blue and white Chelsea civilisation tangled up with suddenly detached pennants, banners, flags, rosettes and badges.

The scores were level at 2-2... but Leeds had the look of a vanquished team. Peter Lorimer, Billy Bremner and Mick Jones... their fallen heroes, lying momentarily on the divot-riddled turf, spirits sapped by Chelsea's late revival.

We're gonna win the cup, we're gonna win the cup...

Now it was the turn of Chelsea supporters to sing the song.

And now you're gonna believe us...

A couple of minutes lapsed and referee Jennings blew for full-time. An additional 30 minutes would be played, which team would prevail? Both were fatigued but the momentum, psychological if nothing else, right now was with Chelsea.

The Blues did have a potential problem... skipper Ron Harris, whose fitness had always been in question going into the game, was being replaced by substitute Marvin Hinton. Would this upset the balance of the side or would a fresh pair of legs be beneficial? Leeds, for their part, chose to continue into extra-time as they were.

Given the trying conditions, in the modern era, not that pitches would ever be as bad now, both teams would almost certainly have worked their way through the permitted allocation of three subs in normal time with a fourth being an option in extra-time. With seven players on the bench to choose from, including of course a reserve goalkeeper, managers are able to plan tactical changes as well as cater for injuries.

In 1970, one sub was permitted per team and that would typically be an outfield player. Substitutes were still a relatively new concept having been introduced in the 1965/66 season and then only permissible as a replacement for an injured player. The rule was relaxed for the 1967/68 season when substitutions were allowed for tactical reasons.

'I don't mind Hinton,' said George. 'Decent defender. We need more energy at the back.'

'It's a shame Chopper can't go the distance yet,' replied Fred. 'It's Webby who really should be coming off. He's had a mare against Gray. Sexton needs to change things or he'll keep running us ragged.'

Four heads nodded in agreement with Fred as they watched the players on the pitch readying themselves for more action.

'If Johnny Boyle is the answer, what is the question?' asked George, rubbing his hands along his cheeks and smiling.

Keith put his hand up, schoolboy-in-classroom style… which was funny. 'Is the question, which current Chelsea player was born on Christmas Day please George?'

George clipped Keith across the top of his head. 'Don't be a smart arse son.'

'But I'm right aren't I,' replied Keith indignantly.

George nodded. 'Yeah, okay. I'll give you that… but Johnny Boyle is also the answer to a different question.

'He could be the answer to a lot of questions though couldn't he,' said Rick. 'Like who is the only Chelsea player to have scored the winner on his debut in the first leg of a League Cup semi-final? (20 January 1965, Aston Villa 2 Chelsea 3, Bobby Tambling, Barry Bridges, John Boyle).

George was getting irate now… 'Chelsea have only ever played one first leg of a League Cup semi-final in their history though.'

Tommy laughed, it was like pulling the wings off a butterfly teasing his father… but he only had himself to blame.

With the players taking up formation for the kick-off, and George still wanting his riddle solved, it was Fred who came up with the question that was the answer.

'Who was Chelsea's first ever player to get subbed on?'

George gave the thumbs up. '28 August 1965… Boylers came on as a sub for George Graham in 3-0 win over Fulham at the Cottage.'

'I went to that game with you,' said Tommy. 'Bert Murray, Barry Bridges and Graham himself scored for us.' He was just about to add that the following season, he'd seen Peter Houseman become the first

Chelsea substitute ever to score a goal when he'd replaced Peter Osgood early on in a 5-2 rout of Charlton Athletic in a League Cup Second Round tie at Stamford Bridge (14 September 1966, Ian King own-goal, George Graham, Bobby Tambling, Peter Houseman, John Hollins) when Eric Jennings blew the whistle to get the first period of extra-time under way and the chant *Chelsea! Chelsea! Chelsea!* took hold of the end. Some songs people swerved joining in with, but *Chelsea! Chelsea! Chelsea!* was all-embracing and anthemic.

Chelsea! Chelsea! Chelsea!

'Come on! This way,' shouted Keith, beckoning as the Blues broke up Leeds' passing game.

The *Chelsea! Chelsea! Chelsea!* chanting stopped completely when Terry Cooper handled midway inside his own half.

HAND BALL!

Eric Jennings awarded a free-kick which Johnny Hollins lofted into the Leeds penalty area. Jackie Charlton headed clear and the ball was shuffled on by Allan Clarke but there was Peter Houseman to play it out to Eddie McCreadie advancing down the left flank.

'Cross it Eddie, cross it.' Keith shouted and whistled instructions, just like every other Chelsea supporter around him was doing.

McCreadie knew exactly what to do and flicked the ball into the Leeds penalty area. With his back to goal, Ian Hutchinson nodded it down into the path of John Dempsey.

SHOOT!

Having been taunted mercilessly by Blues supporters for his earlier mistake, Sprake pulled off a superb save tipping Dempsey's fierce shot over the bar.

'That was our chance... that was our chance.' George appeared disconsolate, contemplating Nick Hill in the Nell Gwynne laughing as he watched the game on television perhaps.

Houseman took the resultant corner which Leeds cleared away up the field, breaking in numbers. Following good work by Paul Madeley and inevitably Eddie Gray who took the ball to the byline and crossed into the Chelsea penalty area, it was Johnny Giles who almost broke Blues supporters hearts.

Giles volleyed hard and low.

George covered his eyes.

Tommy didn't. 'Yes! Webby. You fucking beauty!'

David Webb may have been given the run around all afternoon by Eddie Gray, but he was in the right place at the right time to divert Giles' goal-bound shot over the bar.

Leeds were in the ascendancy again but when Allan Clarke crashed a shot off the bar shortly after Webb's heroics, Tommy convinced himself they weren't going to score again though his attempts to persuade his father to think the same positive way fell on deaf ears. Chelsea were clinging on and end of the first period of extra-time couldn't come soon enough.

Even when the game was level at the end of 90 minutes, nobody had considered the outcome of the match might be a draw… but now it was becoming a real possibility and comments along the lines of 'I'll take a draw now' were being uttered as Jennings blew his whistle and pointed at the center circle.

The teams switched ends swiftly and without any tactical intervention from their managers. Playing out the remaining 15 minutes without taking any risks might have been something Dave Sexton and Don Revie would have drummed into their players had they had a decent chance to do so… but the way the game initially continued in end-to-end fashion suggested caution was still being thrown to the wind.

Houseman chipped a cross over for Osgood who headed just wide and then Madeley delivered a similar ball for Jones which Bonetti clutched from under the bar.

It was perhaps energy, or a lack of it now, rather than motivation that eventually slowed the pace. All the games key players were feeling the effects of the longevity of the contest and cramping up. Just as Tommy was contemplating the draw… there was Tommy Baldwin squaring the ball to Peter Houseman in the Leeds penalty area…

Hit it Mary…
Hit it Tiger…
Hit it Nobby…
FUCKING HIT IT!

The action may have been at the other end of the ground, but Chelsea supporters still surged down their terrace as Houseman fired off a shot which looked bound for the bottom right-hand corner. Gary Sprake, proving he was as agile as his feline opposite number, and not as careless as many joked he was, dived spectacularly to tip the ball round the post.

BASTARD!

Not Houseman, Sprake. Why couldn't he have done something clown-like and conceded the goal. George and Fred's long-running bets were shredded. The game was at an end.

Chelsea! Chelsea! Chelsea!

2-2. A draw. The only winner today was Nick Hill, the corpulent clot would be doing cartwheels in the Nell Gwynne now. Nobody would have backed the draw. Hill might have been bent over when Gay Trip won the Grand National... but he was rolling in clover now and he'd have another bite at the cherry. For the first time since 20 April 1912, when Barnsley drew 0-0 with West Bromwich Albion at Crystal Palace, the FA Cup Final needed a replay. On that occasion, the second game was played four days later at Bramall Lane with Barnsley prevailing 1-0.

Despite their heroics on the pitch, the players doing a lap of honour and clambering up the steps to greet Her Royal Highness Princess Margaret left Tommy feeling a bit hollow. Plenty said that Wembley was no place for losers, and that was certainly true in 1967 after Chelsea lost to Tottenham Hotspur. You don't want to still be in the ground when the opposition captain lifts the cup... it's voyeuristic. You feel like an uninvited guest. No thank you, exit stage left. A draw wasn't a defeat, but it wasn't victory either... celebrating it felt strange. Tommy held back, his father was reserved as well.

'We could quite easily have lost if Bonetti hadn't been on top form,' said Fred, perplexed by the curious sight of both teams doing a joint lap of honour round the pitch. 'So maybe we should be happy... well happier than Leeds anyway.'

George pointed at Alan Hudson walking down the tunnel deep in conversation with Dave Sexton. 'If Huddy had been fit, we might have won today. If he makes the replay it might give us the edge.'

'Are we having a bet then?' asked Fred.

Tommy laughed, everything was back to square one and it would be all to play for... and bet on... but unlike the usual scenarios where cup replays took place a few short days after the initial match, Chelsea and Leeds would have to wait almost three weeks to lock horns once again.

With England scheduled to play Northern Ireland at Wembley on 21 April in a 'British Home Championship' tie, the venue of the FA Cup final replay, should one be required, had already been decided as Old Trafford. Given its 60,000-plus capacity, the home of Manchester United was the logical alternative to Wembley.

'Stan 'king of the spivs' Flashman and his touts will be at it again,' said Fred, as they waited for the crowds to clear. There was no point rushing... the queues outside the stadium would be lengthy.

'First the 'Fat Stan Final', now the 'Fat Stan Replay', replied George. 'Mind you, I think both clubs get 20,000 tickets each instead of 16,000.'

'It's still not enough,' said Tommy. 'Fat Stan's just taking advantage of market forces. I blame the FA. There should be more tickets made available for the supporters of the clubs that reach a final.'

The thought had crossed his mind more than once after the Wembley ticketing fiasco had come to light that he could surreptitiously make use of the skills he'd learned in the printing trade and take advantage of the out-of-hours access he had to his work premises to print fake tickets that would stand up to the most rigorous of scrutiny, but somehow it felt wrong. For a start, betraying Ted's trust and kindness would be bang out of order and then there were other considerations. If he got caught, there would a fine, jail maybe... what would his parents think? What about Sophia?

But what if it was just small-scale... really small-scale? That would be okay wouldn't it? Maybe a test, a one off? The FA Cup Final replay... just to see if it was possible to get away with it? Then what? Just one small job perhaps... yeah... just one small job.

'Penny for your thoughts son,' said George.

'Nah, nothing.' Tommy shrugged his shoulders, lit a cigarette and started a conversation unrelated to what he'd been thinking about. 'There's a lot of football still to be played. It's funny isn't it, the FA Cup final's usually the last game of the season but we've still got three league games to play...'

'In a bloody week!' interrupted Fred. 'Stoke away on Monday night, Burnley away on Wednesday night and then Liverpool at home next Saturday.'

'At least there's almost two weeks then to the replay,' said Rick. 'The early date for the final's down to Alf Ramsey and his England squad needing to get away to Mexico early in May.'

'How many games have Dirty Leeds got then?' asked Tommy, as Keith, impatient to get back to the Prince of Wales Feathers for a drink, beckoned them from across the now almost deserted terrace. It was amazing how quickly football grounds emptied despite all the bottlenecks at the exit points.

'Three the same as us,' replied Fred, giving a thumbs up signal to Keith. 'Celtic at Hampden Park in the second-leg of their European Cup semi on Wednesday and then couple of league games. Home to Man City and away to Ipswich.'

'Imagine if they lost them all,' replied Tommy, that would be funny.

George shook his head. 'I don't mind if they win them all... provided they lose the replay to us.'

Tommy took one last look at the Wembley pitch and flicked his half-smoked cigarette down the empty terrace before following the others up the steps to the exit.

'When's the European Cup Final? Be handy if Leeds got through if it's before the replay,' said Rick.

'Nah. It's after,' replied Fred. '6 May in the San Siro against Feyenoord or Legia Warsaw. Would mean their players in the England squad would be heading out to Mexico late.'

Rick nodded at his father. 'What about if the Celtic / Leeds tie ends in a draw though... they'd have to have a replay.'

'All these replays are a right royal pain in the arse,' said Tommy. 'I bet Princess Margaret doesn't go to ours. The FA should come up with a better idea...'

Editor's note: At this point, Tommy shared his knowledge about what happened in the near term regarding replays. It's a lovely bit of general football nostalgia / trivia and worth sharing here.

"FIFA and UEFA adopted the penalty shoot-out procedure for the 1970-71 campaign and the good old Watney Cup which was contested pre-season between 1970 and 1973 was the English FAs guinea pig.

The premise behind the Watney Cup was great. The two top scoring teams in Divisions One to Four who had not been promoted or qualified for Europe were invited to participate. Man U, Derby County, Sheffield United, Fulham, Reading, Aldershot and Peterborough played in the first competition and the first penalty shoot-out came at the end of a 1-1 semi-final draw between Manchester United and Hull City.

The game was played at the Tigers old Boothferry Park ground on 5 August 1970 and Georgie Best, who else, was the first player to score in the shoot-out... and his teammate Denis Law the first player to miss. Man U prevailed 4-3, but lost 4-1 to Derby in the final."

Tommy then continued...

"Chelsea never contested the Watney Cup though they did participate in another classic pre-season tournament from the same era that will make older readers go a little misty-eyed... the Anglo Scottish Cup. As you know, times and fortunes changed swiftly at Stamford Bridge and a relegated Blues team took part in 1975 and 76 and also in 1977 as a top-flight club again.

Somewhat bizarrely, despite playing nine fixtures across the three tournaments, they never played a Scottish team!! In fact the furthest they had to travel was 10 miles to the East London home of Leyton Orient!! (14 August 1976, Orient 2 Chelsea 1, Micky Droy)

Sorry for getting distracted there, but these little details are important. You want more little details? Well the team that faced Orient contained only one player who featured prominently in the Blues 1970 FA Cup run... John Dempsey who had by now taken the Bobby Charlton / Ralph Coates combover hair-do to an entirely new level.

*****

The highlight of the evening in the Prince of Wales Feathers was watching the pub's colour television... not the highlights of the cup final on *Match of the Day* but a live transmission of the Apollo 13 space mission rocket taking off from the Kennedy Space Centre on Merritt Island, Florida.

George joked that Norman Long should have included a line about man walking on the moon when he wrote his song about preposterous things happening on the day that Chelsea won the cup.

'Sexton's got plenty of time now to come up with a plan to stop Eddie Gray,' replied Fred. 'That's what he'll need to do to make that

Norman Long song redundant once and for all.'

They all agreed that Gray deserved his man-of the match award but that Peter Bonetti perhaps wasn't too far behind him.

The biggest laugh of the evening came when another group of Chelsea supporters in the pub told a story about their journey from Wembley on the underground and how there'd been a scuffle between Danny 'Eccles' Harkins and his gang of Shed boys and some lairy Leeds supporters in their carriage. Eccles settled matters by punching the gobbiest one in the face and then made him say 'thank you' for doing so.

As they laughed, Keith remarked that by the next home game the story would have gone round all the pubs and been embellished a few times. It was always the way. There was as much banter these days about what was happening on the terraces or down dimly-lit avenues and alleyways as there was about what was occurring on the pitch and Eccles exploits, real and imaginary, were firmly establishing him as a cult hero among many Blues supporters.

Tommy thought about telephoning Sophia, he remembered she'd said she was staying in to spend the evening with her parents, but changed his mind at the last minute. He knew he was edging towards being drunk but he hadn't reached that point of drunkenness where common sense so often gets compromised.

As the bell for last orders rang, his father suggested that they head back to the Wetherby for a couple of after-hours drinks... that was the clincher to forget about Sophia. It was a smart move and besides he was dog-tired. It had been a long enjoyable day, why run the risk of spoiling it?

LIVERPOOL
Saturday 18 April 1970

The week that followed the final had been an illuminating whirl for Tommy. Away from the football, on Tuesday and Wednesday evening he'd gone with Sophia to the Royal Albert Hall to see Booker T. & The MG's who were supporting Creedence Clearwater Revival.

The gigs were a sell-out. Creedence, on the back of last years chart hits *Proud Mary* and *Bad Moon Rising* were a massive draw in London, but it was the musicianship of Hammond organ superstar Booker T. Jones, guitarist Steve Cropper, bassist Donald 'Duck' Dunn and drummer Al Jackson, Jr... collectively known as Booker T. & The MG's, that had hooked plenty of people into attending on both nights.

Tommy could tell by the positive audience reaction to their set, a mix of self-penned instrumental hits including *Green Onions*, *Hip Hug-Her*, *Soul Limbo* and *Time Is Tight* (currently being used as the theme music to the Radio 1 *Pick of the Pops* chart show hosted by Alan Freeman and broadcast every Sunday from 5 p.m. until 7 p.m.), and covers of hits which they gave their own R&B / Memphis soul flavour to such as Mrs Robinson (Simon &Garfunkel), *Lady Madonna* (The Beatles) and *Light My Fire* (The Doors), that showed how well thought of the band were.

On Wednesday at work, Tommy had mentioned the gig to his boss Ted and been surprised to hear he was also attending the show that evening as he'd been discussing the supply of secure stationery with the director of finance and administration at the Royal Albert Hall who'd invited him and a guest to watch from a private box.

'Come and find me during the intermission,' Ted had said. 'Bring that charming fiancée of yours with you and join us for a drink.'

"Intermission". That made Tommy laugh. Imagine calling half-time at football the intermission. Mind you, what did you call the time between a support band finishing their set and the headliners coming on?

That night, Booker T. & The MG's absolutely smashed it. They played a slightly different set to the previous evening including a medley comprised of tracks from their new *McLemore Avenue* album, a homage to The Beatles LP *Abbey Road*. *Golden Slumbers*, *Carry That Weight*, *The End*, *Here Comes The Sun* and *Come Together* got the Southern soul treatment. The sound was truly extraordinary, Booker's dexterity on the keyboards and Steve Cropper's guitar playing were a revelation.

During the "intermission", Tommy and Sophia went up to the second

180

floor and found the private box Ted had been invited to. There, Tommy was astonished to find his boss was standing arm-in-arm and sharing an expensive-looking cocktail with the shop assistant from the jewellers he'd bought Sophia's engagement ring from! It was one of those 'fuck me you're a bit of a dark horse aren't you' moments when it was best not to say 'fuck me you're a bit of a dark horse aren't you.'

Tommy was speechless. Sophia of course had no idea why, but Ted soon put her straight when he introduced the shop assistant as Verity whom it transpired he'd asked out on a date the day he'd sorted out the paperwork for the engagement ring. They had a couple of drinks together and made polite small talk.

The next day, a beaming Ted called Tommy up to his office at close of business and thanked him saying he'd asked Verity to marry him and she'd accepted his proposal. A double case of love at first sight then they agreed before briefly discussing business, the FA Cup Final and Chelsea's midweek games.

In the background, a news bulletin on the office television relayed the latest information about the Apollo 13 space mission which had run into difficulties following the explosion and rupture of one of its oxygen tanks a couple of days or so after launch.

"Houston, we've had a problem," astronauts Jack Swiggert and Jim Lovell had said to NASA Mission Control. Plans to land on the moon were aborted, instead the crew now faced a major challenge to return to earth alive. It was gripping stuff, the moon was over 200,000 miles away from earth. Could the Yanks find a solution and bring their boys home?

Somewhat closer, well the Victoria Ground, Stoke to be exact... on Monday, just two days after their exertions on the boggy Wembley marshland, Chelsea had seen action again (13 April, Stoke City 1 Chelsea 2, Ian Hutchinson, Eric Skeels own-goal).

Manager Dave Sexton might have been excused for resting all 12 players that had featured against Leeds, but instead it was almost a case of as you were with only Peter Bonetti (sore knee), Ron Harris (hamstring) and Eddie McCreadie, who'd played through the pain barrier and was waiting to have surgery on minor stomach obstruction, missing from his Wembley starting XI.

Tommy Hughes, Marvin Hinton and Paddy Mulligan deputised admirably, and the victory edged Chelsea above Derby County and back into third place. Charlie Cooke created both Blues goals. The first, with a deft chip that landed at the feet of Ian Hutchinson who beat England keeper Gordon Banks with ease principally because the Stoke backline had given up on Hutch thinking he was offside. The second, with a centre that surprisingly flummoxed Banks and defender Eric Skeels, the latter accidentally diverting the ball beyond his goalie.

The same day, Alan Hudson had gone back into hospital to have further treatment. There was some optimism that he might be fit for the cup final replay, though Ted made a valid point that Leeds might target

Huddy for some serious roughhouse treatment if he played at Old Trafford.

While Tommy and Ted were at the Royal Albert Hall, Chelsea were at Turf Moor playing foes as familiar this season as Leeds United... Burnley. Sexton restored the warrior McCreadie to his side at the expense of Mulligan and gave Ian Hutchinson and Peter Osgood the evening off bringing in John Boyle and Alan Birchenall. It made sense to give Chelsea's key strike force a rest, but without them the Blues were clearly toothless up front and newspaper reports of the game said they also looked jaded... which was understandable.

Burnley seized the opportunity to avenge January's Fourth Round FA Cup replay defeat and were two goals to the good inside 15 minutes thanks to Martin Dobson and Steve Kindon. Johnny Hollins pulled one back for Chelsea with a 25-yard piledriver that apparently would have graced Wembley, but Chelsea were lagging by half-time and it was no surprise when Kindon scored again after the break.

The Blues losing wasn't the main football news of the evening... up in Scotland, Leeds United were beaten 2-1 by Celtic in the second leg of their European Cup semi-final. A 3-1 aggregate defeat meant that Don Revie's side's last remaining hope of winning silverware this season hinged on beating Chelsea at Old Trafford.

Ted said that Leeds were fortunate they had a fortnight to get the disappointment of losing to Celtic out of their system. They'd be fully focussed on beating Chelsea and desperate to give their fans something to cheer at the end of the season.

For a short while, Tommy was concerned but then he soon realised it wasn't worth worrying about. In his mind, Leeds had blown their chance of victory at Wembley. At Old Trafford, Lady Luck simply had to favour Chelsea. He walked over to the office window and looked up at the star-speckled night sky, eyes drawn to the shimmering slither of crescent moon clearly visible in the inky blackness. Somewhere up there were Jim Lovell, Jack Swigert and Fred Haise, the astronauts of the stricken Apollo 13 space mission. A different perspective on the need for good fortune permeated his thoughts...

*****

'Did you see the gate at Hampden the other night for the Celtic / Leeds game,' said George to Fred, leaning back on the crush barrier behind him and looking around Stamford Bridge.

'Well over 100,000 wasn't it,' replied Fred, scratching his head as he tried to remember what the attendance was.

'Well over... yeah! It was 136,505.'

'That's incredible...makes you wonder how many were actually in the ground... I bet it was more than that.'

'I'll tell you what's incredible. Celtic asked for the game to be played at Hampden because their ground only holds 60,000 and they knew more supporters would want to go. How many would want to go to the

FA Cup final... and the replay come to think of it? I know we talk about it all the time, but it really ain't fair on the supporters down here the way the English FA go about their business.'

'What are you saying then? That the replay against Leeds should be played at Hampden Park?'

'Well it's only another 200 or so miles on from Manchester to Glasgow isn't it. The extra journey time wouldn't really make any difference to our supporters travelling up from London and pretty much everyone who wanted to go to the game would get in to see it.'

Tommy listened to the conversation his father and Fred were having with interest without offering an opinion. As expected, most of the discussions being had in The Shed ahead of the last league game of the season against Liverpool were concerned with ticketing arrangements for the Leeds replay.

There was an application form in the programme for today's game... which no doubt 'Fat Stan' and his army of touts had been buying by the satchel-load as 40,000 had been printed. Tickets were going on sale at Stamford Bridge to non season ticket holders at 10 a.m. the next morning with a four-hour window to make a purchase on a one ticket per completed form basis. No more than two forms per person would be accepted meaning the queue at the main gates would begin forming this evening with plenty of supporters prepared to stand in line over night!

Season ticket holders had it slightly easier with an option to buy after today's game, tomorrow or on Monday and Tuesday. Terrace tickets were priced at 12 shillings and sixpence for the ground, 15 shillings for the paddock and 25, 50 and 80 shillings for seats. The ticket selling arrangements had been common knowledge for a few days and Keith's enterprising 15-year old cousin, Mark Meehan, who lived in Cedarne Road just across the road from Fulham Broadway underground station had already offered to queue on his behalf at a rate of £1 for every two hours. Fair play to the kid. He wasn't alone. There were also plenty of enterprising urchins from the World's End offering a similar service.

Editor's note: *Although this was way before most Blues supporters recall nasally whining Scousers giving it large with their long-deemed homophobic Chelsea Rent Boys jibe, in later years Tommy would tell an amusing anecdotal story that the chant originated when a group of Liverpool fans, without scarves identifying them as such, were approached after the game by local kids offering the £1 for every two hours cup final ticket queuing service. This was a much more palatable version of events than the urban myth peddled by Scousers during the 1980s which suggested that police making a dawn raid to arrest a ringleader of the notorious Chelsea Headhunters hooligan firm had found their suspect in bed with a male prostitute.*

FIRST DIVISION
Chelsea 2 Liverpool 1
Stamford Bridge
Attendance: 36,521
Referee: Mike Kerkhoff

Chelsea: Peter Bonetti, David Webb, Eddie McCreadie, John Hollins, John Dempsey, Marvin Hinton, Tommy Baldwin, Charlie Cooke, Peter Osgood, Ian Hutchinson, Peter Houseman.
Scorers: Osgood 21, 68 (pen).

Liverpool: Clemence, Lawler, Yeats, Smith, Lloyd, McLaughlin, Callaghan, Livermore, Evans, Graham, Thompson.
Scorer: Graham 26.

Stamford Bridge had filled up nicely, but it was by no means packed out as the players ran out onto the pitch for what was a rearranged fixture. Plenty of Liverpool supporters were in attendance and making themselves heard on the North Stand terrace.

We love you Liverpool, we do...
We love you Liverpool, we do...
We love you Liverpool, we do...
Oh Liverpool we love you!

The Reds chant, that pretty much every club including Chelsea had its own version of, originated from the 1960 Broadway musical *Bye Bye Birdie* which contained a song entitled *We Love You Conrad.* In 1964, an all female group of Beatles fans, amusingly called The Carefrees, borrowed the melody and came up with the track *We Love You Beatles.*

A very modest hit in 1964, *We Love You Beatles* beget *We love you Liverpool...* and not long after *We love you Chelsea...* the singing of which wasn't how The Shed chose to respond to the chant coming from the North Stand terrace... instead... they aired what would become another timeless classic.

If you're standing on a corner with red scarf round your neck...
Chelsea fans will come and get you...
And we'll break you're fucking neck.

The first series of now popular BBC sitcom *The Liver Birds* had been screened last year and the show's catchy theme tune written and performed by Merseyside band The Scaffold, whose songs *Lily The Pink* and *Gin Gan Goolie* had already spawned tributes to Charlie Cooke and Peter Houseman, had been reworked by Chelsea's choristers into an altogether more threatening version. It was funny how these professional

Scousers had their worked transformed. Tommy wondered briefly if it bothered them and concluded it wouldn't because it was free publicity for their music.

With Alan Hudson out of hospital and Ron Harris responding extremely well to treatment, Chelsea manager Dave Sexton had every reason to be optimistic about his side's chances in the cup final replay. The showdown with Leeds was still 11 days away and so the Blues boss had no hesitation about fielding the strongest team possible for the visit of Liverpool knowing that a point against the Reds would be enough, even if Chelsea lost the replay with Leeds, to bring European football in the guise of the Inter Cities Fairs Cup back to Stamford Bridge.

From the first whistle, it was clear that Sexton wanted his team to play to win and the game was played at full throttle with no quarter given in any challenges, blocks or tackles.

Chelsea deservedly took the lead in the 21st minute when Osgood, too sprightly for Liverpool centre-half Ron Yeats, got into position to make the most of a Tommy Baldwin cross from the right wing. Reds keeper Ray Clemence came out, but Ossie, clearly having no fear or maybe even a thought about injuring himself in a 50/50 tangle with Clem, volleyed the ball into the net without allowing it to bounce. Ossie saluted The Shed who responded with a chant of *Osgood for England!*

Having arrived early for the game to avoid a forecasted torrential downpour which came and went 20 minutes or so before kick-off, George, Fred, Tommy, Keith and Rick were stood half-way down the middle section of the covered part of The Shed and the atmosphere was cracking.

We're gonna win the cup, we're gonna win the cup...

'Ossie's back on form,' shouted Fred to George. 'That's 29 goals for the season now. We should back him to score in the replay.'

And now you're gonna believe us...

Fred was just about to reply when Liverpool equalised and muted The Shed.

'Fuck's sake,' cursed Rick, shaking his head as a lame punched clearance by Peter Bonetti caught out John Dempsey who hesitated and allowed Reds striker Bobby Graham to catch sight of the Blues goal.

Li-ver-pool, Li-ver-pool...
Chelsea! Chelsea! Chelsea!

Two gaps opened... one in the murky heavens from which dirty great stair rods of rain fell and one in the middle of the North Stand terrace where a numerically small Chelsea mob made their presence known... and felt.

A, G... A, G, R... A, G, R, O, AGRO!

The chant sounded tribal. It had its origins in *Hold Tight,* a 1964 chart hit for Dave Dee, Dozy, Beaky, Mick & Tich that had spawned the three-clap / klaxon *England!* chant at the 1966 World Cup and had been picked up on by pretty much every club throughout the land.

'What's the point of doing that?' asked Fred, pointing at the ruck ensuing on the North Stand.

He didn't get an answer. The gap on the terrace closed up within seconds and at half-time the Chelsea mob involved were back in The Shed collecting money to help pay for the fines they were likely to incur should they be arrested in Manchester trying to further their nascent reputation as football's maddest firm.

The pitch, while not as bad as some that the Blues had played on during the course of the season, had become puddled and increasingly pitted as the game progressed. The ground staff had taken pitchforks to the surface in a bid to improve drainage, but to no avail. This didn't dim the players enthusiasm for the contest but it sapped the quality out of the match which looked to be heading for a draw until 20 minutes or so before full-time when there was a massive shout for a penalty.

A speculative in-swinging Chelsea cross was handled by Liverpool defender Larry Lloyd under pressure from Ian Hutchinson. Referee Mike Kerhoff didn't see it, but the whole of The Shed did... and, more importantly, so did linesman Michael Thorpe who waved his yellow flag insistently until Kerhoff came across to have a chat with him.

PENALTY!

Liverpool players protested, in particular Tommy Smith and Ron Yeats... but Kerkhoff heeded Thorpe's observation that the ball had struck Lloyd's arm and pointed at the spot.

'Go on Ossie!' Tommy clenched his fists as Peter Osgood readied himself in front of the Scouse hordes gathered on the North Stand terrace. As Kerkhoff blew his whistle, Clemence moved to his left and turned to see the ball crashed into the back of the net off the middle of his crossbar. 2-1 to Chelsea and the end of the goal action.

The Shed were soon in full flow singing *You'll Never Walk Alone...* the North Stand was silent. Tommy looked on with some concern as Osgood appeared to twist his ankle late on, but the striker saw out the game. 30 goals for the campaign was his best ever haul for Chelsea and brought him level with Jeff Astle of West Bromwich Albion.

'I've seen enough today,' said Fred, distracting Tommy's train of thought. 'I'm betting £20 on Osgood to score in the replay.'

Of course it was a gamble. They'd all lost money to Nick Hill backing

Chelsea to win the final... but they all felt the same way about Ossie scoring at Old Trafford.

The queue for tickets for the replay was already snaking from the main gates down the Fulham Road when they made their way out of the ground at full-time. Keith's cousin Mark was around 50 people from the front and he was standing there looking well-prepared for the damp chills of the night ahead wearing a heavy overcoat, carrying an umbrella and with a knapsack on his back which contained sandwiches, a packet of biscuits and a flask of tea.

The two tickets that Mark would be able to buy were going to be for George and Fred, it was the respectful thing to do. Tommy, Keith and Rick would return first thing in the morning and gauge from the extent of the queue if they stood a chance of getting tickets. If that failed, Nick Hill knew 'Fat Stan'. There would be a heavy premium to pay on the face price... but if that's the way things worked out so be it.

Tommy insisted they went to the Lord Palmerston after the game though he failed to persuade George and Fred who went to the Nell Gywnne instead to discuss bets for the replay. The Palmerston had several televisions and there they could watch the extended BBC *Match of the Day* highlights of the afternoon's 1-1 draw between Wales and England in the British Home Championship. That's how he'd sold it in. The screening was at 7.30 p.m. but he was more interested in watching any news bulletins that evening which would have footage of the Apollo 13 command module re-entering the Earth's atmosphere and splashing down in the South Pacific Ocean.

'They're coming in at 8,970 miles an hour,' he said to his friends. 'You could get from London to Manchester in one minute and 20 seconds at that speed... imagine that.'

'Be handy for getting to Old Trafford then wouldn't it,' replied Keith.

'Be a bit more expensive than the 60 shillings we'll be paying British Rail to go up there,' added Rick laughing.

Tommy was peeved that his friends trivialised the information he'd shared with them even if it was second-hand from the BBCs font of all knowledge Cliff Michelmore. He cheered loudly as the network's live coverage presented by James Burke and Patrick Moore showed the command module emerge from the clouds suspended from a parachute and land in the ocean. It was 6.07 p.m. the astronauts were safe. Mission accomplished.

'You'll be asking Santa for a fucking telescope for Christmas this year I bet,' joked Rick, but Tommy's mind by now was miles away... the Isle of Wight to be precise. He'd had an idea yesterday evening that had kept him awake until the small hours... all he needed was a simple plan... but that could wait. It was Saturday night and the sight and sound of Mick Greenaway clambering on a table in the far corner of the pub, necking the pint he had in his hand and belting out *Zigger Zagger, Zigger Zagger... Oi, Oi, Oi* was a unifying distraction for everyone.

LEEDS UNITED AT OLD TRAFFORD
Wednesday 29 April 1970

'So this is what it feels like to take the famous Stretford End,' said Tommy, laughing as he stood at the top of the famous terrace that normally played host to Manchester United's staunchest fans. When they'd been to Old Trafford in December to watch Chelsea play the Red Devils, he'd looked across the pitch at the Lowry-esque faces bobbing up and down on a sea of red and white scarves and wondered if they could ever be scattered.

Those were the days my friend, we took the Stretford End...

Rick, thinking the same thoughts, burst into song and Keith joined in. Why not? It was the obvious thing to do... they'd done it before.

We took the Kop, we took the fucking lot...

At the same time, George and Fred shook their heads and mouthed the word 'wankers' at them.

We'd fight and never lose, then we'd sing Up the Blues...
Those were the days, oh yes those were the days.

The replay was being screened live by the BBC and it must have been chastening for the 20,000 or so Man U fans that regularly packed out the Stretford End to see it bedecked in blue and white.

La, la la, la la la la, la la la la... Chelsea!
La, la la, la la la la, la la la la... Chelsea!

Now that was beautiful. Music to the ears of everyone, even George and Fred. The Beatles track *Hey Jude* reworked. Tommy liked the link between the Mary Hopkins hit *Those Were The Days* and *Hey Jude.* Both songs had been released on the same day, 26 August 1968, to launch the Apple record label and, a couple of months later, *Those Were The Days* replaced *Hey Jude* at the top of the charts. Of course, both tracks had been played during *Pre-match Spin* and The Shed had made some changes, not so subtle in one case, subtler in the other, and that was that.

It was a introspective moment which Tommy kept to himself. He was buzzing for the game but had been in a reflective and largely uncommunicative mood all day.

On the train up from Manchester, while the others were discussing Alan Hudson's wretched fortune, Leeds' continued failings and Chelsea's chances of winning the cup, he'd been pondering a gamble far more spectacular than anything his father George and Fred ever contemplated in the Nell Gywnne.

Huddy's dreams of making Dave Sexton's starting XI for the replay had been shattered by the stark reality he still hadn't regained sufficient mobility in his ankle. Yesterday, he'd run a couple of laps at Chelsea's training ground at Mitcham and pulled up limping. It was heartbreaking for the kid and being told he would still get a medal was scant consolation no doubt.

Leeds had followed up their European Cup exit to Celtic with defeats in their last two league games, losing 3-1 at home to Manchester City and 3-2 away at Ipswich Town. It was as he'd imagined. How would the mood be in Don Revie's camp now? If the Yorkshire club's rank form wasn't enough of a concern for their supporters, goalkeeper Gary Sprake getting injured added to Revie's troubles.

Sprake had damaged his knee ligaments in a collision with Celtic striker John 'Yogi' Hughes during Leeds' 2-1 defeat at Hampden Park and been stretchered off. David Harvey had replaced him and kept his place in the side. Like Hudson, Sprake had failed a late fitness test for the FA Cup Final replay and so it was Harvey who would be the man under the bar for the Whites.

Fred joked that Leeds were probably a better side without *Careless Hands* in goal, but nobody laughed mainly because the memory of Eddie Gray traumatising David Webb was still fresh in the mind. Luckily, skipper Ron Harris was 100% fit and raring to go and a tactical switch by Dave Sexton was likely meaning Harris would now be on Gray's case allowing Webb to move to central defence and also roam forward... for everything else, Chelsea had Peter Osgood!

Tommy listened to what was being said, but pretended to be reading a newspaper so he didn't get drawn into the conversation. In his jacket pocket he had two tickets for the replay. One he'd bought legitimately from Stamford Bridge when he'd queued up with Keith and Rick for five hours the morning after the Liverpool game... the other an exact reproduction that he'd created the front and reverse plate for at work and printed on powder-blue, stock weight, pre-perforated paper!

It had been an extraordinarily and somewhat alarmingly easy process because the ticket had no serious security features and was a very basic three-colour job. First the stock paper had to be printed with Manchester United in faded red letters with a blue halo effect, then the match details in black and finally a sequential number added along with the word CHELSEA rubber-stamped at a slight angle for complete authenticity.

It took some work to precise the colour matches, but by the fourth attempt, Tommy considered himself as skilled a forger as Flt Lt Colin Blythe RAF, the character portrayed by Donald Pleasence in one of his favourite films *The Great Escape*. Even with a magnifying glass, there was no discernable difference between the genuine ticket and the counterfeit. Should there have been, it probably wouldn't have been a risk as turnstile operators never scrutinised tickets. It wasn't in their minds to do that and the sheer volume of people clicking through must be mind-numbing.

On the night, the worst that could happen would be a conversation along the lines of, 'sorry son, this is a fake ticket you can't come in on this... you shouldn't buy from touts'... and he would just go to another turnstile and gain admission by presenting his valid ticket.

Tommy had a simple plan. He wanted to make enough cash to pay a sizeable deposit on a house for him and Sophia to live in. £1,500 was the target, and he wanted to raise the money by the end of the summer. Once achieved, that would be the end of it because when he'd looked at the ticket he'd just reproduced, and considered all the possibilities and eventualities, he quickly realised it could get out of hand and the downside was too significant to contemplate.

Stories abounded that last year's Isle of Wight Festival had drawn an attendance of 200,000! For this August's event which had The Who, Jimi Hendrix and Joni Mitchell on the bill, rumours were circulating that as many as 500,000 people were expected at Afton Down. A weekend ticket cost £3... 500 counterfeit tickets = £1500 = job done! It would be easy... it would be profitable... it would be safe because security would be poor just like it had been last year. In all probability, thousands of people would arrive ticketless and find a way to break through the flimsy fences anyway.

Tommy considered selling on to touts without disclosing the tickets were fake. Fat Stan, Johnny 'The Stick' Goldstein and One-armed Lou were the main players and Nick Hill knew these people... getting an introduction would be easy... but he'd be giving away margin and he didn't want anybody asking questions... and that included Sophia, Keith, Rick and their girlfriends.

They were all planning to attend the festival together and he'd already said he would sort the tickets out and purchased a bona fide pair by mail order from the promoters.

Replicating them would be easy and he would be an anonymous, one-stop-pop-up-shop selling them in singles and pairs at gigs he went to over the next few months. Any left over he would sell at the Southsea ferry terminal on the Wednesday and Thursday leading up to main headline days of the festival.

CHHHHHHEEEEE – ELLLL – SEA! (clap, clap, clap)

Tommy refocused on the matters at hand. All eyes were on referee Eric Jennings as he put his whistle to his lips. Wembley was meant to have been his swansong before he retired, but he was having another crack at the whip tonight and if matters weren't settled a further replay had already been scheduled for the coming Saturday at Highfield Road the home of Coventry City where Jennings would be the man in the middle once again.

Here we go, Here we go, Here we go…

The Leeds fans packed in the Scoreboard End… were making themselves heard as the teams formed-up for kick-off, but a repeated chant of *Chelsea! (clap, clap, clap)* didn't mute them, it just made them impossible to hear above the cacophony in the Stretford End.

FA Cup Final Replay
Chelsea 2 Leeds United 1 (after extra-time)
Old Trafford
Attendance: 62,078
Referee: Eric Jennings

Chelsea: Peter Bonetti, Ron Harris, Eddie McCreadie, John Hollins, John Dempsey, David Webb, Tommy Baldwin, Charlie Cooke, Peter Osgood (Marvin Hinton 112), Ian Hutchinson, Peter Houseman.
Scorers: Osgood 78, Webb 104.
Booked: Huchinson 65.

Leeds United: Harvey, Madeley, Cooper, Bremner, Charlton, Hunter, Lorimer, Clarke, Jones, Giles, Gray.
Scorer: Jones 36.

The white sock clash which had seen Leeds wear red socks in the first game at Wembley was reversed for the replay at Old Trafford except Chelsea opted to wear yellow socks with two blue stripes in the tops.
'There's no white in our kit,' said George pointing at John Dempsey who was the nearest player in view. 'Yellow stripe and numbers on the shorts and the number on the back of the shirt's yellow as well.. and the crest on the front.'
'It's funny Dirty Leeds play in white,' replied Fred. 'I remember when they played in blue and yellow halved shirts. Now that would have made for a colour clash probably. Revie copied the Real Madrid kit as he thought they were a team to aspire to.'
'Were Real Madrid dirty as well then?' asked Rick, giving his father a playful dig in the ribs.
As Mick Jones kicked off for Leeds, a stream of toilet rolls, pinched from the lavatory facilities on the ten football specials that had departed

Euston for Manchester earlier in the day, were launched from further along the Stretford End behind Peter Bonetti's goal. Catching the stiff evening breeze they fluttered impressively through the air before landing on the pitch which despite the fact it had been raining in Manchester all afternoon looked in decent condition especially when compared to the Wembley quagmire.

Leeds took the early initiative. With barely a minute gone Peter Lorimer got away from Ron Harris and squared a pass into the penalty area for Allan Clarke... keeping running to the by line, Lorimer picked up the return ball which he drilled hard and low into the six-yard box aiming for Mick Jones. The ball cannoned backwards off John Dempsey, but fortunately Peter Bonetti was well placed to scoop it up.

'They're all over us again,' said George, shaking his head. 'I hope Sexton's switch of Chopper and Webby works out.'

Keith laughed. 'Give it a chance George, the game's only just started.'

'Go on Webby, get stuck in!' Tommy shouted as the defender, mindful of the roasting Eddie Gray had given him at Wembley, challenged the Leeds winger for the ball as he advanced in the Chelsea half. As Gray went to ground a huge cheer went up from the Blues fans in the Stretford End. It may have been Ron Harris who had been given the task by Dave Sexton of trying to shackle the flying Scotsman, but Webb's tackle was an indication that he'd also been ordered to stop Leeds by fair means or foul. Eric Jennings had erred on the side of leniency in the first game and this was a marker to check out his degree of patience in the replay.

'Any other ref would've booked Webby for that,' said Tommy, laughing as Jennings awarded Leeds a free-kick and Webb skipped away unpunished.

'Thank God, we ain't got any other ref then,' replied Keith.

Here we go, Here we go, Here we go...

The Leeds contingent were getting excited again as Billy Bremner lofted the free-kick into the Chelsea penalty area, but the ball was caught cleanly by Peter Bonetti.

Revie's men had the bit between their teeth, but it wasn't all one-way traffic. Shortly after, the Blues counter-attacked and Ian Hutchinson screwed a decent shot just wide of David Harvey's post. The attendant surge down the terrace almost took George's breath away. As he recovered his composure, he regretted they hadn't positioned themselves against a crush barrier. Fred grabbed him, and together, with equilibrium restored, they jostled there way back up the steps and kept jostling until they reached a barrier to lean against.

'Go on Tiger... That's the way to do it.' Keith's comment about a feisty Peter Houseman tackle on Billy Bremmer drew laughter and applause in equal measures from those stood nearby.

'I keep telling you,' said George. 'Peter Houseman is a proper Chelsea player now... he can reduce those Dirty Leeds bastards just as well as Chopper and Webby.'

Jennings awarded Leeds a free kick which was again lofted into the Blues penalty area and comfortably dealt with by Bonetti who immediately set his side on a counter-attack which the Whites broke up clearing the ball for a throw-in.

Chelsea! (clap, clap, clap) Chelsea! (clap, clap, clap)

'Hutch is going to do one of his windmill specials,' said Tommy, lighting a cigarette and taking a deep drag as Ian Hutchinson launched a looping throw which saw the ball drop down from a height into the Leeds penalty area. David Harvey was equal to it, coming out and catching cleanly under pressure but it was a sign of what was possible.

'Better luck next time.' Tommy exhaled as he spoke, plumes of smoke trailing out of his nose making him look like a mythical fire-breathing beast.

We are Leeds, We are Leeds, We are Leeds...

Encouraged by their supporters who unimaginatively appeared to be using the same melody (John Philip Sousa's *The Stars and Stripes Forever* which had spawned the ubiquitous *Here We Go* chant), Don Revie's side upped the ante with Terry Cooper and Eddie Gray probing and passing. Hard tackles were in order as a means for Chelsea to regain possession.

'Cooke's looking a lot sharper than he did at Wembley,' said Keith as the Blues winger went on a mazy run that ended with a pass to Johnny Hollins that was miscontrolled and ran out of play. 'Ossie seems to be playing deeper in midfield though... Oi fuck off Giles.'

Keith's commentary ended abruptly with a stream of expletives as Johnny Giles clattered into Peter Osgood to remind the striker he was keeping tabs on him and there was no hiding place. John Dempsey hoofed the resultant free-kick up field and there was Ossie... kicked again... and this time in the penalty area...

PENALTY!

BOOK HIM REF!

Eric Jennings wasn't interested. Instead of his notebook, he took his handkerchief out of his pocket, blew his nose and waved play on.

Peter Osgood's counterpart at number 9, Mick Jones, was also being closely monitored with John Dempsey in particular doing a good job of marking him and getting to the ball first when his teammates sent it his way.

As the first-half progressed, the sun began to dip over the horizon behind the Stretford End and the players began to cast increasingly long shadows down the pitch. It was a beautiful evening, and a few feet down the terrace Tommy noticed a young lad twirling his blue and white scarf in the air. He seemed happy just to be in the ground, savouring the atmosphere… watching the game appeared to be a bonus to him.

The lad turned round briefly and Tommy recognised him. Outside the ground earlier when he'd taken the decision to use his repro ticket at the turnstiles, he'd seen the lad who was in his early teens holding a sign saying 'ticket wanted please'. The politeness of the request and the fact the kid had bunked school and quite probably the train as well to go and support Chelsea with no real chance of getting into the ground struck a chord with Tommy.

'There you go son. It's your lucky day.'

'I've not got any money.'

'I don't want any.'

Tommy gave the lad a thumbs up… but he couldn't be sure he saw it not that it mattered. He would remember the kind act forever, especially if Chelsea won the cup. It made him feel better about the offence he'd committed… yeah it was fraud, but so what… it was hardly the crime of the century.

'Done a proper job on Gray so far ain't he,' said Rick, nudging him as another Leeds attack down the left flank was broken up with the Leeds winger dispossessed by Ron Harris. 'X-rated tackles going in all over the pitch. Hutch on Giles. Charlton on Baldwin. Hollins on Bremner.'

'And still no bookings by the ref… that's why,' replied Tommy.

'I reckon this game's going to go the distance as well,' said George, immediately wishing he'd kept his mouth shut as for once Gray got the better of Harris and sent a teasing ball across to Jones who brought a good save out of Bonetti at the near post.

Leeds pressed relentlessly. A defensive mix-up at the back by Chelsea allowed Peter Lorimer to screw a ball back across the area which deceived Bonetti who was thankful, just as the Blues crowd were, that Eddie McCreadie was behind him to clear away the danger off the line. Moments later, Allan Clarke sent a shot just wide.

DIRTY LEEDS BASTARD!

The whole of the Stretford End seemed to curse in unison as Mick Jones, running into the Chelsea six-yard box looking to get on the end of a long, teasing Terry Cooper cross, clattered into Peter Bonetti leaving the Blues goalkeeper prone on the deck. Referee Jennings spoke to Jones... but did nothing. Eddie McCreadie and Ron Harris remonstrated with both of them but were ignored.

'Doesn't look good for Catty,' said Keith, as Chelsea trainer Harry Medhurst came onto the pitch to tend to the stricken goalkeeper's left knee. Medhurst's treatment didn't involve the famous magic sponge as such, it was more a case of repeatedly bending the Cat's leg at the knee, which understandably made him grimace.

'If this is bad, it might mean Webby has to go in goal,' said George in a concerned voice.

The Leeds supporters were totally unsympathetic to Bonetti's plight and lazily re-worked *The Stars and Stripes Forever...*

Let him die, let him die, let him die...

Chelsea fans, annoyed that Jennings had taken no action against Jones, countered with a corrupted version of the nursery rhyme *The Farmer's In His Den...*

We want a ref, we want a ref... Eee Aye Addio... we want a ref...

The minutes ticked by... one... two... three... four... long enough for Tommy to burn through yet another cigarette. Eventually, Bonetti was hoisted to his feet and a huge cheer rippled across the Stretford End.

Peter Bonetti, Peter Bonetti...

Medhurst continued to massage the goalie's knee before giving it the 'magic spray' treatment and asking him to try walk off the problem... and all the while Eric Jennings kept checking his watch.

'That's decent,' said George, as Leeds trainer Les Cocker arrived on the scene to offer his help. It was an unexpected sporting gesture which was applauded and whistled in equal measures.

After what felt like an eternity, a limping Bonetti, still clearly struggling from the knock, signalled he was ready to continue and the game restarted.

'We're in the shit if they keep the pressure on,' said Fred, shaking his head. 'I'm really worried now.'

Nobody else spoke. There was creeping sense of unease that Leeds were going to take advantage of the situation, and it came as no surprise when in the 36th minute they scored the first goal of the game.

Allan Clarke waltzed forward from the half-way line and ghosted through Chelsea's midfield before playing the ball neatly to Mick Jones who was bearing down on the Blues penalty area. Evading the attentions of John Dempsey, Eddie McCreadie and John Hollins, the Leeds striker let fly from just inside the box. Peak Bonetti, without the wounded knee, might have had enough spring in his step to launch a cat-like dive that would have given him the momentum to reach the ball... but unfortunately the crippling injury he'd just sustained prevented this and the net behing him bulged.

Tommy looked on... first at Bonetti, back on his feet after his valiant but failed dive, limping forward to the edge of his box... and then beyond him at the jubilant Leeds fans still surging and swaying in the Scoreboard End. 'Bastards!'

We're gonna win the cup, we're gonna win the cup...
And now you're gonna believe us...

In the ten minutes or so that followed before half-time, Eddie Gray and Terry Cooper were given well-applauded doses of career-compromising treatment by Ron Harris every time they went near the ball. Chopper kicking Mick Jones up in the air would have been equally well received but John Dempsey and David Webb were both on his case.

Shortly before the break, Harris rattled Gray again... sending him to the ground with the type of boot-on-flesh tackle that would normally earn the aggressor an early bath. Les Cocker was on the pitch again tending to one of his own this time while Eric Jennings looked on.

Now it was the turn of Chelsea supporters to sing *Let him die...* and Leeds fans to question Jennings' parentage in song. At last a new melody... Western folk balled, *Oh My Darling, Clementine...*

Who's your father? Who's your father? Who's your father referee?
You ain't got one... never had one...
You're a bastard referee.

'Shame Princess Margaret isn't here tonight,' said George during the half-time break.

Tommy laughed. 'I'll tell mother you said that.'

'Why? I'm talking about royalty presenting the cup to Chopper when we come back and win it.'

'Who's presenting the cup then?' asked Keith.

Rick looked up from the match programme he was reading. 'It says in here, Dr. A Stephen, Chairman of the Football Association.'

Fred nodded. 'Andrew Stephen... he was the doc at Sheffield Wednesday for years before he became their chairman and now the FA's as well. If you remember the game when we beat Wednesday to win the league in '55, Stephen treated their goalie Dave McIntosh after he collided with Roy Bentley.'

'I honestly don't know how you've remembered that,' replied George. 'I thought I had a good memory,'

'Maybe Sexton could've done with getting Stephen to look at the Cat's knee at half-time,' said Keith.

Fred laughed. 'McIntosh was carried off on a stretcher in that game against us... maybe he's not that good a doc.'

As the players came out for the second-half, Tommy narrowed his eyes and peered across the pitch at Peter Bonetti who was now keeping goal in front of the Leeds fans massed in the Scoreboard End. The goalkeeper's knee was bandaged up and he still didn't look to be moving all that freely.

Jennings got the game underway again and almost immediately Leeds were testing Bonetti. Mick Jones forced the Cat to make a smart save, but it wouldn't have counted had he scored as the ref signalled he'd handled the ball when bringing it down to shoot.

'It's good Catty can get some distance with a throw,' said Tommy, as Bonetti repeatedly opted to clear the ball in this way from open play only relying on John Dempsey to take goal-kicks. 'Wonder who can lob it further, him or Hutch?'

The game soon evened-up as a contest and, as the second-half progressed, Chelsea were making frequent inroads deep into Leeds territory with Peter Osgood, now playing in a more advanced role, linking up well with Peter Houseman. Don Revie's side still had a 1-0 advantage and were cramping the flow of the game and running the clock down with every set piece.

'Time-wasting Yorkshire ponces,' shouted Tommy, as Billy Bremner and Jackie Charlton took an age to size-up a long-range free-kick which Charlton then hoofed aimlessly wide.

The first serious flare-up between the players came soon after when Osgood snapped at Charlton's heels. The duo had been trading digs in the first-half and this time the Leeds centre-half lost patience with his new England teammate, turning around and barging him to the floor.

Linesman Bob Matthewson swiftly intervened and as both sets of supporters jeered, Eric Jennings came across and spoke to the warring duo... but his notebook remained in his pocket.

'He'd need to see a knockdown from a punch before he booked anyone,' said Tommy.

'He's old-school ain't he Jennings. A man's game and all that,' replied George. 'Mind you he's in danger of losing control if he's not careful.'

A few minutes later John Dempsey floored Charlton with a tackle from behind. This time, instead of having a go at Dempsey he seemed more concerned that Allan Clarke hadn't made a forward run for him.

The skirmishes continued. Ian Hutchinson and Billy Bremner were the next duo to mix it in the tackle, and once again Jennings remained lenient.

Chances were few and far between. Hutch launched a long throw into the Leeds penalty area that was well defended while Johnny Giles saw a shot deflected wide of Peter Bonetti's post.

During the passage of play from the resultant corner, it became clear that Bonetti's knee injury was still causing him major problems. Leeds crowded the box, the Cat clawed at the corner-ball and missed it but fortunately an alert Eddie McCreadie was there to clear it off the line.

Even though Jennings awarded a free-kick to Chelsea for a foul on Bonetti, McCreadie was applauded by Blues fans. This was the second time in the game he'd cleared the ball off the line... his Wembley sin was absolved.

We're gonna win the cup, we're gonna win the cup...
And now you're gonna believe us...

There was an increasingly confident tone to the Leeds chant... full time was in sight. Old Trafford was now floodlit, day had turned to night... and Chelsea were chasing shadows.

Dave Sexton had tweaked his tactics at half-time and asked John Hollins to move across midfield so he could link up more effectively with Charlie Cooke and Peter Osgood. The plan was working... slowly. The Blues first decent chance in a long while came when Hollins lofted a forward ball to the edge of the penalty area which was nodded on by Osgood. Baldwin was close in on goal, but his header was saved by David Harvey who was rewarded for his endeavours by having a toilet roll thrown at him.

CHELSEA! CHELSEA! CHELSEA! CHELSEA! CHELSEA!

The mood of all the Blues supporters stood on the vast Stretford End terrace lifted. Their team now looked like they had the wherewithal to score. Anthemic chanting had to help... and then a strange thing happened...

After yet another clash, this time between Billy Bremner and Peter Osgood, the ensuing fracas saw Ian Hutchinson wade in and push Bremner to the ground. The Leeds skipper rolled around theatrically in front of Eric Jennings who was so impressed he promptly booked Hutchinson.

If this was an intended warning to the players that any further misdemeanours would be punished it went unheeded. The tit-for-tat spats continued. Bremner kicked Hutchinson. Charlie Cooke kicked Norman Hunter. Significantly perhaps, one man being spared a kicking in the second-half was Eddie Gray. The Leeds winger, hobbled by Ron Harris in the opening 45 minutes, looked out of sorts and had drifted out of the game.

For all their endeavour, Chelsea were still without a precious goal. In a bid to speed things up, Peter Bonetti attempted to clear his lines with his boot... but the kick lacked distance and direction and he went back to throws which required greater concentration to monitor on the part of his teammates. It was dangerous and nerve-jangling. With 15 minutes left, Tommy Baldwin misread a short throw and his chest down was intercepted by Terry Cooper. The Leeds full-back let fly a left foot shot from the edge of the box which Bonetti just managed to turn around the post for a corner. What a let off. At 2-0, Chelsea would have been finished.

CHELSEA! CHELSEA! CHELSEA! CHELSEA! CHELSEA!

The squandered opportunity to score buoyed Chelsea.

'Just one chance... one chance,' pleaded Keith as the ever-industrious Johnny Hollins, controlling possession just inside the Leeds half, played a short pass to Peter Osgood who sent the ball wide to Ian Hutchison and ran forward. Hutch passed to Charlie Cooke who advanced a few yards to the inside-right position, looked up and saw Ossie hadn't been tracked as he'd marched blind-side into the opposition penalty area. If Cooke's dipping pass was sheer pinpoint-precision artistry, then Osgood's horizontal diving header was the brush stroke of a grand master.

OSSSSSSSSSSSIE...

Directed by Osgood's head, the ball flew past David Harvey into the back of the Stretford End net. Ecstatic Chelsea supporters surged down the terrace... toilet rolls were launched... and a straw hat hurled in joy sailed serenely through the air from one side of the terrace to the other.

On the pitch, Ossie saluted the crowd and was mobbed by his teammates. The sense of relief was palpable. The Blues were back on level terms. 1-1... a little over ten minutes left... game most definitely on.

'Looked well rehearsed that move,' said George, raising a clenched fist as Tommy, Keith and Rick returned from their little flying trip. 'Cooke and Ossie, fucking brilliant,' he continued. 'Scored in every round of the Cup now has Ossie... not many have done that.'

'Jeff Astle did it for West Brom a couple of years ago,' replied Fred. 'I read that in the paper on the way up here,' he continued, laughing as he embraced George. 'It also puts Os on 31 goals for the season one ahead of Astle funnily enough. The country's number one hotshot.'

CHELSEA! CHELSEA! CHELSEA! CHELSEA! CHELSEA!

Leeds were rattled... their supporters silenced. Having seized the initiative, would Chelsea go for broke to try and score again before the 90 minutes were up or would they settle for keeping it tight at the back and then go for it in extra-time?

Tommy considered the possibilities and just as he was contemplating a possible replay at Highfield Road, Paul Madeley clattered Ian Hutchinson to the ground. Boos rang out from the Stretford End...

You dirty Yorkshire bastard...

Whatever happened, peace wasn't about to break out between the two teams... if anything the tackles were now getting harsher. Tommy Baldwin went in hard on Norman Hunter and then Eddie McCreadie attempted to decapitate Billy Bremner in a high scissor-kick move that wouldn't have looked out of place in a martial arts contest.

Terry Cooper darted down the left flank and zipped over a cross aimed for Mick Jones who had Eddie Mac in close attendance. The loose ball bounced up at shoulder height towards Bremner and McCreadie launched himself to clear it... his boot connecting with the left side of the Leeds's player's head!

FUCK!

Bremner went to the ground. The Leeds fans in the Scoreboard End who were closest to the action screamed...

PENALTY!

Tommy covered his eyes and cursed. Referee Jennings did absolutely nothing.

'Reckon we've got away with that,' said Rick. 'How Eddie's not been sent off is a mystery to me.'

'Never a penalty,' replied Keith laughing. 'My lucky coat is working its magic again,' he added, rubbing the lapels of the Aquascutum mac he'd worn to every Chelsea cup tie this season.

With Bremner still on the deck, the game continued at a frenetic pace. Jack Charlton tried to scythe down Peter Osgood, and then at the end of a Blues counterattack Ian Hutchinson fired a shot into the side netting of David Harvey's goal.

At the break in play, Eric Jennings allowed Les Cocker onto to the pitch to treat Bremner... his ministrations clearly had mystical powers unlike McCreadie's act of contrition which involved rubbing the Leeds skipper's head... with his hand this time instead of his flying boot!

'I'll buy the ref a pint if we win this,' said Tommy, as Bremner got to his feet and gambolled away like a sping lamb.

'I'll buy him a pub,' joked George.

'You'll be able to with the amount of money you'll win off Nick Hill,' said Rick.

Bremner was soon on the receiving end of more rough treatment, this time from Hutchinson. Given he'd already been booked, Hutch might have considered himself lucky to be still on the pitch but he probably wasn't thinking along those lines... he wanted to get the job done. That was commitment for you. *Come on Chelsea!*

Jennings awarded a free kick. Lucky! Tommy kept looking at his watch and it seemed to tell the same time. Leeds kept pressing. Once again Bremner went down in the Chelsea penalty area and once again

Jennings did nothing... perhaps he was tired of the flame-haired Scotsman's histrionics.

Tommy put his fingers to his mouth and whistled... and plenty more Chelsea supporters did the same as Eddie Gray finally slipped the shackles Ron Harris had placed on him and fizzed a shot inches over Peter Bonetti's crossbar.

'Come on ref... how about full-time?' screamed Rick. The whistling around him was incessant now.

Leeds squeezed Chelsea back, but the Blues held firm. Mick Jones got on the end of a cross but couldn't keep his header down. Enough was enough. Finally... three shrill beeps of Eric Jennings' whistle cut through the noise. Full time. 1-1.

'How are we getting to Coventry on Saturday?' asked Fred, rubbing his hands together and blowing on them as Leeds kicked off the first period of extra-time attacking the Stretford End. The temperature had dropped, and a cold, stiff breeze was blowing into the faces of Chelsea supporters packed across the terrace.

'We ain't going Dad... we're going to win the cup tonight,' replied Rick, raising his hands above his head to applaud Charlie Cooke as he went on a mazy run before linking up with Peter Osgood.

'Cookie and Ossie have been brilliant,' said George, joining in the clapping. 'We look a lot more confident now... we've shut the Leeds lot up as well.'

Tommy thought about his father's words. He was right. Perhaps the Leeds supporters, having experienced so much disappointment over the past few weeks, were sensing that it wasn't going to be their night... again. No longer the champions of England, no longer in with a chance of being champions of Europe... and, quite possibly, now seeing the chance of their team winning the oldest national football competition in the world slipping away from them. Whatever happened, there was going to be a new name inscribed on the cup... please God, let it be Chelsea!

Chelsea! (clap, clap, clap) Chelsea! (clap, clap, clap)

Houseman took a throw just inside the Leeds half which released Osgood, but Charlton was all over him and quick in the tackle... the ball skidded out of play three or so yards from the corner flag.

'Perfect for Hutch this,' said George clapping his hands.

Come On Chelsea! roared the Stretford End.

'Ha ha... look Charlie thinks it a free-kick,' said Tommy, as the Blues number 8 trotted over and went to set the ball up. Referee Jennings signalled once again for a throw-in and Hutch duly picked the ball up.

Tommy sucked in lungfuls of air and held his breath. Hutchinson was like a machine. Two steps, a whirling motion of the arms which appeared to defy the law of physics... and the ball went looping high into the air. Down it came... but Leeds were well prepared and Bremner was able to clear it.

Tommy exhaled and reached in his jacket pocket for his cigarettes.

'I'm convinced if we can get a couple more opportunities for Hutch to lob a long one in we might fuck Leeds up properly,' said Keith.

The tackles were still flying in. Ten minutes into the first period of extra-time, Tommy Baldwin reminded Terry Cooper he wasn't going to get too far away from him with or without the ball. A yard outside the penalty area wasn't the best of locations however to concede a free-kick especially as Peter Bonetti was still hobbling.

Johnny Giles sent over the kick which caused panic... and when the loose ball fell to Peter Lorimer, Tommy covered his eyes with his hands.

Bonetti may have lost some of his agility... but his superb sense of positioning was intact and he was able to deal with Lorimer's volleyed shot with consummate ease.

All the players were starting to show signs of fatigue as the wear and tear of the contest, coming at the end of a long arduous season, began to take its toll. Norman Hunter went down with cramp, Jack Charlton looked like he had a thigh problem and Peter Osgood trouble with his ankle.

Les Cocker had come on to tend to Hunter and sorted him out, but the Leeds player was soon on the deck again... this time felled by Peter Houseman!

'I thought Hunter was meant to be the Leeds hard-knock,' said George laughing. 'Doesn't look that tough now.'

'Tiger's done him good and proper there,' replied Tommy, the unlit cigarette at the corner of his mouth bobbing up and down as he spoke.

'It's probably still the cramp,' said Keith.

'Don't spoil the moment,' replied George as Les Cocker came on and got to work again.

Come On Chelsea! Come On Chelsea!

Blues supporters found their voices to back the team. The minutes and seconds remaining in the first-half of extra-time were ticking away... that trip to Coventry on Saturday now seemed a real possibility.

'Look at Eddie,' said Tommy, pointing down the field at the Chelsea full-back who was sitting on the ball down the far left touchline just inside his own half chatting to the linesman. 'He just needs a snout and a pint! And Ossie and Cooper, lying down like they want to be tucked up for bed.'

'If you didn't know any better, you'd think they'd agreed to call it a draw,' said Fred. 'No chance of that though. *COME ON CHELSEA!*'

Jennings eventually managed to get the game back under way and, through a series of throw-ins and poor clearances, Chelsea made ground down the left flank and into the Leeds half. The ball went out of play again and Tommy looked on hopefully as Ian Hutchinson picked it up… another opportunity perhaps to launch one of his flying bombs.

'Go on Hutch… this is the one mate.' shouted George.

Time stood still. The Stretford End held its breath as the Blues striker readied himself, wiping the ball with the sleeves of his shirt. There was a beauty to the routine that was mesmerising. He stepped forward, whirled his arms and propelled it high into the dank Manchester night sky. All eyes followed its trajectory… like the Apollo 13 Command Module returning to earth!

Dropping down towards a gaggle of rising heads and the firsts of goalkeeper David Harvey, it was Jackie Charlton who met the ball first under pressure from Peter Osgood who was at his shoulder. Charlton couldn't get sufficient purchase with his header and only succeeding in re-directing it dangerously across the six-yard box.

With Harvey now stranded having gone to ground following his failed clearance attempt, if a Chelsea player could get any part of his body on the ball, the goal was gaping wide open. David Webb rose the highest at the far post… Tommy Baldwin was there with him, muscling Eddie Gray out of the way…

YESSSSSSSSSSSSSSSSSSSSSS!

It wasn't clear whether Webb had headed the ball or it had come off his chest, his shoulder or his face… but it didn't matter, it was in the back of the net and Eric Jennings had given the goal. Chelsea supporters went ballistic!

As he watched his son, Keith and Rick surge down the terrace, George caught sight of the straw hat that had gone sailing through the air previously when Peter Osgood equalised come flying back in the direction from where it originally came. He hadn't noticed before just how many Chelsea supporters were in the ground. Blue and white scarves were twirling merrily along three sides of Old Trafford… just the Scoreboard End, where the goal had just been scored, was mortuary-like in its stillness.

We're gonna win the Cup, we're gonna win the Cup…
And now you're gonna believe us…
And now you're gonna believe us…
And now you're gonna be-lieve us… we're gonna win the Cup!

For the first time in both matches, Chelsea were ahead… and for the first time also their supporters were able to sing with conviction the shared belief their team was going to win the cup… even though there was still the second-half of extra-time to get through.

Before the break, Charlie Cooke went in hard on Billy Bremner who got up and flew at his Scottish countryman. Don Revie's side were on strings now and it was probably just as well for Eric Jennings, from a 'keep the peace' perspective, that the 15 minutes were up.

Here we go, here we go... here we go

Chelsea supporters, sensing a glorious victory were in full cry... scarves aloft, brim-full with enthusiasm as Ian Hutchinson kicked off the second period of extra-time with the Blues attacking the Stretford End.

Going behind may have been a punch to the guts for Leeds, but Don Revie had clearly rallied his troops during the brief break. The Whites had to go for it now and soon Allan Clarke, Johnny Giles, Terry Cooper and Eddie Gray were hogging possession, playing neat give-and-go passes and frustrating Chelsea.

'We need another goal,' said Keith, stating the obvious.

Tommy laughed. He still had the unlit cigarette stuck at the corner of his mouth which had survived the wild goal celebrations intact. It was a sign... lucky like Keith's coat... he wasn't going to light it until Ron Harris lifted the FA Cup.

CHELSEA! CHELSEA! CHELSEA! CHELSEA! CHELSEA!

'Our end is mustard tonight,' said Rick as the repetitive *Chelsea! Chelsea!* chant ebbed slightly. 'I bet we look good on television.'

'Should get that *are you watching White Hart Lane?*' chant going,' replied Keith. 'Mind you, we don't wanna tempt fate eh... never hear the end of it.'

'It said in the paper, there'll be nearly as many people watching this game live on TV as watched the World Cup Final,' said George.

'How many was that?' asked Tommy.

'Over 32 million.'

'I do wonder how they work that out because I also read that there are only 15 million homes with television sets.'

It was interesting point to ponder... but only very briefly. With play confined at the far end of the pitch for much of the time, nerves were getting frayed again. Tommy couldn't think of another game he'd been at when time seemed to pass so slowly. Tick-tock-tick-tock.

Finally, Chelsea managed to break out of their own half. Peter Bonetti overarm-bowled the ball out to Peter Osgood...

Come on Ossie!

The Stretford End were unified in their encouragement as Osgood, reinvigorated for one last hurrah perhaps, made lung-bursting strides towards them... and the Leeds penalty area.

'Go on my son!' roared George, as Osgood kept running. Jack Charlton was left for dead. Paul Madeley and Norman Hunter tried to keep tabs, but Ossie was too quick. His side-foot pass to Ian Hutchinson who'd kept pace with him left David Harvey on his backside scrabbling at thin air...

'Go on Hutch!' The veins on George's neck were bulging as he screamed at the top of his voice... 'YESSSSS!'

Hutchinson reached the edge of the six-yard box and stabbed the ball into the net. Chelsea supporters celebrated wildly once again... but in vain... the 'goal' was flagged offside.

'Bollocks! I can't see how Hutch was offside there,' said Fred as play restarted with a Leeds free-kick.

'Still winning though ain't we,' replied George. 'Looks like Marv's coming on,' he continued, pointing at the Chelsea technical area where Blues substitute Marvin Hinton, who'd replaced Ron Harris at the end of the regulation 90 minutes at Wembley, was preparing to enter the fray.

'Ossie! Bloody hell!' There was a collective expression of surprise as Peter Osgood was replaced by Hinton... but there was no dissent. Manager Dave Sexton had learned from the first game and got his tactics spot on so far for the replay. Hinton would be a level head and fresh legs... he would help shore up the Chelsea defence for the expected final onslaught from Leeds.

CHELSEA! CHELSEA! CHELSEA! CHELSEA! CHELSEA!

Leeds tried their damnedest... Chelsea tackled their damnedest... Ian Hutchinson continued to show scant regard for the risk he was running of being sent off... a bone-shaking challenge on Terry Cooper the latest addition to a long list of misdemeanours that Eric Jennings let go.

'The game's been going on so long, Hutch has probably forgotten he's been booked,' said George.

'How much time's left now?' asked Tommy, knowing the answer was about five minutes. It was funny, you always knew how long was left in a game but it never stopped you looking at your watch or asking the question.

Leeds pressed and won a corner, but the ball was scrambled away. It was better the goalmouth action was at the other end of the ground, it would be even more unbearable seeing it close up... especially when Jennings awarded the Whites a free-kick just outside the Chelsea penalty area. Peter Lorimer sized it up... but sent his shot wide.

We shall not, we shall not be moved,
We shall not, we shall not be moved.
Just like a team that's gonna win the FA Cup...
We shall not be moved.

'How long's left now?' asked Tommy, knowing he was repeating himself as Leeds won another corner and Jack Charlton, now being deployed as a striker by Don Revie, made a menacing presence of himself on the Chelsea goalline.

'You should smoke that bloody cigarette,' replied George. It'll calm your nerves.

Tommy shook his head and applauded as the corner-kick was wasted, the ball landing on the roof of Peter Bonetti's net. Even at a distance, Charlton looked infuriated and his consternation continued as Chelsea held firm and Bonetti, the last man, caught every speculative ball that was punted into his goalmouth.

Come On Chelsea! Come On Chelsea!

Chanting took the edge off Tommy's nerves, and he cheered as Charlie Cooke cleverly held the ball up and running with it to waste more seconds that were precious to Leeds. The canny Scot was laying a trap which was sprung by Norman Hunter who couldn't resist the temptation to foul his opponent.

We're gonna win the Cup, we're gonna win the Cup...
And now you're gonna believe us...
And now you're gonna believe us...
And now you're gonna be-lieve us... we're gonna win the Cup!

As the song gained momentum, and Hunter realised he'd been hoodwinked, Eric Jennings blew his whistle three times. Dissonant and short it may have been... but Jennings' last act as a football referee sounded like an orchestral symphony to Tommy. Finally, the game was over. Chelsea had won the FA Cup.

The celebrations felt unique for all of them. George, Fred, Tommy, Keith and Rick embraced and shook hands with those around them. On the pitch, some of the players swapped shirts. Ian Hutchinson was wearing Norman Hunter's while Peter Osgood had donned Billy Bremner's... the spoils of war!

'Imagine us lot doing that outside with Leeds supporters,' said Rick.

'Fucked if I'm swapping my lucky Aquascutum coat for a coalminer's donkey jacket,' replied Keith.

Tommy laughed, lit the cigarette that was still at the corner of his mouth and took a long drag before exhaling and standing stock still to soak up the atmosphere. Emotionally, he felt drained.

Without the same fanfare and formality that there would have been at Wembley, it wasn't long before Ron Harris was leading the victorious Chelsea team up the steps to be presented with the FA Cup by Dr. Andrew Stephen. Harris, with Bonetti and Hollins following him, raised the trophy briefly above his head and every Blues supporter at Old Trafford cheered and joined in the song...

We've won the cup, we've won the cup…
Eee Aye Addio… We've won the cup!

The victorious Chelsea team were soon back on the pitch starting their lap of honour and dodging the prying lenses of press photographers who were as doggedly determined to get money shots of them as the Leeds players had been to tackle them.

The cup changed hands a few times and it was Tommy Baldwin and Eddie McCreadie who were running with it when the ramshackle party of players, press, officials and hangers-on reached the Stretford End.

Chelsea! (clap, clap, clap) Chelsea! (clap, clap, clap)

Peter Osgood, a blue and white scarf now tied around his neck contrasting nicely with Bremner's shirt, held the cup aloft with Ron Harris who was still wearing his Chelsea shirt.

'Look Webby's wearing Eddie Gray's shirt,' said George. 'Wonder if he tore it off him?'

As the players continued their parade around the pitch, Blues supporters in the Stretford End began to sing *You'll Never Walk Alone…* It was spine-tingling. Briefly, Tommy looked across at his father and thought back to his childhood days and his first experience of going to watch Chelsea. Then, now and everything in between… what an epic journey and he was still only 20-years old. The future was unwritten, but already he felt he had a lot to be thankful for.

EPILOGUE
Friday 7 September 2019

Tommy Walker passed away in his sleep on 30 August 2019, 50 years to the day since he first met his wife Sophia on that sunny summer afternoon at the Isle of Wight Festival. Now they were together again, sharing everlasting peace after so much time apart.

The last conversation I had with Tommy was a few days prior to his death after I'd finished going through this snapshot of his life with him. At the end, he had this to say and his words will always resonate with me.

'My days are numbered, the time has flown... and as I listened to you reading, I realised how quickly. It only seems like yesterday I was a young man experiencing all the joys life has to offer for the first time. So many faces and places mentioned are long gone and I feel sad I didn't appreciate them as much perhaps as I should have done. I missed that chance and now there's no going back.'

Tommy's words saddened me. I understood exactly what he meant. Even more so now, sitting at a table on the olive-grove-bordered terrace at Villino Lo Zaffiro, the place that meant so much to him, making the final edits to his memoir and re-reading it while listening to the playlist we'd compiled.

Come On – The Rolling Stones
I Can't Explain – The Who
Sgt. Pepper's Lonely Hearts Club Band – The Beatles
Purple Haze – Jimi Hendrix
Jet Boy – New York Dolls
Did You No Wrong – Sex Pistols
I Want Everything – The Godfathers
My Generation – The Who
Space Oddity – David Bowie
Pinball Wizard – The Who
Liquidator – Harry J. All Stars
Debora – Tyrannosaurus Rex
Bad Moon Rising – Creedence Clearwater Revival
Oh Well – Fleetwood Mac
Hurry On Sundown – Hawkwind
Na Na Hey Hey Kiss Him Goodbye – Steam
Time Is Tight – Booker T. and the MG's
Those Were The Days – Mary Hopkin
Let It Be – The Beatles
Who Knows Where the Time Goes? – Fairport Convention (Sandy Denny)

I remember years ago, Tommy telling me that Sophia always said 'music was a ladder for the soul'. The power of music to evoke reminiscing can trigger deeply nostalgic emotional experiences that elevate our spiritual station.

Listening to Sandy Denny singing *Who Knows Where the Time*

Goes? ghostly negatives of Tommy and all the departed heroes and heroines of this book fill my mind... in particular, those, like his wife Sophia, whose lives were cut short in tragic circumstances.

My father who took me to my first football match was only 50 when he died in 1987. Peter Houseman (31), Ian Hutchinson (54), Peter Osgood (59), Jimi Hendrix (27), Marc Bolan (29), Keith Moon (32)... sadly, the list could go on and on. Sandy Denny herself was just 31-years old when her life ended in 1978. Tommy was so right about the passage of time and sometimes leaving it too late to show appreciation to the people that we love.

The swirling organ and rhythmic reggae-infused beat of *Liquidator* lifts my mood from deep melancholy. Now I envisage Tommy in his prime... stood shoulder-to-shoulder with Keith and Rick on a packed Shed terrace giving it the large one with George and Fred looking on...

(clap, clap, clap, clap) Chelsea!

I'll see Keith and Rick next week at Tommy's funeral. He asked for *The Liquidator* to be played at the end of the service and said we should box the ears of anyone who shouts out *we hate Tottenham* (even though it's true) during the *clap, clap, clap, clap* bit. He never liked the way the tune was 'contaminated' as he put it, in that way.

Breakfast arrives. Eggs Purgatorio. Oh the taste! Truly exceptional!!! Tommy was 100% correct. Eggs Purgatorio, Villino Lo Zaffiro-style, are the best in the world... even better than my Nonna Dirce's!

'Meraviglifuckingoso!'

If you're wondering why I'm here, well Tommy had one last revelation to share with me. He and Sophia married in 1971 and moved to Anne Boleyn's Walk in Cheam to be close to Nonsuch High School where she'd secured her next teaching role. As planned, a sizeable deposit on their £4,450 house came from the proceeds of his entrepreneurial creativity... which also funded the outright purchase of Villino Lo Zaffiro!

Property was dirt cheap in Calabria in the early '70s and Sophia's father Enrico had long dreamed of returning home and eventually retiring there. A generous donation from Tommy facilitated the move. He said the £500 he gave his father-in-law had come his way via an inheritance. Nobody questioned it. Why would they?

It was Sophia's mother Frances who had the idea to turn Villino Lo Zaffiro into an up-market bed and breakfast that would be attractive to adventurous tourists and it proved successful. When her parents tired of the day-to-day running of the property, they hired a local manager to take care of the business and that's how things remained to the present day.

At the same time, Tommy shared the truth about his connection with the place he also gave me an envelope... inside was a key to a self-contained, two-bedroomed lodge that Enrico built adjacent to the main building where he and Frances lived to their dying days.

'Yours for you to use whenever you want it,' he said to me. 'Thank you for being my friend and telling my story.'

Now it's entirely possible some people might take a dim view of the criminality related to Tommy counterfeiting tickets, but consider these three facts.

Firstly, as expected, the 1970 Isle of White Festival ended up attracting way more people than the promoters planned with well over 600,000 attending... some estimates put it as high as 700,000! As increasing numbers of ticketless music fans continued to arrive during the weekend, perimeter fences were inevitably torn down as the site was swamped forcing the festival to become a free event. In the grand scheme of things, Tommy's 500 fake tickets were tiny little fishes swimming in a big blue anarchic ocean in which he certainly wasn't a cash-obsessed shark.

Secondly, true to his personal vow, Tommy never engaged in any fraudulent activity again and in his will he bequeathed a significant sum of money to charity. In his final months, Villino Lo Zaffiro had been signed over to the family that had managed it for years with a proviso that it be converted for use as a respite care home... that work was already underway.

Thirdly, and perhaps most importantly, the reason Tommy wanted to tell his story was not to champion his guile but to advocate love and to show gratitude to the people whom he treasured as well as sharing memories of a magical time in Chelsea's history that meant so much to so many people.

Tommy Walker was a giant among men, a true legend in my eyes. His like I will never encounter again and I miss him terribly.

*****

The music has stopped now. The only sounds I can hear are gentle waves breaking on the sandy shore before me and a flock of iridescent-plumed swallows chirping as they soar overhead, distinctive long tail streamers trailing behind as they begin their migration south to the Sahara for the winter.

Out of the corner of my eye, I catch sight of my young daughter Misty Blue standing at the water's edge, skimming stones on the shimmering sapphire Tyrrhenian Sea that stretches out before her. I love her madly. She's nine-years-old, carefree and with a whole life to live and look forward to. I remember being nine like it was yesterday... it was 1970! Where did all the time go? Who knows?

I wonder what great experiences await Misty and how she will remember them. As George once did with Tommy, and my father once did with me, I'm taking her to Stamford Bridge to watch Chelsea for the first time this season... and so a new version of a story many Blues supporters could tell will begin once again.

GATE 17
THE COMPLETE COLLECTION
(DECEMBER 2019)

FOOTBALL
Over Land and Sea – Mark Worrall
Chelsea here, Chelsea There – Kelvin Barker, David Johnstone, Mark Worrall
Chelsea Football Fanzine – the best of cfcuk
One Man Went to Mow – Mark Worrall
Chelsea Chronicles (Five Volume Series) – Mark Worrall
Making History Not Reliving It –
Kelvin Barker, David Johnstone, Mark Worrall
Celery! Representing Chelsea in the 1980s – Kelvin Barker
Stuck On You: a year in the life of a Chelsea supporter – Walter Otton
Palpable Discord: a year of drama and dissent at Chelsea – Clayton Beerman
Rhyme and Treason – Carol Ann Wood
Eddie Mac Eddie Mac – Eddie McCreadie's Blue & White Army
The Italian Job: A Chelsea thriller starring Antonio Conte – Mark Worrall
Carefree! Chelsea Chants & Terrace Culture – Mark Worrall, Walter Otton
Diamonds, Dynamos and Devils – Tim Rolls
Arrivederci Antonio: The Italian Job (part two) – Mark Worrall
Where Were You When We Were Shocking? – Neil L. Smith
Chelsea: 100 Memorable Games – Chelsea Chadder
Bewitched, Bothered & Bewildered – Carol Ann Wood
Stamford Bridge Is Falling Down – Tim Rolls
Cult Fiction – Dean Mears
Chelsea: If Twitter Was Around When… – Chelsea Chadder
Blue Army – Vince Cooper
Liquidator 1969-70 A Chelsea Memoir – Mark Worrall

FICTION
Blue Murder: Chelsea Till I Die – Mark Worrall
The Wrong Outfit – Al Gregg
The Red Hand Gang – Walter Otton
Coming Clean – Christopher Morgan
This Damnation – Mark Worrall
Poppy – Walter Otton

NON FICTION
Roe2Ro – Walter Otton
Shorts – Walter Otton

www.gate17.co.uk

Printed in Great Britain
by Amazon

37054980R00128